In the Field, Among the Feathered

In the Field, Among the Feathered

A HISTORY OF BIRDERS & THEIR GUIDES

Thomas R. Dunlap

OXFORD
UNIVERSITY PRESS

OXFORD
UNIVERSITY PRESS

Oxford University Press, Inc., publishes works that further
Oxford University's objective of excellence
in research, scholarship, and education.

Oxford   New York
Auckland   Cape Town   Dar es Salaam   Hong Kong   Karachi
Kuala Lumpur   Madrid   Melbourne   Mexico City   Nairobi
New Delhi   Shanghai   Taipei   Toronto

With offices in
Argentina   Austria   Brazil   Chile   Czech Republic   France   Greece
Guatemala   Hungary   Italy   Japan   Poland   Portugal   Singapore
South Korea   Switzerland   Thailand   Turkey   Ukraine   Vietnam

Published by Oxford University Press, Inc.
198 Madison Avenue, New York, NY 10016

www.oup.com

Oxford is a registered trademark of Oxford University Press

Library of Congress Cataloging-in-Publication Data
Dunlap, Thomas R., 1943–
In the field, among the feathered : a history of birders and their guides / Thomas R. Dunlap.
p.   cm.
Includes bibliographical references and index.
ISBN 978-0-19-973459-7
1. Bird watching—United States—History. 2. Bird watchers—United States—History.
3. Birds—United States—Identification—History. I. Title.
QL677.5.D83   2011
598.072'3473—dc22   2011009169

3 5 7 9 8 6 4 2

Printed in the United States of America
on acid-free paper

*For my brother Dave and my sister Martha,
my constant family readers*

Contents

Acknowledgments

The History Department and the College of Liberal Arts at Texas A&M University provided me a fine situation in which to work, and I thank them, and my department head, Dr. Walter Buenger. For an uninterrupted year in which to write—a precious commodity indeed—I thank the National Science Foundation for its support under SES grant 0550268, and Dr. Ronald Rainger, the project officer who steered the proposal from rough idea to clear application. During the writing I had what I have come to think of as my usual conversations with Bill Cronon. This book would not have been the same without his friendship, advice, and analysis. I shared birding field trips with Kurk Dorsey at the American Society for Environmental History, and he reviewed the manuscript. I tried out my ideas on far too many friends to mention each by name, but they all have my deep thanks.

Like all researchers I rely on archives, and I thank the following not only for permissions but also for staff assistance, invariably friendly and helpful: the Wisconsin State Historical Society for a copy of my taped interview with Joseph J. Hickey; the Roger Tory Peterson Institute in Jamestown, New York, for access to Peterson's extensive correspondence, library, and specimen collection; the Museum of Vertebrate Zoology in Berkeley, California, for its correspondence files, which I have been using for research for more than twenty years; the American Museum of Natural History in New York for the correspondence of Frank M. Chapman; the Cornell University Library for access to the Ludlow Griscom Papers; and the Thomas J. Dodd Research Center at the University of Connecticut for the Edwin Way Teale Papers. I also thank the editorial team at Oxford University Press for the alchemy that turns manuscript into book, with my special thanks to Susan Ferber, whose editorial talents forced me to sharpen my ideas and improved my expression of them. Errors and remaining infelicities are all my own.

Birders, naturally, want to know if I am one of them. By hard-core standards, no. I began with the standard child's guide of the postwar years, Gabrielson and Zim's little Golden Guide, *Birds*, went on to Mom's "Peterson," and have at least one guide to every country I have ever visited. Birds fascinate me far more than listing does, though, and while out birding I am happy to be distracted by snakes, turtles, frogs, regrowth in burned-off pastures, and almost any other evidence of the changing world around us.

In the Field, Among the Feathered

Introduction

Field guides to the birds sit in their millions on shelves and windowsills near bird feeders, and in cars with the spare set of binoculars. They fill the "Nature" or "Environment" section of bookstores, always the lead volumes in the series of field guides that line the shelves. Familiar and ordinary, they are also the essential tool for one of the most popular outdoor activities in the country, a hobby supported by clubs, local and national festivals and workshops, and ecotourism. Publishers have added new guides or new editions of classic guides at the rate of about one a year since Florence Merriam published *Birds through an Opera-Glass* in 1889.[1] For more than a century field guides have been Americans' commonest means of informal nature education, their variety and continued popularity the most conspicuous evidence of their continuing quest to connect their lives in an industrial, urban society to nature.

While books about birds date from antiquity, and amateur natural history volumes to early nineteenth-century Britain, the story told here begins with Merriam and her cohort because they wrote not for science or education but to help people enjoy identifying birds in the field, and because they were the vanguard of what became Americans' favorite way to learn about nature. The field guide genre developed over the decades at the intersections of outdoor recreation, fine art, commercial art, science, and business, and its history tells us much about how Americans have used science to understand the world around them and how commercial realities have both enabled and restrained the passage of knowledge from small groups of scientists and enthusiasts to the general population. Guides reflect changes in scientific understanding, for they use the ornithologists' taxonomies and names, but they also embody and pass on the craft knowledge of field identification. Early guides ignored some species or some forms the authors said could not be identified by sight; a later generation said all could be named, largely by differences in plumage; recent guides commonly include all species, all plumages, and teach identification by call, flight patterns, and overall impression.

The hobby of identifying birds in the field began as part of the late nineteenth-century reaction against the industrial city, a movement that sent millions of middle-class Americans (as well as people in other industrialized countries) back to "nature" to hunt, fish, canoe, hike, ski, and climb mountains. Before the Industrial Revolution, people found nature each day as they worked, and they learned what they wished, often what helped them find fish or furbearers or berries; in the process they learned where certain birds nested or when they raised their young. Living in cities with electric lights and plumbing, taking trolleys to work in offices or factories, they lost day-to-day contact with nature. Many, seeking to retain some tie, took up outdoor recreations, as strenuous as mountaineering or as leisurely as a walk in the park with opera-glasses, some new, others pioneer work turned into play. Sport hunting, for instance, emphasized woodcraft and harked back to the frontier past, while sport fishing appealed to an idealized rural life and, often, memories of rural childhood.

Outdoor recreations soon built national networks, often through magazines that educated readers on techniques, set standards of competence or conduct, and rallied enthusiasts for political action to save their sport. Sporting magazines, for instance, said quail and grouse were game birds, robins and chickadees, often shot for pies, were not, and they poured scorn on poor sportsmanship. Shooting sitting ducks was definitely not done. They rallied sportsmen against market hunting and in support of closed seasons, bag limits, and wardens—to ensure that the next generation would have game to hunt. Other outdoor sports faced less urgent problems and had less ambitious goals, but all had an agenda.

Birdwatching was one of these activities, but with its own unique characteristics. All outdoor recreations supported conservation, but rather than conservation programs emerging to serve the hobby, birdwatching as a recreation developed, in large part, as a way to encourage conservation. Get women interested in birds, ran the logic, and they would rally to end the shooting of songbirds and the slaughter of other species for their plumes. It was women who established the hobby and are by some definitions still in the majority. The early watchers included a cohort of naturalists, particularly at the expert end, and nature education added children, mainly boys, but upper- and middle-class women interested in nature and humane ideals organized and ran the early clubs, boosted the hobby, and even wrote some of the guides. Compared to other outdoor sports, birdwatching had much closer ties to science. Naturalists passed on field skills to the amateurs, and the amateurs' growing skill and numbers made them increasingly valuable to ornithologists. Uniquely, birdwatching relied on books, not simply kept and read at home but used in the field. With more enthusiasm than knowledge, early watchers needed field guides and found lists the best way to measure their growing competence. Birdwatching let them re-create—on a small scale and in a humane way—natural history's program of arranging, classifying, and mapping on the land the life around them.

Because many ornithologists were interested in birdwatching, the relationship between amateurs and professionals remained unusually close. Scientific disciplines typically confined membership in professional societies to those with professional credentials and positions, but so many of the founders of the American Ornithologists' Union (AOU) had begun as bird-struck teenagers and remained enthusiasts and amateur observations continued to be so useful that the professionals did not strictly enforce the usual ban on amateur involvement. Scientists who stayed in the lab (the only acceptable site for respectable science in the late nineteenth century) talked to their peers, but field workers encountered women and children. Some, certainly, ignored these interlopers, but others encouraged them by writing guides, teaching courses, and aiding the Audubon movement, that coalition of humane reformers and nature lovers who, around the turn of the century, set out to defend birds. By the 1920s, about the time birdwatchers had methods to identify all the North American species, ornithologists began to study living populations in the field and found it necessary to add birdwatching skills to their professional toolkit. As birdwatchers' numbers and expertise grew, along with the need for bird conservation, the ornithologists enlisted them to gather data. The line between scientific research and popular study, a well-marked and guarded border in most fields, here remained a meeting place.

Birdwatchers' central activity—listing birds by their species—came from natural history, a term now associated with amateur nature study or elementary school science, but from the eighteenth century to the late nineteenth century the leading edge of what became the biological and earth sciences. A product of the age of exploration, the field encompassed animals, vegetables, minerals, weather, landforms, and societies lacking what Europeans then considered high civilization, a mixture still on display in modern natural history museums. In the nineteenth century, naturalists set out to catalog and arrange all the "productions of nature," an ambitious intellectual project that drew in amateurs around the world.[2] It was open to all, for it relied on recording observations and generally dealt with things you could see without a microscope or telescope. The program required care and attention but not mastery of theory.

Natural history gave birdwatchers a comfortable frame in which to work. They could put the correct names on birds, decide one was, say, an immature male Northern Cardinal, another a mature female Cooper's Hawk, without knowing anything about taxonomy or the scientists' sophisticated understanding of species. They could also go beyond facts to appreciate nature's wonders. Natural history emphasized accurate observation, but it developed alongside, and often as part of, natural theology—the study, as the Victorians put it, of Creation to understand the attributes of the Creator—and so included what they would have capitalized as Higher Truths. When Christian understandings dwindled, secular ones took their place; finding transcendence through close, down-to-earth observation underlay much of twentieth-century nature writing and amateur nature study, and birds were ideal subjects—varied, often beautiful, and flying. Birdwatching began with science, conservation, and self-improvement, but it also rested on a deep, often unacknowledged and never clearly articulated feeling that there was something magical about birds.

Natural history, taking in all nature across the globe and concerned with organisms and the distribution of life across the land, gave birdwatching a broad view of nature and tied nature to society. Other outdoor recreations looked to the land outside cities and homes and took place in areas set aside for their sport. Practitioners presented nature as an arena for testing physical skills and character. Birdwatching, however, intertwined nature with society. Birds on the Ramble in Central Park were as wild, and counted as much for watchers' lists, as those in an Arctic wilderness. With lists and notes—the methods of natural history—watchers traced the bird life of their territories through the years. Enthusiastic and methodical hobbyists recorded decades of migrations arranged in field notebooks, while ordinary birders used the margins of their field guides to note when and often where they found a new species, and they transferred notes from battered, worn-out copies to new ones, shelving the old as souvenirs of their lives outdoors.[3] The places birdwatchers looked for birds changed with technology and social standards. Early guides often passed over species found in swamps and other locations not considered suitable for ladies, but the decline of gentility and the recruitment of school boys (often through Junior Audubon clubs) put less savory but bird-rich areas—garbage dumps, sewage farms, landfills—on birdwatchers' maps. Cars let birdwatchers expand their range and made spring migration the occasion for day-long expeditions; better cars and roads after World War II, coupled with longer vacations, let middle-class birdwatchers dream of seeing birds across the country; and in the late twentieth century, specially organized bird tours allowed enthusiasts to go birding around the world and encouraged even homebound birders to dream of faraway places with strange-sounding names. That lists contained only free, wild birds remained a constant.

Field guides became an indispensable adjunct to birdwatching. While other hobbies kept their books at home, this one took them to the field and consulted them at every turn. Changing knowledge and new conditions produced new guides, and the developments between Florence Merriam's *Birds through an Opera-Glass*, published in 1889, and David Sibley's *Sibley Guide to Birds* (2000) reveal much about the hobby and the community. The history of the field guide can be roughly divided into three stages: the pioneer period, the mature form, and the environmental age. The first guides reflected the confused state of the hobby. Not sure who they were writing for or how best to help their readers, authors experimented with text, pictures, and layout. To show birds they tried wood engravings, color reproductions of fine art paintings, photos of stuffed birds, and drawings in black and white or color. Their descriptions ran from scientific to sentimental, sometimes in the same book, and included everything from physical appearance to incidents in nature. Publishers produced volumes suited for library shelves or shirt pockets. A new era began with the publication, in 1934, of the first edition of *A Field Guide to the Birds*. Commercial artist as well as enthusiastic birder, Roger Tory Peterson created the first guide whose illustrations could be reliably used to identify species, with arrows highlighting distinctive features. In the postwar years, "Peterson" in its eastern and western editions made birdwatching a recreation for the masses. While not a guide or even a bird book, Rachel Carson's *Silent Spring* ushered in environmental conservation and a third phase of field books. The new guides paid more attention to birds' connections to the world and also demonstrated the community's increasing expertise in identification.

This book tells the story of birdwatching and birdwatchers through the prism of their field guides. It begins with the guides that brought people out into the parks, then looks at the problems of making a book that was truly useful in the field. Early authors faced the daunting task of introducing an audience to a still-undefined activity and giving them enough information to make their first excursions enjoyable enough that they would continue. That demanded a new kind of book. Volumes of natural history, or ornithology, described birds, but in the hand, not as the birdwatcher saw them, in the bush. They located the birds by taxonomy, as things within a class, but not by the characteristics that could be used to tell them apart. Field guides, obviously, needed pictures, but reproductions tended to be either too expensive for mass-market books or too crude to help the birdwatcher. Readers' enthusiasm made up for the books' deficiencies; within a generation birdwatching grew from a fad for genteel ladies into a recognized, if somewhat eccentric, hobby. A few of the early guides moved beyond taxonomy and stories about birds to focus on distinctive features or arranged text and pictures to make comparison of similar species easy. While they did not look like modern guides, these books pointed toward their form.

During the next forty years, roughly 1920 to 1960, the modern guide took form, and birdwatching became a popular hobby. Chapter 3 looks at the people, most of them residents of the Northeast, who worked out ways to identify all the species by sight. Ludlow Griscom, birdwatcher and ornithologist, took the lead there and in spreading information and methods up and down the East Coast. His most famous student was Roger Tory Peterson, and chapter 4 follows him from his childhood in upstate New York through writing his first guides to his striking out, after World War II, on a career as freelance writer, artist, and illustrator. In 1947 he published the third edition of his *Field Guide to the Birds*, the focus of chapter 5. This third edition was the book that lured millions out of doors and made Peterson a household name and the field guide Americans' standard form of informal nature education.

The last two chapters deal with birding in the environmental age: the ways the gospel of environmental conservation changed the balance between conservation and recreation in the hobby and the ways ecological insights changed field guides. By making conservation a moral and urgent matter, involving human survival as well as nature's beauty, the environmental movement made checking birds off on a list seem at best a diversion from the urgent work of saving the planet, at worst a waste of time. Even as they pushed their skills to new heights and field guides pushed identification past Peterson's plumage patterns, recreational birders felt their activity was being pushed to the margins. As it became apparent that industrial civilization was not in danger of imminent collapse, conservation and recreation struck a new balance. To get the information they needed to manage continental bird populations, ornithologists recruited more aggressively among the large and often expert group of recreational birders. They designed programs that allowed them to gather and process amateur observations from experts and backyard birders. Meanwhile, birding continued to grow in popularity. In 2001 a survey by the U.S. Fish and Wildlife Service found 46 million Americans over the age of sixteen were birders, a group it defined as people who either took a trip a mile or more from home or closely watched and tried to identify birds around home. It revealed that birding generated $32 billion in retail sales and created over eight hundred thousand jobs in such areas as tourism and nature stores.[4] All that activity, and all those people, depended on field guides—even the birders who memorized field marks culled them from books. The entire hobby rested on volumes presenting the accumulated knowledge of generations of amateur observers, organized by science, and produced for sale. While the form of the guides evolved, they held to the same mission: to pass on a body of craft knowledge within a national community of interest and give people a way to interact with nature in their everyday lives.

A final note concerns terms. The word "birding" for this field hobby goes back to Merriam's *A-birding on a Bronco* in 1896, but for the next fifty years the people out in the park with binoculars called themselves "birdwatchers" and went "birdwatching." "Birder" and "birding" came into use around World War II, gained traction in the 1970s, and dominate now. While some apply "birder" and "birding" to all amateur bird study, others see peering out the back window at the feeder or strolling through the park as mere "birdwatching" and reserve "birding" for their own passionate pursuit. Since no single set of terms will satisfy everyone, I simply try to avoid anachronism by using "birdwatching" into the 1970s and "birding" thereafter.

PART I

Getting Started

ONE

Shooting Birds with Opera Glasses

These are great migration times . . .
the parks are full of birds . . .
and people shooting them with opera glasses.

—FRANK DAGGETT (1904)

sunset, sitting on a branch in the softened light
and whispering a little song to himself, his sentiment is the wholesome every-day sort, with none
of the sadness or longing of his cousins, the
thrushes, but full of contented appreciation of the
beautiful world he lives in.

Unlike some of his human friends, his content
does not check his activity. He is full of buoyant
life. He may always be heard piping up above
the rest of the daybreak chorus, and I have seen
him sit on top of a stub in a storm when it seemed
as if the harder it rained the louder and more ju-
bilantly he sang. He has plenty of pluck and
industry, too, for every season he dutifully accepts
the burden of seeing three or four broods of bird
children through all the dangers of cats, hawks,

I t takes a pile of guides to give the flavor of birdwatching's early days, for no one was quite sure what this new activity was or was for—the first step toward a career in science, natural history without collecting, informal nature education, a search for nature's wonders, or just a way to pass time out-of-doors? Taking the scientific approach, Florence Merriam Bailey's *Handbook of Birds of the Western United States* and Frank Chapman's *Handbook of Birds of Eastern North America* were chunky volumes, eight inches by five inches, bristling with an array of typefaces and scientific terms. They presented birdwatching as bloodless ornithology and kept one foot in traditional natural history by giving directions on collecting and preparing specimens. The books aiming to lure ladies out to the park included Florence Merriam's *Birds through an Opera-Glass* and *Birds of Village and Field*, Neltje Blanchan's *Bird Neighbors*, and Mabel Osgood Wright's *Birdcraft*. In contrast to the handbooks, which covered all the birds of a region in scientific detail, these treated a selection of birds seen in the yard or the park, paid little attention to taxonomy, used few technical terms, and viewed the birds as, to use Blanchan's phrase, our neighbors. John B. Grant's *Our Common Birds and How to Know Them* and Edward Knobel's *Field Key to the Land Birds* took an even more basic approach. Small books concentrating on the identification of common species, they had pictures and short descriptions, omitting both sentiment and science.[1]

This chapter looks at the fruits of their labor, the guides and their picture of nature. The books come first, for they taught people the

1.1 · *Merriam's Robin* · The first guide had a conventional look, the text did not describe the birds well, and the picture, a wood engraving, decorated the page rather than aiding identification. From Florence Merriam, *Birds through an Opera-Glass* (Boston: Houghton Mifflin, 1889).

b^1. Smaller (wing less than 2.50); bill small, nearly as broad as high at base, and tapering rapidly to the slender, slightly hooked tip. (Color olive-green or russet-olive above, with top of head and neck ash-gray or else with tail russet; lower parts neither yellow nor green.)

Hylophilus. (Page 478.)

b^2. Larger (wing not less than 3.00); bill stout, much deeper than wide at base, the culmen curving rather abruptly toward the strongly hooked tip.

c^1. Depth of bill at base only about half the exposed culmen. (Lower parts green, becoming yellow on throat, or else white with rufous band across chest; upper parts bright green, with top of head sky-blue, or else olive, the sides of head striped with yellow, slate-color, white, and black.)... *Vireolanius.*[1]

c^2. Depth of bill at base much more than half the exposed culmen. (Lower parts yellow; upper parts plain olive-green, becoming ash-gray on head and neck, the forehead and broad superciliary stripe rufous.)

Cyclorhis.[2]

GENUS **VIREO** VIEILLOT. (Page 468, pl. CXV., figs. 1–3, 5.)

Species.

COMMON CHARACTERS.—Above plain olive-green or olive-grayish, with or without white wing-bands; beneath whitish or yellowish, or both. *Nest* a very beautiful basket-shaped structure suspended from a forked twig, composed of mosses, lichens, fine strips of bark, etc. *Eggs* white, usually more or less dotted or sparsely speckled round larger end with brown and blackish.

a^1. Spurious primary, if present, very narrow and pointed, and decidedly shorter than tarsus.

b^1. Wing without light bands or other distinct markings. (Subgenus *Vireosylva* BONAP.)

c^1. Without any spurious primary, or else, if present, the exposed culmen .50, or more.[3]

d^1. Exposed culmen .50, or more; middle of chest white.

e^1. A distinct dusky streak along each side of throat.

Above plain dull olive-greenish, becoming gray on top of head, which has a more or less distinct dusky streak along each side of crown; a conspicuous superciliary stripe of dull whitish, bordered below by a distinct dusky streak through the eye; cheeks dull grayish white or pale brownish gray (whole side of head, including superciliary stripe, sometimes strongly suffused with dull brownish buffy); lower parts white,

---

[1] *Vireolanius* BONAP., Consp. i. 1850, 330. Type, *V. melitophrys* DU BUS.

[2] *Cyclorhis* SWAINS., Zool. Jour. iii. 1828, 162. Type, *Tanagra guianensis* GMEL.

[3] The exception is *V. olivaceus*, which is said to have *sometimes* (but very rarely) a spurious primary.

hobby, and within that group the ones that adapted scientific knowledge to observing rather than shooting birds and tackled the problems of making a book people could use in the field. Birdwatching depended on and cultivated a craft skill, identifying birds by sight, and the books served the purpose, but people went to nature not just for diversion but to make it a part of their lives. After the guides come these influences, beginning with the possibly genetic attraction that made nature a fascinating subject for humans back, at least, as far as the ones who painted animals on cave walls, and on to American bird studies, and then the elite late Victorian genteel culture out of which birdwatching emerged. It came as part of Americans' search for a relation to nature from within an industrial society. Moving to the city, they lost nature as the context of life and work, and many people sought a replacement in play, in outdoor recreations, including identifying birds. In the century since, Americans have defined and redefined their ties to the world beyond the sidewalk, but two constants remain: they approach nature in their leisure hours and understand it through science.

The Early Field Guides

On any spring morning in 1889, a respectable young Victorian lady named Florence Merriam might be found in the pastures of her Uncle Gustavus's ranch near San Diego, California, treating her fashionable malady, an attack of "nerves," with the equally fashionable remedy of a retreat to nature. Rather than rambling over the hills admiring the flowers, she sallied forth, "armed with opera-glass and notebook, and Ridgway's *Manual* to turn to in all my perplexities," to see if she could put a name to all the birds she saw.[2] She was as prepared as anyone for the task. Sister of the naturalist C. Hart Merriam, she had spent her childhood exploring her family's rural acres. As a student at Smith College she watched birds, organized a college Audubon Society, and even arranged for a three-day visit to campus by the nation's leading nature writer, John Burroughs. After leaving college, she taught bird classes at a summer school in Rockford, Illinois—part of Jane Addams's social work at Hull House in Chicago—and in the winter in Grace Dodge's clubs for working girls in New York. She wrote a series of articles about

1.2 · *Ridgway's Vireos* · When Merriam turned to Ridgway for help "in all my perplexities," she found this confusing mass of type—taxonomy as hierarchy, the successive indentations recording more and more minute distinctions, the whole arranged for use in testing possibilities on a specimen in the hand. From Robert Ridgway, *Manual of North American Birds* (Philadelphia: J. B. Lippincott, 1887).

watching birds and turned them into the first book on field identification for amateurs, *Birds through an Opera Glass.*[3]

Despite her considerable knowledge, she failed Emerson's challenge
to "name all the birds without a gun." She "made the acquaintance of
about seventy-five birds, and without resort to the gun was able to name
fifty-six of them. . . . The fact of the matter is, you can identify perhaps
ninety percent of the birds you see, with an opera-glass and patience;
but when it comes to the other ten percent, including small vireos and
flycatchers," she wrote, you cannot."[4] Her declaration makes sense if we
look at what she had for a guide, Ridgway's *Manual,* more formally *A
Manual of North American Birds.* It is a handsome book, nine and a half
by seven inches, two inches thick, weighing four pounds, and filled with
information, but organized to help those studying dead specimens.
Suppose she spotted a generally olive-colored vireo with a broken eye-
ring. Turning to "Order Passeres—The Perching Birds," and the subdi-
vision Family Vireonidae—The Vireos," which began on page 468, she
would have found descriptions of the various genera (the taxonomic
unit in which ornithologists grouped closely related species), distinguished by such measures as "Wings shorter than tail, extremely
rounded, the fifth or sixth quill longest," and an extensive key to species
and subspecies, organized by these measurements. Since Ridgway took
no account of what stood out or visibly marked one species off from
another, Merriam would have to wade through his beak-to-toe descriptions. Eventually she would have found one that began: "Lores and or-
bital ring dully whitish, the latter interrupted on upper eyelid. Above
plain olive or olive-grayish, becoming more decidedly olivaceous on
rump, upper tail-covets, and edges of secondaries and tail-feathers . . ." It
went on for another dozen lines, but Merriam had seen a Hutton's Vireo,
and by the range would have identified it as the subspecies *V. huttoni
stephensi* Brewst.[5]

Besides attending to details invisible at a distance, Ridgway and his
fellow ornithologists approached birds in a way hardly suited to birdwatching and quite horrifying to genteel ladies. Ornithology in the late
nineteenth century meant collecting specimens. Ridgway did not deal
with that, but the other standard work of the period, Elliott Coues's *Key
to North American Birds,* did.[6] Its "Field Ornithology" section did not
discuss birds in the field but how to get them out of the field and into
the specimen drawer. The first necessity, Coues said, was a double-barrel
12-gauge shotgun, and since a decent collection required enough specimens of each species to show the plumages and the major variations in
plumage and coloring across the geographic range, he advised readers

to get as many specimens as possible, "with some reasonable limitations; say fifty or a hundred of any but the most abundant and widely diffused species.... Begin by shooting every bird you can, coupling this sad destruction, however, with the closest observations upon habits." There was no need to take birds like robins or bluebirds, which every collection had, but in a new area, where what was common might be rare in collections, "seize the opportunity and get good store,—yes, up to fifty or a hundred; all you can spare will be thankfully received by those who have none." He devoted six pages to "The Regular Process" of turning a bird corpse into a specimen and six more to "Special Processes; Complications, and Accidents." The collector cut the skin from breastbone to vent, took out the internal organs, scooped out the eyes, removed the brain through the bottom of the skull, treated the remaining soft tissues with solutions to harden them, then dusted the skin with powdered arsenic to keep the bugs at bay. "Shovel in arsenic. . . . The simple rule is, put in as much arsenic as will *stick* anywhere." After that, he tied a label to the feet showing where and when the bird was killed, and put the skin into a drawer, periodically treating it with "insect powder" from the druggist. Otherwise insects would consume skin, feathers, and all.[7]

Birdwatchers clearly needed another sort of approach. Just what it was no one quite knew. Early guides commonly spoke of gaining knowledge or enjoying beauty. Frank Chapman's *Handbook of the Birds of Eastern North America* and Florence (Merriam) Bailey's *Handbook of Birds of the Western United States,* for example, used science. They had close descriptions of all the birds of the area, directions on preparing specimens, and many pages on taxonomy but little on how to identify birds in the field. One frustrated user, the young Roger Peterson, complained that Chapman's *Handbook* "would describe a bird from its beak to its tail, but wouldn't give you the clue you needed to identify it quickly."[8] Other books aimed to introduce readers to the world of birds for their own enjoyment. Most, aiming at beginners with little interest in science, described some common birds and helped the novice sort them out by descriptions, keys based on color or size, and lists of what might be found in different habitats. None really helped in the field, but names, pictures, descriptions, keys, and lists, even if they did not allow instant identification, at least organized the confusing mass of colors and forms they saw in the fields and woods.

Science ruled, with a light touch in the basic books, openly in Chapman and Merriam's chunky volumes, but it was science geared to the public, not the experts. Chapman said he included "what personal experience with students of birds has led me to believe would meet their wants" in a text "so free from technicalities that it would be intelligible without reference to a glossary . . . in a volume which could be taken afield in the pocket." An ad for Bailey's book saw it as a western counterpart of Chapman's *Handbook*, presenting information in "a scientific, yet not unduly technical form, descriptions and life histories of all the birds of the West."[9] Both stressed bird study and not birdwatching, as in Chapman's subtitle: "With Keys to the Species and Descriptions of their Plumages, Nests, and Eggs, their Distribution and Migrations and a Brief Account of their Haunts and Habits with Introductory Chapters on the Study of Ornithology, How to Identify Birds and How to Collect and Preserve Birds, their Nests, and Eggs." They included taxonomy and systematics, the great concerns of the nineteenth century, and pointed toward ecology and ethology, the field's frontiers in the twentieth, leaving out only the laboratory sciences of anatomy and physiology. Even collecting was deemphasized. The plumage of eastern birds, Chapman said, was "well-known to science," and in getting specimens for "self-education" it was "not necessary that you should acquire the large series of specimens found in museums. From two to five specimens of each kind are enough."[10] Bailey included an essay titled "Collecting and preparing Birds, Nests, and Eggs" (written by her husband, Vernon) but did not see collecting as essential or even particularly useful for most. To show the new practices of field identification she included local bird lists compiled by western ornithologists.

Bailey's and Chapman's handbooks could easily appeal to science because ornithology—by then an academic, fully professional discipline—still had much of natural history's wide-ranging curiosity and its search for beauty as well as facts. These handbooks used a format common to ornithology until just a generation before, a mixture of technical material and personal observations. Chapman, for instance, began his discussion of the American Robin, as he did all the birds, with its number on the AOU's list, 761, and scientific name, *Merula migratoria*, followed by five lines of small type giving a physical description with measurements of the adult male, several more on the female and young, and finally information on range and nest. He continued in a

1.3 · *Chapman's Ducks* · Chapman laid out this book like a natural history text, with each species' number on the AOU list and its Latin name first, followed by a description in small type and a discursive entry in a larger font. Only its small size (7 ½ x 5 ½) marks it as a book for the field. Frank M. Chapman, *Handbook of Birds of Eastern North America* (New York: Appleton, 1895).

Washington, not rare, W. V. Long Island, A. V. Sing Sing, A. V., Apl. Cambridge, casual; one instance, Nov.

Nest, on the ground, in grassy sloughs or marshy lake sides. *Eggs*, six to twelve, similar in color to those of the two preceding species, 2·28 × 1·63.

This is more of a fresh-water bird than either of the preceding. It is not common in the Atlantic States north of Florida, where during the winter it is abundant on fresh-water lakes.

151. Glaucionetta clangula americana (*Bonap.*). AMERICAN GOLDEN-EYE; WHISTLER. *Ad. ♂.*—Head and throat dark, glossy *green*, a circular white patch at the base of the bill measuring, along the bill, less than *half an inch* in height; neck all around, breast, belly, exposed part of wing-coverts, speculum, and most of the scapulars white; rest of plumage black. *Ad. ♀.*—Head and throat cinnamon-brown, fore neck white; upper breast, back, and sides ashy gray bordered with grayish; wing-coverts tipped with white; speculum, lower breast, and belly white. L., 20·00; W., 9·00; B. from anterior margin of white patch to anterior margin of nostril, 1·00; from anterior margin of nostril to tip, ·75.

Range.—North America, breeding from Manitoba and Maine northward, and wintering from the southern limit of its breeding range to Cuba.

Washington, not rare, W. V. Long Island, common T. V. and W. V., Nov. 15 to Apl. 15. Sing Sing, common T. V. and W. V., Nov. to May. Cambridge, rather common, Oct. and Nov.

Nest, in a stump or hollow tree. *Eggs*, six to ten, pale bluish, 2·35 × 1·75.

The rapidly moving wings of most Ducks make a whistling sound, but this species excels in wing music. As a diver it can also claim high rank.

152. Glaucionetta islandica (*Gmel.*). BARROW'S GOLDEN-EYE. *Ad. ♂.*—Head and throat dark, glossy, *purplish blue*, an irregular, somewhat *spread-wing*-shaped white patch at the base of the bill measuring, along the bill, about *one inch* in height; neck all around, breast, belly, speculum, lesser wing-coverts, ends of greater ones, and the shaft part of the scapulars white; rest of the plumage black. *Ad. ♀.*—Resembles the ♀ of the preceding species in color; there is some difference in the size and proportions of the bill, but the two birds can not always be distinguished with certainty. W., 9·25; B. from anterior margin of white patch to anterior margin of nostril, ·80; from anterior margin of nostril to tip, ·66.

Remarks.—The males of this and the preceding species may always be distinguished by the difference in the color of the head and size and shape of the white spot at the base of the bill.

Range.—Breeds in the far north—Greenland, Iceland, and Alaska—and southward in the Rocky Mountains; winters as far south as Illinois and Virginia.

Washington, A. V., one record. Long Island, A. V.

Nest, in a stump or hollow tree. *Eggs*, six to ten, pale bluish, 2·40 × 1·70.

9

larger typeface: "While the few Robins that have the courage to winter with us are seeking protection from chilling winds in the depths of friendly evergreens, their comrades who extended their journey to the south are holding carnival under sunny skies."[11] Below her description of the Bobwhite Quail and a photo of a museum study skin, Bailey had a description of quails' lives in the spring and summer (another of Vernon's contributions).[12]

These two handbooks addressed people already interested in birds; other early guides spoke to those who lacked much knowledge but were attracted to nature or the Audubon movement. Bailey wrote her early books for them, as did Wright and Blanchan. The books spoke of bird-watching not as an introduction to science but the way into "a new world of interest and beauty" or a way to learn about our "bird neighbors."[13] In *Birds through an Opera-Glass* Merriam described some seventy eastern birds, mainly familiar sparrows and warblers, the Blue Jay, and the "Yellow Hammer: Flicker," leaving out twelve of the seventeen orders of birds, "the divers, all kinds of swimmers, waders, herons, cranes, parrots, and others that most of us never see outside of museums." Blanchan aimed to give the reader an "introductory acquaintance with one hundred and fifty of our common birds." *Birds of Village and Field* had about that number, but Merriam still focused on the ones genteel women could see in respectable places like parks.[14] She offered basic advice, some of which remains a staple of novice guides.[15] Readers were to "begin with the commonest birds. . . . Classify roughly at first,— the finer distinction will easily be made later." Sort the songs by those that have melody and tune and those that are "only monotonous trills." Use size to decide among species, taking the robin for a standard measure. Remember the different kinds of land where different birds may be found, and from there move on to remembering all the characteristics of any new bird—"its locality, size, color, details of marking, song, food, flight, eggs, nest, and habits"—and you will "come easily and naturally to know the birds that are living about you."[16] She introduced taxonomy only after describing a dozen species, and then only to answer the question of how anyone "could be expected to remember such a medley long enough to know the birds out of doors."[17] Her illustrations, small black-and-white wood engravings, decorated the pages but did not particularly help readers identify species.

The guides generally mixed moral sentiments and aesthetic reactions, for they presented birds in the context of the women's sphere of home and family, and even used birds to comment on people. Merriam called the robin "a domestic bird with a marked bias for society. Everything about him bespeaks the self-respecting American citizen . . . his sentiment is the wholesome every-day sort . . . full of contented appreciation of the beautiful world he lives in." Blanchan, meanwhile, spoke of bird-watching as a social obligation. "Not to have so much as a bowing acquaintance with the birds that nest in our gardens or under the very eaves of our houses, that haunt our wood-piles; keep our fruit-trees free from slugs; waken us with their songs, and enliven our walks . . . seems to be, at least, a breach of etiquette toward some of our most kindly disposed neighbors."[18] Moral standards applied in the bird's world as they did in human society. Blanchan spoke of the Mourning Dove as "a shy bird, attached to its gentle and refined mate with a devotion that has passed into a proverb," but the mate hardly deserved that devotion, for she was "a flabby, spineless bundle of flesh and feathers, gentle and refined in manners, but slack and incompetent in all she does."[19] The Cowbird, which left its eggs to be hatched by other birds, stood for the breakdown of family life. While Elliott Coues found its selection of smaller birds to foster its eggs "a wonderful provision for the perpetuation of the species," Merriam condemned it for "foist[ing] its offspring upon its neighbors," saying its behavior does "such violence to the one redeeming instinct of the lower types of man and beast that it is hard not to regard the bird with unqualified loathing." In *Birdcraft* (1895) Wright described the species as "the socialists among birds, and are like their human prototypes, who send their young to free kindergartens and mission schools that they may be fed and clothed at the expense of others, then drawing back, with their inherited principles unchanged."[20]

All associated the introduced House (or as it was called in those years the English) Sparrow (*Passer domesticus*) with the unwashed immigrants with whom it shared the city streets. Wright particularly lamented its effect on the Purple Martin, "unable to cope with [this bird, which was] steadily and persistently appropriating his houses. The Sparrow has the advantage of being more prolific, as well as more gross and brutal in its methods, and represents in the bird world a class of emigrants whose human prototypes the native American can hardly withstand."[21] There was a certain irony in Wright's describing her Puritan ancestors as "native American," but she seemed unconscious of it. Blanchan approvingly quoted H. E. Parkhurst's declaration that "no self-respecting ornithologist would condescend to enlarge his list with [the sparrow], too pestiferous to mention."[22] Predation they accepted, describing the Osprey as a hard-working fisherman and praising buteos like the Red-tailed Hawk as the farmers' friends for their diet of rodents. The Goshawk, Sharp-shinned, and Cooper's Hawks, on the other hand,

PLATE XXV. PURPLE FINCH.

1.4, 1.5 · *Grant's Purple Finch* · An early attempt to use photography for identification shows, more clearly than the bird, the limits of black and white photos of stuffed specimens for identification. From John B. Grant, *Our Common Birds and How to Know Them* (New York: Scribner's, 1891).

they regarded with horror, for they ate other birds. Merriam ended her description of the group in *Birds of Village and Field* by calling the Cooper's Hawk "the last of the three brigands of the family," and saying that "after following their gory records it is pleasant to turn to citizens of better repute." Wright, deeply committed to humane values, thought the Sharp-shinned Hawk "a worthy target for rifle practice."[23]

Other guides steered between science and sentiment, or included a dose of each, taking as their task introducing readers to common species. John B. Grant's book *Our Common Birds and How to Know Them*, for example, discussed ninety species found around the home and in city parks, in its descriptions emphasizing distinctive plumage patterns. For the "White-throated Sparrow," also identified by the local name "Peabody Bird," Grant offered: "Head with one central white stripe, then two black ones, and then two stripes which are yellow from bill to eye and white beyond; cheeks dark ash shading to white

PLATE XXV.—PURPLE FINCH.

Carpodacus purpureus.

Body crimson, paler on rump and belly; back streaked with brown; wings, brown, some of the feathers edged with reddish; tail, the same color as the wings, forked; bill conical, horn-color; feet brown. Length, 6.20 inches.

Resident. Nests in trees, sometimes rather high in the branches. It is difficult to say why this bird has been called purple. Dr. Coues writes: "The shade of red is very variable, almost anything but purplish." Mr. Burroughs has caught the purple tint; he says: "The color is peculiar, and looks as if it might have been imparted by dipping a brown bird in diluted pokeberry juice. Two or three more dippings would have made the purple complete."

The song of the Purple Finch is a charming one, which coupled with the gentle deportment and trustful and social disposition of the bird, renders it a general favorite.

During the breeding season it pairs; but after parental duties are over, it is generally seen only in small flocks.

109

- Grant gave readers the fundamentals for identification, a picture and a description.

- The limits of cameras and printing confined field guides to posed shots in black and white. This stuffed and mounted specimen gives little help in learning the plumage pattern of this small bird.

- Grant leaves out the American Ornithological Union number, giving the English-language name top billing.

- The text, like Chapman's following natural history works, begins with obvious characteristics but then wanders off into less useful material.

on the belly; back streaked with black, reddish-brown and pale yellow; rump ash; wings reddish-brown, with two transverse white bands; tail reddish-brown, slightly rounded; bill dark, feet lighter. Length 6.75 inches."[24] That hardly met modern standards, but it served the bird-watcher much better than Ridgway's *Manual*. For sixty-four of the birds Grant included four- by five-and-a-half-inch black-and-white pictures of a mounted specimen—which at least gave a rough idea of what the bird looked like. He gave the usual advice to beginners: dress in clothes suitable for the field, take a pocket notebook and a pair of binoculars, and in the summer at least, go out as early as possible. In the spring and fall midday may be good, and in winter sometimes best. Walk quickly in fields, where you will scare up birds; slowly in the woods, checking the treetops. To attract birds, try "sundry chirps and whistles," for birds responded to even poor chirping.[25] It had its flaws, but Ludlow Griscom received a copy in 1896, along with a pair of three-power field glasses, for his sixth birthday, and went on to become the dean of American birdwatchers.[26]

Merriam's second book, *Birds of Village and Field* (1898), followed Grant's format on a slightly higher level. She treated 154 birds, drawing on her "years of experience with field classes of . . . beginners," people who did not know a Crow or a Robin, boys interested in starting "bird-work," and teachers in "this increasingly popular branch of bird study." She presented "only necessary statistics from the ornithologies, giving untechnical descriptions, and illustrated keys based on such colors and markings as one can note in the field." She organized birds by categories such as "Red Conspicuous in Plumage," further broken down by the color of body, wings, and throat, and included two pages of wood engravings showing the patterns on the heads and breasts of the males of fourteen species of warblers in spring plumage and two more showing the heads of ten finches and sparrows.[27] Like other guide writers, she assumed people could tell a sparrow from a thrush, know if a bird was a hawk, oriole, blackbird, duck, or gull, and recognize some species on sight. That let her concentrate on diagnostic features. Only the Catbird, for example, appeared wholly gray and had a black cap above the eyes, while only the Indigo Bunting had its body entirely that color. Range and season helped as well. Knowing that the Scarlet Tanager bred "from southern Illinois and Virginia to Manitoba and New Brunswick" gave birdwatchers something to go on when they glimpsed a red bird in the forest in May.[28]

Although experienced birdwatchers often relied on calls and songs, neither Merriam nor other writers gave them much space, as they were hard to put them into print. The Ovenbird's call of "Teacher, teacher, teacher" identified it as clearly as its golden crown, and—given its retiring habits and forest home—more often. While it and some others, like the Bobwhite and the Whip-poor-will, had unmistakable notes that translated easily into words, most did not, and as Peterson noted a generation later, a "'sizzling trill' or a 'bubbling warble' conveys but a wretched idea of the real effect produced by the voice of any particular bird."[29] As early as the 1880s authors tried to represent calls by musical notes, and in 1904 F. Schuyler Mathews, in *Field Book of Wild Birds and*

Their Music, arranged the calls of 127 birds to his own system of notation and musical terms.[30] The book sold well enough that a revised and enlarged edition appeared in 1921. Even Mathews never tried to extend his system to all the birds, and he included seventy pages of color and black-and-white illustrations to supplement his descriptions of sounds.

None of the guides worked very well, but their deficiencies hardly mattered. Science could seem daunting, but in a society coming to see it as truth, putting the correct name on a bird gave the satisfaction of sharing at least a bit of the culture's authoritative knowledge. The catalog could make identifying a bird more difficult by giving a long list of species it might be but almost certainly was not, because of their ranges, but it had a satisfying air of completeness, and listing the birds had its own deep satisfactions. Many people felt the lure of the list and the pleasures of completing it. In a society where science was becoming academic, professional, objective, and materialist, the books spoke of an older scientific vision, the Humboldtian one that so occupied Henry David Thoreau in the last decade of his life. Facts led on to meaning, understanding linked together beautiful things, and the deep structures of nature might be glimpsed in small events—a thrush's song in the woods, a wren or phoebe's nest at the door.[31] A little advice and basic information did not make people experts but did encourage them to learn, and soon the parks were filled with people shooting birds with opera glasses.

Birdwatching's Roots in Human Nature and Victorian Culture

On one level, the rise of birdwatching is the story of a book that allowed urban Americans to engage the world around them, on another of an interest fueled by deep human drives and interests and guided by late Victorian elite culture. Field guides got people out to the parks, but they went back, took their friends, and formed bird study clubs because they had fun. At bottom, birdwatching appealed to humans' curiosity about the life of the world around them, an urge so common and strong that biologist E. O. Wilson believed it genetic and called it biophilia.[32] Most societies, anthropologists tell us, name between six hundred and a thousand different organisms, even if they place no particular value on nature or nature knowledge, and sort and arrange them in the same ways: mark off living things off from nonliving ones, plants from animals, divide animals into kinds by body shapes, make categories corresponding to birds, mammals, and reptiles, and commonly have a catchall category for small, squirmy, slimy things, what

Carolus Linnaeus, the father of Western taxonomy, put in the category "Vermes" (worms). This dividing of the world held as far down as the level Western science called the "species," so an ornithologist from New Jersey and a tribesman from New Guinea would categorize the birds they saw in the New Guinea forest in the same general way, even though they would call them by different names.[33]

Birds had unique advantages for an outdoor hobby. They could be seen anywhere and almost anytime; many had distinctive plumage; and some sang sweetly. In addition, they flew, which has fascinated people from ancient times to today. Small mammals hid, and large mammals were scarce; frogs and fish stayed in ponds and snakes in the grass; insects were small and, except for butterflies and moths, not very attractive. Plants just sat there, and when they bloomed it was usually for a short time. Birds' characteristics also made them easy to sort out, or at least easier than most organisms. They came in a small number of shapes. The roughly eight hundred species in North America fell into some three dozen families, and most people could recognize some, forms like thrushes and seagulls and jays, before they began birdwatching. Further simplifying identification, most individuals of a species, once out of the nest, looked much alike and were roughly the same size. These characteristics gave birdwatching one of the central attractions of any good game. It was easy to begin and impossible fully to master. Birdwatchers found many easy tests of skill, and as they achieved mastery, more challenging problems. Once they could name all the species, they could go on to seasonal plumages (many warblers were far more difficult to name in the fall than the spring), aberrant individuals, hybrids, or simply birds higher in the sky. If their enthusiasm for identification waned, they could take up some problem in bird behavior, become an expert on woodpeckers' food or warblers' nesting habits, even turn their hobby into field ornithology by writing for a local or regional journal.

Birdwatching had roots in nature and human nature but more immediately in culture. Listing birds by species represented natural history's devotion to gathering data and cataloging nature, and birdwatchers' interest in beauty and meaning represented natural history's inheritance from natural theology. While the pious search for the attributes of the Creator in the wonders of Creation faded in the early nineteenth century, a secular search for meaning took its place; natural history's great figure in the early nineteenth century, Alexander von Humboldt, combined a passion for quantification and rigor with the Romantic ideal of exploration and the search for beauty, and he inspired the collecting of

Charles Darwin and Alfred Russel Wallace, the landscape paintings of Frederic Church, and Thoreau's explorations of Concord.

Even as science became objective, professional, and, firmly grounded in materialism, dismissed the search for understanding and beauty in nature, Elliott Coues, even as he helped organize the AOU and formulate a rigorous avian taxonomy, could scorn the mere collector who "looks at Nature, and never knows that she is beautiful." The AOU held regular exhibits of bird art at its meetings and even included an article on progress in that field in its retrospective *Fifty Years Progress of American Ornithology, 1883–1933*.[34] Field guides would become banks of data, crammed with observations and free of emotional language, but, like Humboldtian naturalists, birdwatchers looked beyond the data. They still do. Kenn Kaufman, who began as bird-struck teenager in the 1970s, recalled a California birding guru who believed birds were "magical, and . . . searching after them was a Great Adventure . . . [with the list] just a frivolous incentive for birding."[35]

Birdwatching adopted the practice of keeping lists from the British amateur natural history movement of the early nineteenth century. Scientific knowledge conveyed through inexpensive handbooks allowed people to learn about the world at their own pace. The hobby offered a combination the Victorians found irresistible: self-improvement, piety, status, accumulation, and high-minded recreation. A few, including Wallace and Darwin, began as amateurs and forged careers in the field, but most stayed close to home physically and intellectually, taking advantage of the railroad's holiday excursion fares to go out with their local natural history society. Between 1830 and 1880, a series of popular collecting fads swept Britain, for flowers, birds' eggs, stuffed birds, minerals, seashells, beetles, butterflies, moths, ferns, and almost anything else that could be preserved and displayed or kept alive in garden, herbarium, terrarium, or aquarium.[36]

Birdwatching built on the American version of this movement but also, quite consciously, on the view of America as Nature's Nation, its wonders as a source of national pride and a touchstone of national identity. American bird studies began in the early nineteenth century with Alexander Wilson, a Scottish immigrant, who worked as a printer, peddler, and schoolteacher while gathering specimens and selling his books by subscription. The first volume of his *American Ornithology* appeared in 1808, the last two in 1813. He described 278 species, forty-eight new to science.[37] Thomas Nuttall, an English immigrant, traveled from northern New England to the Southeast and on through Arkansas Territory and the Rockies out to California and Hawaii to compile his *Ornithology of the United States and Canada* (1832, second edition 1840). It described roughly twice as many species as Wilson. Like his predecessor, Nuttall spoke of an expanding bird frontier. Of the "Arkansa [*sic*] Kingbird," now known as the Western Kingbird, he could only say: "We are indebted to Mr. Say, the well known naturalist, for the discovery of the recently known species of Flycatcher, which appears to inhabit all the region west of the Missouri River."[38]

New editions of Nuttall appeared, with new illustrations, into the 1890s, but the only name remembered today is that of John James Audubon, who painted all the species then known in North America. His four double-elephant folios, *Birds of America,* mingled art, science, bookmaking, and painting in 435 prints, showing all the species life-size (which required painting some of the larger species in contorted postures to fit them on even these pages) and in color. The smaller, octavo edition became America's first nature book best seller. Audubon spent thirteen years making these huge books, dividing his time between shooting and painting birds in the United States and supervising the production of prints in Britain. He painted every feather, and his printer reproduced his every detail, but the immediate popularity of the prints owed less to their faithfulness to life than their composition and his carefully cultivated legend of himself as an American frontiersman. Although he did not work from birds in life but from dead birds pinned to boards, his pictures seemed to give a window onto the American wilderness, offering a vicarious experience of the adventure of exploration and the pleasures of discovery. Mockingbirds defended their nest from a rattlesnake, Peregrine Falcons fed on ducks they had killed, a Bobwhite covey scattered before a hawk, and robins fed their nestlings.

The books, high art in the service of science, had to be made in London, as no American city had enough people skilled in the crafts needed to produce them.[39] An artist traced the lines of Audubon's original painting onto a sheet of paper; then a printer transferred them to a copper plate. Engravers cut the lines into the metal or etched them with acid, adding shading by another process involving heating powdered rosin on the plate and treating it again with acid. The printer inked the finished plate and ran it through the press to produce a black line print that watercolorists—Audubon's printer had fifty in his shop—filled in according to a master drawing. The result was exquisite art at exquisite prices. Audubon estimated it cost $115,640, in modern terms more than $2 million, to make 170 to 200 complete sets.[40] The smaller and less expensive octavo editions for the mass market used a new process, lithography: the lines of the painting were traced with crayon on a specially prepared stone, which was then treated with ink; the stone absorbed the ink only on the crayon marks, and a paper was pressed on the stone to make the image. Lithography did away with the difficult skilled labor of cutting lines into metal and allowed quick repairs, but each color still required its own stone and careful alignment of the paper. The process remained, at least for good-quality reproductions, too expensive for general use.[41]

Science supplanted Audubon's observations, but his art fixed him in popular memory as America's great bird painter, and the bird conservation movement found in him a symbol of a precious and vanishing wild America, helping to make nature preservation something close to a patriotic duty and the preservation of American history. Reformers campaigned for urban parks and national ones, an end to market hunting, and clean water for fishing—seen as a contemplative activity to escape society or bring back the joys of rural childhood. They went canoeing and camping as a way of returning to their ancestors' virtues and paying homage to them.[42] Men reproduced pioneer virtues in the chase and on the stream. Women and children could watch birds.

Sportsmen and naturalists began the campaign for bird protection, but women made it a mass movement and popular reform—with the field guide the reformers' primary recruiting tool. Bird protection developed as a reaction to the great slaughter of wildife in the two decades after the Civil War, when Americans took advantage of railroads and firearms to bring nature to market. The buffalo, shot for their hides, vanished in a generation, followed by the wolves that preyed on them, killed for bounties or fur. The flocks of Passenger Pigeons that darkened the skies over Audubon's America dwindled to a few birds, then one captive in the Cincinnati Zoo, finally to the specimens. Even today, you can open cabinet drawers in the back rooms of natural history museums and find them, their colors still bright and their feathers soft. Deer almost vanished east of the Mississippi, and many other species suffered less drastic fates or just disappeared without fanfare. In 1886 George Bird Grinnell, editor of the pioneer sportsman's journal *Forest and Stream*, called for a society for bird conservation, and within a year thirty-nine thousand people had pledged not to molest birds. He eventually abandoned the club as too great a drain on his time, but reform-minded women took up the cause, reframing it in domestic and patriotic terms. Saving songbirds meant saving the beauties of the country's homes and parks and spreading humane values, women's distinctive contributions to the public sphere. Interest was strongest in the Northeast and upper Midwest, among educated upper- and upper-middle-class women.[43] Harriett Hemenway rounded up the nucleus of the Massachusetts Audubon Society by paging through her copy of *The Boston Blue Book*, the city's social guide; Mabel Osgood Wright drew on her social circle to organize the Connecticut Audubon Society; and "over 200 of the leading women" of the city, members of the Chicago Women's Club, established an Audubon society there in 1897.[44] Scattered groups became a national presence. In 1899 Frank Chapman, curator of birds at the American Museum of Natural History in New York, founded the magazine *Bird-Lore* to print the movement's news as well as information about birds (it became National Audubon's official journal, renamed *Audubon*), and in 1905 the state organizations formed the National Association of Audubon Societies, usually referred to as Audubon.

Bird protection began with two great goals, saving songbirds and ending the slaughter of birds for feathers to decorate women's hats and dresses. Both were seen as women's unique contributions to the defense of home and family and an extension of their private virtues into public life. Scientists began the work through the AOU's Committee on the Protection of North American Birds, but women turned a discreet gentleman's lobbying campaign into a state-by-state crusade, and they prosecuted the campaign against commercial traffic in feathers for fashion, a demand that decimated many species.[45] Birds like the Snowy Egret suffered the most, for their long-shafted, white-feathered breeding plumes made dramatic accent pieces on hats, and their communal rookeries made them vulnerable.[46] Audubon presented horrible tales of starving nestlings dying under the hot sun as the bodies of their slaughtered parents drifted in the water below.[47] Humane values anchored the campaign, but Audubon appealed as well to social status. A 1903 article in *Bird-Lore* rejoiced that stuffed birds and wild bird feathers were now found only on the "wearer of the molted garments of her mistress" or the "'real loidy' who . . . with hat cocked over one eye, pink tie, scarlet waist, [and] sagging automobile coat . . . haunts the cheaper shops . . . and in summer rides a man's wheel, chews gum, and expectorates with seeming relish."[48]

Women who led the campaign for bird protection usually had money or family support. Mabel Osgood Wright, a clergyman's daughter, married a rare book dealer who shared her interest in nature, and she published nature essays in the New York papers that became her first book, *The Friendship of Nature* (1894). She founded Connecticut Audubon, established Birdcraft Sanctuary near her home in Fairfield, and became a member of the AOU in 1895.[49] Neltje Blanchan, like

Wright, had support, in her case her husband, Frank Doubleday, a publisher. Florence Merriam, sister of Clinton Hart Merriam, head of the federal Bureau of Biological Survey, established herself by writing several guides and became the AOU's first female associate member. She later married a Survey naturalist, Vernon Bailey, and they worked together as a scientific team. Besides guides, she wrote state ornithologies, authoritative summaries of information on all the species in a state.[50]

Reflecting the stronghold of women's reform, birdwatching's heartland ran along a line from Boston south to Washington, D.C., and west to the Mississippi. While all states eventually had state societies, the eighteen listed in the first volume of *Bird-Lore* were, with four exceptions, in New England, the Middle Atlantic, and the upper Midwest.[51] Field guides reflected this in their coverage. Readers in the East found a reasonable amount of information, and Houghton Mifflin found a large enough market to support Ralph Hoffman's guide to the birds of New England and eastern New York state, but the West received only passing attention. Reed devoted two volumes to the East and one to the West, which had more species and recognizable subspecies. Until Peterson's western guide in 1941, birdwatchers in that region had only Bailey's ornithologically oriented *Handbook* and, after 1927, Hoffman's *Birds of the Pacific States*, which did not cover the inland West.[52] Even the Audubon guides to western birds published after World War II omitted descriptions of species found in the East, forcing western readers to buy those volumes to supplement their own.

The combination of women's clubs and amateur nature study made birdwatching an individual but also a community activity, with outings a combination of competition, friendship, and informal instruction in the fine points of identification. Women's emphasis on home and neighborhood fit natural history's study of a local area, a home range known through the seasons and the years. That formed the basis of natural history's first literary classic, Gilbert White's *Natural History of Selbourne* (1787), and informed Thoreau's *Walden* and the essays of John Burroughs, "John o' the Birds," as popular in his lifetime as his contemporary John Muir, "John o' the Mountains." Bird-watching substituted neighborhoods and local parks for White's parish, Thoreau's Concord, and Burroughs's farm and added a national vision. That combination of a local range embedded within a larger whole still forms birdwatchers' understanding of the land.

Women also made birdwatching part of children's nature study, a program that served at once to recruit a new generation, teach it humane values, preach the virtues of rural America to the immigrant masses of the industrial cities, and make nature a central part of American identity. Educators embraced the program because it fit the prevailing educational dogma that children learned best when they studied what already interested them by working directly with it; teachers found material for lessons all around and field outings a useful break from indoor routine; and parents supported it to give their children contact with nature, or at least teach them that milk came from cows and not bottles. By 1900 most American states included nature study in the elementary schools, and the Audubon Society provided pamphlets and posters for the classroom, sponsored essay and birdhouse-building contests, published a children's section in *Bird-Lore*, and helped teachers set up Junior Audubon clubs.[53]

Birdwatching began with listing, which was to lead to sympathy with birds and so to bird conservation, but it also led toward a lifetime interest in nature. Nature study encouraged that, and Anna Botsford Comstock's *Handbook of Nature Study*, an extraordinarily popular and influential text—still used in its 1986 revision by home-schooling parents—showed the pattern that birdwatchers could follow.[54] Seeking to cultivate "in the children powers of accurate observation and to build up within them, understanding," her book described everything from plants to the sky, the wild and the tame, in open-ended lessons that began with the familiar, led to the unknown, and could be followed as far as the student wished.[55] Birdwatchers had books—in that generation Comstock or the smaller, less organized nature guides, after World War II the Peterson Field Guides—and action, from putting up a bird feeder in the backyard to helping band birds to, in the last thirty years, working on scientist-citizen projects. A general interest in nature, focused by birdwatching, led to lifetime study and action.

Beyond giving people a simple and enjoyable activity in nature and encouraging conservation, field guides made birdwatching a competitive and self-competitive game.[56] This element, until the environmental revolution of the 1960s the more visible part of the hobby, encouraged the cultivation of identification as a craft skill, which gave field guides an instrumental function that has shaped their form down to the present day. The early guides encouraged people by showing how common birds could be identified but offered no systematic help in eliminating possibilities. Was the Harrier the *only* soaring bird with white at the base of the tail? How many warblers had yellow on their bellies, and was a lack of yellow ever diagnostic? To flourish, the hobby needed a guide that helped newcomers in their first, confusing days in the field, gave advanced students a firm sense of what could be known on sight, and addressed problems in identification. Many years and books, though, lay between *Birds through an Opera-Glass* and the first edition of Peterson's *Field Guide to the Birds.* The next two chapters cover that period, first taking up the early guides that consciously tackled the problems of helping birdwatchers in the field and the growth of a community devoted to field identification, then relating how a part of that community, determined to know all the birds, found the information and methods Peterson put into a book for the masses.

TWO

A Book for a Hobby, 1889–1920

The illustrations . . . are designed to aid
the student in identifying birds in their haunts
by giving, in color, those markings which
most quickly catch the eye. They do not pretend
to be perfect reproductions . . . but aim
to present a bird's characteristic colors as they
appear when seen at a distance.

—FRANK CHAPMAN (1903)

Chapman arranged the birds in taxonomic order, which often grouped similar species, and the arrangement of six or eight species to a two-page spread made it easy to compare them at a glance.

These line drawings, all done by Chester Reed, were colored in blocks, which cut production costs but also, as Chapman realized, showed the birds as people saw them, not feather by feather but as blocks of color.

Woodpeckers.

402. Yellow-bellied Sapsucker (*Sphyrapicus varius*). L. 8.5; W. 4.8. *Ad.* ♂. Crown and throat red; a *whitish* band from eye to eye across nape; belly washed with yellow; breast patch black. *Ad.* ♀. Similar, but throat white; crown rarely black. *Yng.* Breast grayish with internal dark rings or bars; crown dirty yellowish margined with dusky; red feathers soon appear on throat and crown. *Notes.* A clear ringing *cleur* repeated; a low snarling cry resembling *mew* of Catbird. (Brewster.)

Range.—Eastern North America; breeds from Massachusetts and northern Illinois north to about Lat. 63° 30'; south in Alleghanies to northwest Georgia; winters from southern Illinois and southern Virginia to Central America.

402a. Red-naped Sapsucker (*S. v. nuchalis*). Similar to No. 402, but slightly larger. W. 5; the nape band *red*; red of throat encroaching on black bordering streaks; female the same but chin white.

Range.—Rocky Mountain region; breeds from Colorado and northeastern California (?), north to British Columbia; winters from southern California south to northwestern Mexico.

403. Red-breasted Sapsucker (*Sphyrapicus ruber*). L. 9. *Ads.* Crown, whole throat and *breast* dull red; in other respects resembling No. 402. *Notes.* Jay or *chaē, peeye, pinck, and peurr*. (Bendire.)

Range.—Breeds in mountains from northern Lower California north to southern Oregon.

403a. Northern Red-breasted Sapsucker (*S. r. notkensis*). Similar to No. 403, but colors deeper, red brighter; belly yellower.

Range.—Pacific coast region from Santa Cruz Mountains, California, north to southern Alaska.

404. Williamson Sapsucker (*Sphyrapicus thyroideus*). L. 9. Belly *bright* yellow; rump white. *Ad.* ♂. Above black; a red stripe on throat; lesser wing-coverts white. *Ad.* ♀. Crown and throat brownish; back and lesser wing-coverts barred black and whitish. *Yng.* Similar to ♀, but breast barred like sides. *Notes.* A shrill *huit-huit* uttered when flying. (Bendire.) The roll of this Woodpecker is not continuous, but is broken or interrupted.

Range.—Higher mountain ranges of western United States; breeds from northern New Mexico, Arizona, and southeastern California north to Wyoming and southern British Columbia; winters from southern California and western Texas into Mexico.

408. Lewis Woodpecker (*Asyndesmus torquatus*). L. 11. *Ads.* Breast and a collar around the neck gray; region about base of bill dark red; belly pinkish red; above shining green black. *Yng.* No gray collar; crown suffused with red. *Notes.* A weak peeping twitter. (Lawrence.) Generally a silent bird.

Range.—Western United States; breeds from New Mexico, Arizona, and southern California north to southern Alberta and British Columbia; winters from southern Oregon and Colorado south to western Texas and southern California.

152

2.1 · *Chapman's woodpeckers* · For a bird book of 1903, a very modern look, text and pictures together, and the birds in color. Frank M. Chapman, *Color Key to North American Birds* (New York: Doubleday, Page, 1903).

406. Red-headed Woodpecker (*Melanerpes erythro-cephalus*). L. 9.7. *Ads.* Whole head and breast red; end half of secondaries white. *Yng.* Whole head and breast grayish streaked with blackish; back black margined with grayish; end half of secondaries white with black bars. *Notes.* A tree-toad-like *ker-r-ruck, ker-r-ruck.*

Range.—Eastern United States west to Rocky Mountains; breeds from Florida and Texas north to New York and Manitoba; local and irregular in northern parts of range; winters from Virginia, and occasionally from New York, southward.

407. Striped-breasted Woodpecker (*Melanerpes formicivorus*). L. 9.5. Breast band *streaked with white*; rump white. *Ad.* ♂. Forehead, white, *crown*, nape, and breast-spot red. *Ad.* ♀. Center of crown with a black band of *same* width as white band on forehead. *Notes.* A loud *tchurr, tchurr.*

Range.—Mexico north to southwest Texas and Arizona.

407a. Californian Woodpecker (*M. f. bairdi*). Similar to No. 407, but black breast-band with white only on its posterior margin.

Range.—Pacific coast region from northern California to southern Oregon.

407b. Narrow-fronted Woodpecker (*M. f. angust-ifrons*). *Ad.* ♂. Similar to No. 407, but smaller, W. 5.2; the throat brighter yellow. *Ad.* ♀. With black crown-band *wider* than white forehead band.

Range.—Cape Region of Lower California.

409. Red-bellied Woodpecker (*Centurus carolinus*). L. 9.5. Center of belly reddish. *Ad.* ♂. Top of head and nape entirely red. *Ad.* ♀. Nape red, crown grayish, forehead tinged with red. *Notes.* A hoarse, *chûh-chûh.*

Range.—Eastern United States, west to the Plains; breeds from Florida and Texas to Maryland, Ontario, and South Dakota; winters from Virginia and southern Ohio southward; casually north as far as Massachusetts.

410. Golden-fronted Woodpecker (*Centurus auri-frons*). L, 10.5; center of belly yellow. *Ad.* ♂. Forehead yellow, crown-patch red, nape orange. *Ad.* ♀. Forehead and nape yellow, crown entirely gray. *Notes.* Loud and penetrating. (Bailey.)

Range.—Mexico, north to central Texas.

411. Gila Woodpecker (*Centurus uropygialis*). L. 10. Center of belly yellow. *Ad.* ♂. Top of head and nape *sooty* gray; a red-crown patch. *Ad.* ♀. Top of head and nape entirely sooty gray. *Notes. Dchûrr, dchûrr;* when flying, a shrill *huit* like call-note of Phainopepla. (Bendire.)

Range.—Northwestern Mexico, north to southwestern New Mexico, and Lower California.

153

406.

407.

409.

410.

411

C.A.REED

Science shaped the entries, from the AOU numbers for the birds to the scientific symbols for the sexes, but the English-language names took precedence.

Chapman moved toward the birdwatchers and away from the naturalists by drastically shortening descriptions, leaving out things that could not be seen in the field; however, range and season, which quickly became central to identification, still appear at the end in small type.

The books described in the previous chapter got people into the field and helped them identify familiar birds and some new ones, but others from the same years aimed more directly to give them the information they needed in a format that met their needs. These pointed the way toward the modern guide, a book aimed solely at field identification. These included the most popular books of the pre-Peterson era, Chester Reed's three pocket-sized volumes: two covering eastern species—*Water Birds, Game Birds, and Birds of Prey,* and *Land Birds East of the Rockies from Parrots to Bluebirds*—and one for the areas west of the Great Plains, *Western Bird Guide: Birds of the Rockies and West to the Pacific,* all three published privately before 1910 and by commercial presses thereafter. There were two others, in more usual sizes, Frank Chapman's *Color Key to North American Birds* and Ralph Hoffman's *Guide to the Birds of New England and Eastern New York.*[1] Reed's, at three and a half by five and a half inches, had tiny pictures and minimal text but showed all the birds in the region. *Color Key,* which steered between Chapman's ornithologically based *Handbook* and his more elementary book, *Bird-Life,* put text and pictures together, used drawings colored in large blocks to show distinctive patterns, and often put similar species on the same page. Hoffman's handsome production, about the size of Peterson's guides but a bit thicker, looked like a book for the study, with its bright blue cover and gilding on title and cover illustration; had the same old-fashioned format Merriam employed in *Birds of Village and Field*—technical descriptions for each species given in small type and a more discursive section in a larger font below; and used some of the wood engravings of birds' heads from that work. All his text, though, dealt with identification and gave information in a standard order, beginning with the seasons when the species could be seen and its range in the region, moving on to habitat, habits, and calls, and ending with distinguishing marks, which were printed in italics. It offered something new: information arranged to answer the birdwatchers' common questions in roughly the order posed in the process of identification. With these volumes, the field guide advanced beyond vague encouragement and toward a systematic presentation of information for the hobby.

This chapter examines the guides, the process of identification they fostered, and birdwatching's emerging approach to nature. Making a book that helped people name the birds required choosing information, arranging it for easy reference in the field, and integrating text and pictures. That required compromises, for the guide had to serve every step as the reader moved from sighting to checkmark: deciding what kind of bird it was (a vireo or a kinglet), separating similar species (Cooper's or Sharp-shinned Hawk), and checking for diagnostic features (did those breast stripes mean it had to be a Palm Warbler?), range or habitat (would a Double-crested Cormorant be here at this time of year?). An arrangement that helped at one step might hinder the next. None of the guides considered here found a perfect or even a complete solution, but each had virtues that later guides adapted. Reed filled birdwatchers' first need, a comprehensive catalog for the area that was portable. But the pictures were tiny and the descriptions sketchy, comparing similar species required flipping back and forth, and size and format made that a little awkward. *Color Key* made it easy to compare similar species but included a lot of information for ornithologists and was designed for the shelf, not the pocket. Hoffman's book was easier to carry, but its main recommendation was an organization and approach that followed birdwatchers' mental sorting processes. The illustrations were of little help, and comparing similar species required, as with Reed, flipping through the pages.

The guides made their way in a market and a community that was still developing and experimenting. To put names on the birds, guides and birdwatchers alike turned to natural history's guide to the perplexed, the dichotomous key; but identification, to the frustration of generations of novices, could not be reduced to a rule. It remained a craft knowledge, a skill that could be described but had to be learned in the field. During these years birdwatching became for many a game, an activity separate from conservation, nature study, or nature appreciation. Field guides played a role here, establishing and passing on the rules of the game and helping form a national community of competitors and friends, whose growing knowledge shaped the next generation of watchers and books.

Birders recognize this layout, an array of species allowing quick comparison, though Seton, a naturalist, emphasized science, not recreation, in his article.

These showed patterns seen in flight, the bird-watchers' great need for birds overhead, where color was often misleading.

Published as part of a scientific article, this lacked the title a field guide would have used, either here or on the facing page.

The use of numbers by the drawings and a key below kept production costs down, but field guides would put the names by the birds.

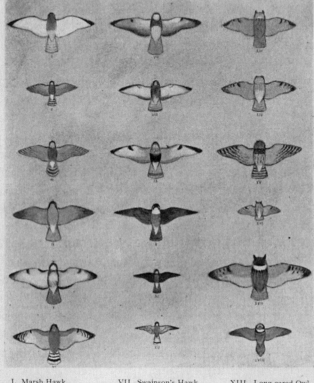

I. Marsh Hawk.	VII. Swainson's Hawk.	XIII. Long-eared Owl.
II. Sharp-shinned Hawk.	VIII. Broad-winged Hawk.	XIV. Short-eared Owl.
III. Cooper's Hawk.	IX. Rough-legged Hawk.	XV. Barred Owl.
IV. Goshawk.	X. Duck Hawk.	XVI. Screech Owl.
V. Red-tailed Hawk.	XI. Pigeon Hawk.	XVII. Horned Owl.
VI. Red-shouldered Hawk.	XII. Sparrow Hawk.	XVIII. Hawk Owl.

While Reed's, Chapman's, and Hoffman's guides strayed into science and sentiment, they aimed primarily to help readers put the right names on what they saw. Reed's books dominated the market, largely because they were complete, small, and inexpensive. They fit into a shirt pocket, and while they did not, despite Reed's promise, do away with the need to write down the bird's "peculiarities and markings" for reference back home, they gave help on the spot.[2] Reed had material on taxonomy and included technical terms, but only in the introduction, where one page showed the "topography of a bird," labeled with specialized but useful terms like scapulars and tertials, and other pages gave the "Characteristics of Form or Habit That Will Determine to What order or Family Birds Belong." In the rest of the book, readers found accounts of all the birds of the region. The eastern volumes gave each species its own page; in the western one, there were often pairs on a page. On the outer edge, a postage-stamp-sized color reproduction of one of Reed's oil paintings showed the species in its habitat; the rest of the page was filled with a description headed by the bird's official English-language name and number and the scientific name, all from the AOU list, then notes on call, nest, and range. In a bow to natural history, recently extinct species appeared in their proper taxonomic places. Reed showed the Great Auk, last seen in 1844, on its island home, and wrote of its having been "killed in countless numbers . . . for food, and in some cases merely for the love of slaughter." Another page memorialized the Labrador Duck, "extinct before anyone realized" it was in trouble.[3] The pictures did not always help. Portraits of shorebirds on the sand, warblers in the trees, and hawks perched on tree limbs failed to highlight distinctive marks. Some ducks stood on shore, hardly a characteristic pose, and the Caspian Tern and the Nighthawk appeared in the air but in contorted positions. Text varied from helpful to useless. Under the Redhead readers were told to "note the shape of the bill as compared to that of the similarly colored Canvas-back"; while the page on the American Egret said that "the hand of man, to gratify the desire of woman, has ruthlessly slaughtered thousands upon thousands of these exquisitely beautiful birds"; and the page for the "Snowy Heron" (Snowy Egret) told the story of Guy Bradley, an Audubon warden who was killed while protecting these birds' rookeries from poachers.[4]

2.2 · *Seton's raptors* · These pattern drawings showing birds' "uniforms," the inspiration for Peterson's plates, come from Ernest Thompson Seton, "Directive Color of Birds," *Auk* 14 (Oct. 1897): 395–96. Compare this plate with Peterson's hawks, shown in chapter four.

Reed had an old-fashioned approach but an up-to-date business model. He and his father published his guides as part of a series in a uniform format that included such popular topics as flowers, birds' eggs, mushrooms, and "Nature Studies—In Field and Wood," a general introduction to common flowers and animals "one finds during a ramble," as well as something new, "Camera Studies" of wild birds. The bird books came in two editions, clothbound for the field (50 cents per volume in 1906) and leather-bound for the study (75 cents). The Reeds sold to the public through advertisements in magazines like *Bird-Lore*, but they had other outlets. The Audubon societies used them for the Junior Audubon Clubs—Roger Peterson got one in the seventh grade, his first guide—and the Boy Scouts for a merit badge in ornithology. The Reeds also sold other useful material. Ads in the back of one bird guide touted a set of forty colored bird pictures, three by four inches, "USED IN SCHOOLS for compositions and decorations. ONE CENT EACH in lots of ten or more," and a pair of three-power binoculars chosen after examining "more than a hundred makes of field glasses" to find those best "adapted for bird study," offered for $5.[5] The books sold well from the first, and even before the western volume appeared in 1913 the Reeds licensed the eastern ones to Doubleday. As late as World War II, commercial publishers were still considering revised editions.

These books' long life was not unusual. Publishers made their money from field guides, as they had from popular natural history, by selling the same book for many years, and they often kept a series, with occasional revisions, in print for decades. Schools were an important market. Elementary school nature study courses used Reed's books, while college instructors assigned Chapman's eastern handbook and Bailey's western one.[6] A few publishers dominated this steady but unspectacular niche market. Houghton Mifflin, which brought out the original edition of Merriam's *Birds through an Opera-Glass,* stood out for its continuing interest and strength. Beginning with Merriam and Hoffman, it went on to the Peterson guides (in print from 1934 to the present) and the Peterson series, begun in the late 1940s, now grown to some four dozen books and finding new media and formats.

Unlike Reed's books, Chapman's *Color Key* and Hoffman's *Guide to the Birds of New England and Eastern New York* helped readers sort through the possibilities. The former experimented with text, illustrations, and their arrangement; the latter arranged information to help readers systematically eliminate some species and look for diagnostic features on the others. Chapman wrote the *Color Key* in response to the "recent remarkable interest in the study of birds which, fostered by

Audubon Societies and nature study teachers, has assumed an ethical and educational importance of the first magnitude."[7] He meant it for birdwatchers, though enthusiasts used his other works. Peterson graduated from the Reed guides to Chapman's *Handbook,* and George Sutton, ornithologist and bird artist, had a copy of Chapman's introductory *Bird-Life,* more about birds than identification, which he "looked at every day, and quite literally wore out."[8] *Color Key* had as "its sole end . . . identification of the bird in the bush."[9] It did away with stories, accounts of birds' lives and—except in the introductory thirty-page "Synopsis of Orders and Families"—ornithology. Useful phrases replaced formal language, for example: "761. [AOU checklist number] American Robin (*Merula migratoria*). L[ength]. 10; W[ing]. 4.9; T[ail]. 3.8. Outer tail-feathers with white tips. Ad[ult male] Breast and belly rich rust-brown; above dark slaty, head and spots in back black. [Adult female] Similar but paler below, little or no black above."[10] That stripped ornithological descriptions to the bare bones but, more important, gave readers information they could use in the field. *Color Key* grouped six to eight birds on a two-page spread, most in taxonomic order, and arranged the more numerous families of perching birds by color. Since related birds often looked alike, that brought similar species together. Pictures marched down the outside edge of the pages, text within, allowing readers to see everything without turning the page.

Chapman took a new approach to illustrations in *Color Key*. Instead of reproductions of fine art, natural history's feather-by-feather drawings, or photographs of museum specimens or stuffed birds, he used line drawings (by Chester Reed), colored without shading, not to save money—though it did—but to help "the student in identifying birds in their haunts by giving, in color, those markings which most quickly catch the eye. They do not pretend to be perfect representations . . . but aim to present a bird's characteristic colors as they appear when seen at a distance."[11] He did not invent the form; that came from the naturalist, writer, and artist Ernest Thompson Seton, who published an article in *Auk* in 1897 titled "Directive Coloration in Birds," illustrated with a plate of eighteen hawks arranged in the same pose on a neutral background, painted in large blocks of color. Four years later Chapman made this available to amateurs by publishing Seton's "Recognition Marks of Birds" in *Bird-Lore,* with the same plate.[12] The format passed into the field guide a generation later in Roger Tory Peterson's work.[13]

The *Color Key* raised questions birdwatchers and guide authors have debated ever since: what kind of illustrations work best for a field guide, and how can their numbers best be balanced against the cost. Field guides, after all, have to be affordable. Photos, paintings, and drawings all had virtues but also drawbacks. Field guides needed inexpensive pictures that showed birds' markings as they appeared at a distance, and *Color Key*'s block-colored line drawings pointed toward that.[14] Translating the principle to the page, though, called for a new kind of art work and printing methods that yielded higher quality at lower cost.

Some early guides opted for a few, exquisite illustrations. Chapman used mainly line drawings in his *Handbook*, then went to the other extreme with *Bird-Life*, first using full-page, black-and-white drawings by Ernest Thompson Seton and in later printings "photographic bromide copies of the original[s] . . . colored by an expert under the author's supervision and . . . reproduced by lithography."[15] Mabel Osgood Wright used color photoreproductions from Audubon and other artists to show the 166 species in *Birdcraft*. The images had to be done on a different paper, ink, and press than the text and the pages sewn in as the book was assembled. That meant few plates, and as a result individual pictures on each plate were small. Wright complained about the quality. The "highly coloured plates are very well done but the neutral tinted ones are too bright. So I have compromised on 19 coloured plates and 3 in black and white as it expressed the gulls so much more clearly than pink and blue attempts at gray." She had had "some of the more nasty colors done in halftones," but still "the Wrens look as if they had taken a bath in ginger tea, and the female tanager was wrongly marked."[16] Others apparently agreed, for a reviewer was pleased to note that in the new edition, "the very poor colored plates . . . [have been] replaced with life-like black and white drawings."[17]

Most authors wanted as many illustrations as possible, even if they were not the highest quality. For that they turned to wood engravings, a variant of the woodcut, popular in the eighteenth century for natural history and revived in the nineteenth. It involved tracing a picture onto the end grain (rather than, as for a woodcut, the plank side) of a block of dense wood and carving away the surface to leave raised lines on a block. A skilled carver could quickly produce a block that could be put in the printer's form and printed in the same pass as the text letters, advantages that made it the newspapers' favorite method from the Civil War until the 1880s, when photoreproduction displaced it. Natural history books continued to use wood engravings for their low cost and good detail, and blocks used in one book often appeared in another. Merriam used them as decorations in *Birds through an Opera-Glass*, and then to show plumage patterns in *Birds of Village and Field*, and Hoffman used some of her blocks in his guide.[18]

Others turned to photographs of birds, printed by photoreproduction technology, but cameras could not capture good pictures of live birds in the field. Authors turned to dead ones. Bailey included shots of museum specimens in *Handbook of Birds of the Western United States*, possibly the least useful approach, for one dead bird on its back with feet and beak in the air looked much like any other. Mounted, stuffed specimens gave some idea of living birds, but taxidermists paid little attention to the way different birds stood, and the patterns, Seton's "uniforms," did not show up well in black and white, even when the photographer chose a good view. Neltje Blanchan included fifty-two full-page color pictures in *Bird Neighbors* by posing stuffed and mounted birds in front of out-of-focus backgrounds. They gave the book a handsome air, but the Red-winged Blackbird stood on one foot on a branch, and it and the Crow looked as if they had been dipped in shoe polish. Printing technologies of 1900 did not serve the field guide well. Chapman's block colorings were, for that generation, state of the art.

Birdwatchers needed pictures, but also other information, and Hoffman organized his *Guide to the Birds of New England and Eastern New York* to help them. With its large blocks of text, wood engravings of birds' heads, color key for the common land birds, and advice—opera glasses were "almost indispensable, a field notebook "indispensable"; bring a handbook to check details on the spot—it looked much like other early guides. The entries had the same form as Merriam's *Birds of Village and Field*, a two-line physical description in small type, followed by a longer section in larger print. Where she had stories and observations, though, he gave "short descriptions with particular reference to their appearance in the field." Each entry began by telling where the bird could be found in the region, at what time of year, and how common and abundant it was. The White-Breasted Nuthatch, for example, was "a permanent resident of southern and central New England and the lower Hudson Valley and a summer resident throughout New England and New York; the Cliff Swallow, or Eave Swallow as it was called then, was "a summer resident of New England and New York, arriving about the first of May, and leaving early in September." Habitat followed: the Pileated Woodpecker was found only in areas "that are still heavily forested," while the White-eyed Vireo "frequents tangled thickets, particularly in the lowlands." Then came behavior and habits, and at the end a review of helpful characteristics. The Brown Thrasher could be "readily told by the *reddish-brown* color of its upper parts and by its long tail," and the meadowlark had a distinctive way of flying—a few strokes, a short sail on outstretched wings, and repeat—as well as white outer tail feathers. Hoffman wove together the various clues of body, voice, behavior, and habitat birdwatchers used to make the first guide organized for field identification.[19]

Between Hoffman's systematic approach and the ornithologists' equally organized information lay the divide separating scientists and hobbyists. Both identified birds, but by different means for different ends. The scientists used form, primarily, to place specimens in a taxonomic system that, ideally, mirrored the relations of descent; birdwatchers used characteristics visible at a distance—form, plumage, and behavior—and in the environment (habitat and season) to put a name on an individual bird. The scientists used taxonomy as an analytical tool to organize birds, including the fossils in the rocks; the amateurs followed the professionals in their parsing of differences down to the level of the subspecies, but only to get the right name for the checklist. They had no interest in the birds in the rocks. Birdwatchers in that generation worked out ways to know all the birds, but they cared little for variations among species—a burning scientific question at that time— unless these could be reliably picked out in the field. Their principle concern as a community was the development and handing on of the craft knowledge of identification. Differences were greatest in this generation, for birdwatching began just as the ornithologists largely finished cataloging the continent's bird life and turned from the field to the laboratory to ask new questions about avian physiology. In subsequent years, as scientists turned again to living birds and their populations, ornithologists acquired the birdwatchers' skills, then began making use of birdwatchers' data.

In their different ways, Reed's little *Bird Guides,* Chapman's *Color Key,* and Hoffman's *Guide* pointed toward birdwatching as a game, distinct from but related to nature study, ornithology, conservation, and humane values. That view shaped birdwatching from the start but by the 1920s came to define it. Birdwatchers paid little heed to the admonitions to carry notebooks and record their observations. Reed's books, with their promise of doing away with the need for "copious notes of all the peculiarities and markings of the bird" and "on our return home [getting] down our bird books [and] carefully looking through the whole library," fit people's needs. They wanted to be able to identify birds when they saw them, preferably by looking them up in a book they could put in their pockets.[20] Chapman tackled the problem of presenting and arranging information to allow easy comparison of plumage patterns of similar species, and Hoffman that of assembling the clues from bird and environment. Here began the making of guides useful for birdwatching as a game, but these first efforts only went part way. *Color Key* included a good deal of ornithology and taxonomy, and it and Hoffman's guide had keys—Chapman's an elaborate color system for the perching birds, Hoffman's tables arranged by color and season, though Chapman did move the ornithology to the front, and Hoffman exiled the keys to the back. Reed's text was often sentimental and discursive, and it included extinct species. His illustrations were more portraits, sometimes poorly posed, than examples of what was seen in the field. The books' failings stemmed largely from the unformed state of the art: no one knew how to identify all the birds by sight or could even be sure it could be done, and no one knew how to put together a book that really helped readers identify even the species that could be known.

Identifying Birds with a Book

Everyone realized that a truly useful guide had to be systematic, and early authors almost always adapted a familiar tool from natural history, the dichotomous key, a form that posed questions that could be answered with a yes or a no (hence the term "dichotomous"). Each answer eliminated one set of possibilities and led to another question, until all but one was eliminated. Keys, developed to allow inexperienced people identify what they saw, served amateurs and experts alike in natural history's great project of cataloging the world's life. People in scientifically unexplored countries like Australia or the United States could find out whether their specimens were new or known to science. If new, they might gain the minor scientific immortality of having their name as part of a Latin binomial on the new species. Ornithologists relied on keys. Coues, recall, titled his book *Key to North American Birds*, and he included an artificial key (that is, one based on characteristics not clearly related to taxonomic classification) to help amateurs sort out orders, suborders, and families. Ornithologists' keys, though, did not serve birdwatchers well. Merriam found in Ridgway's *Manual* a mass of information, most of which she did not need and no quick way to find what she did need. The use, and failure, of keys in birdwatching highlighted the novelty of this new recreation and the difficulties of identification.

Field guide authors adapted natural history's keys by substituting visible characteristics, such as size and color, for the measurements that served taxonomy and descriptions of birds in the bush for those in the hand. They also limited keys to the larger and possibly more confusing families, leaving it to readers to deal with the smaller groups. In *Birds*

CHIPPING SPARROW.

560. *Spizella passerina.* 5¼ inches.

Crown chestnut; forehead black; line through the eye black.

One of the commonest and most useful of our Sparrows, frequenting orchards, yards and bushy pastures. They are not at all timid and frequently nest in vines, covering porches or the side of the house, provided that English Sparrows are not too plenty. They eat great quantities of insects and worms, and some seeds, feeding their young wholly upon the former.

Song.—A very rapidly chanted chip, chip, chip, chip, continued for several seconds; call, a sharp chip.

Nest.—A small cup-shaped structure of rootlets, lined with horsehair; placed in bushes, trees or vines; eggs three to five, bluish green, specked, chiefly around the large end, with blackish brown (.65 x .50).

Range.—N. A. east of the Plains, breeding from the Gulf of Mexico north to Newfoundland and Hudson Bay; winters in the Gulf States. A sub-species is found west of the Rockies.

100

2.3 · *Reed's sparrows* · Reed's shirt-pocket-sized books were easy to carry but not focused on identification. Peterson's first guide quickly replaced them. From Chester A. Reed, *Bird Guide: Part Two, Land Birds East of the Rockies from Parrots to Bluebirds* (1906; reprint, New York: Doubleday, Page, 1912).

through an Opera-Glass Merriam divided birds into three groups by size—smaller than a robin (broken into three subcategories: less than half as large, half as large, more than half as large); about the same size as a robin; and larger—then into color categories, including "striking or bright," "dull or plain," and "brilliant males changing to dull colors of females in the autumn." She also gave lists of birds that might be found "about or near houses," "in gardens or orchards," or in fields and meadows, bushes and clearings, woods, or the edges of woods, and of birds that sang on the wing, had "marked habits," walked rather than hopped, or flocked when not nesting.[21] Knobel's *Field Key* divided 150 land birds by size, then plumage: gay, not speckled, and speckled. Chapman, a museum curator and taxonomist, had many keys. The appendix to his *Handbook* included "A Field Key to our Commoner Eastern Land Birds," based on color, "the most tangible character." He

CLAY-COLORED SPARROW.

561. *Spizella pallida.* 5½ inches.

No reddish brown in the plumage; crown largely black, with a whitish stripe in centre. The habits of these birds are the same as those of the Chippy; they are abundant on the Plains north to Saskatchewan and breed south to the northern portion of the United States. They spend the winter in Mexico. Their nests and eggs cannot be distinguished from those of the preceding, except, perhaps, by the fact that the nest has more grass than hair.

BREWER SPARROW.

562. *Spizella breweri.* 5½ inches.

Like the last species, the general tone of plumage of this is gray. It differs, though, in having the crown finely streaked with blackish. It is a more western species than the last and is rarely found east of the Rockies. It ranges from British Columbia southward into Mexico.

101

- This layout kept picture and text together, but the awkward proportions made it difficult to flip pages quickly in the field to compare species.

- The pictures are photoreproductions of Chester Reed's oil portraits, showing species in their habitats. They were attractive but did not emphasize what birdwatchers needed for identification.

- The AOU number remains, but in other respects Chapman moved toward modern practice. The text remains a mixture of identifying characteristics, including what we would now call "field marks," and comments on the birds.

- The common Chipping Sparrow got the full treatment, but the Clay-Colored and Brewer's Sparrows, living far from most of Reed's readers, only a once-over.

modified this for *Bird-Life* by omitting water birds, hawks, and owls (which people could presumably recognize by form) and giving other groups: birds feeding on the wing for long periods, climbing and creeping birds. He divided the others by color—yellow or orange; red; blue; black or black and white—with a category for those not in any of the others. *Color Key* had seven groups for the perching birds: red; blue; orange or yellow; reddish brown or chestnut; brownish and generally streaked; those without prominent marks; and those with gray, black, or black-and-white plumage.[22] Wright, who consulted Chapman while writing *Birdcraft*, took his system but divided land birds into nine categories, five by color (red or orange; blue; yellow; black, dusky or dark gray; brown or brownish), four by behavior or season: "Daintily plumed small birds feeding about the branches and terminal shoots of trees; Tree-creeping birds of various sizes, seen upon the trunks and branches, feeding upon bark insects; winter birds of meadow and uplands; birds of the air, constantly on the wing, feeding as they fly."[23] Within groups Wright did not give choices but just described each species. Merriam scattered keys to the various families through *Birds of Village and Field* and put others, developed from her years of teaching field classes of beginners, at the end.[24]

For a variety of reasons keys never caught on. The scientists regarded them as mere stopgaps. Chapman said the key in his *Handbook* was "designed simply as an aid to the first steps of the beginner, who will soon graduate from it to the more detailed keys in the body of the book," that is, to ornithological taxonomy. Bailey saw the color key in her western *Handbook* as only to be used until readers mastered taxonomic nomenclature and scientific organization. The use of a key "by any one who has skins to consult is earnestly deprecated, as it is much better to work a little harder and learn more—to begin at the beginning, with 'Keys to Orders,' and follow through to the species, so learning something of the classification of birds, something of their fundamental relations, rather than to find their mere names arbitrarily by the use of purely superficial characters."[25] Most people, though, did not have access to museum specimens, and many birdwatchers did not want to use keys. Joseph Grinnell, head of the Museum of Vertebrate Zoology at the University of California, Berkeley, told Bailey her western *Handbook* had more than people wanted. "From my own experience, I do not believe that the ordinary run of school boys do anything more than look at pictures. In fact, in my school work, I have found it pretty difficult to make mature people use the keys conscientiously, and more so to make them study over the introductory matter."[26] People did not want keys because they were hard to use or just not needed. Consider Chapman's example of how to use the key in his *Handbook*. When readers saw a bird with a flash of yellow, they turned to birds with "yellow or orange in the plumage." That gave six choices: "throat yellow," "throat white," "throat vinaceous," "throat and head black," "throat and upper breast ashy," or whole body "grayish brown." Assume the throat was white and, though he did not say so, that you could see it. That led to "with yellow on the sides" or "no yellow on the sides." A bird with yellow on its sides was a Myrtle Warbler, a White-eyed Vireo, or a Redstart, the first marked by a yellow rump, the second distinguished by having no white in the tail, and the last had tail and wings banded with yellow.[27] In the field observers rarely had all the information the key required. What made birdwatching possible was that in most cases they did not need it. Often they cut through most of the key's steps, quickly identified the bird as, say, a warbler or a vireo, and then turned to the species accounts, where they might find a particular diagnostic characteristic. When they needed other information, it often came from clues the key did not include, such as habitat, behavior, time of year, and range.

Despite people's reluctance to use keys, every generation saw new versions promising to make identification easier for the beginner. In 1935 Florence Dickey's *Familiar Birds of the Pacific Southwest, with Size and Color Key* divided birds by these characteristics. Thirty years later, Lou Blachley and Randolph Jenks's *Naming the Birds at a Glance* used color and a set of categories ranging from "woodpeckers" to "Skimming Insect Hunters in Flight." In 1994 an introductory British guide, *Birds by Colour*, arranged 184 of the most common species by size and color.[28] John T. Elmen and David Archbald produced the most elaborate effort, a "pocket-sized 'computer,'" the *Quick-Key Guide to Birds*, consisting of fifty-three stiff seven- by three-inch sheets, each devoted to some characteristic, such as size, shape, and color, particular kinds of marks ("crown patch" or "eye ring"), location ("when and where"), habitat, behavior ("jerks tail or body"), calls, and type of song.[29] Each card was punched out in a pattern, and a brad in the corner held them together. Birdwatchers selected the cards corresponding to what they saw—say, robin size, seen in marsh, and swimming—and the alignment of the holes told them the bird was a Wilson's Phalarope. Like Hoffman's guide, this put in a physical form the elements birdwatchers used, organized not for each species but as a set of categories. What it lacked was the mental sorting process birdwatchers used. Like the early chess-playing computer programs that calculated all the possibilities for each move before making a decision, it put all the data on the same level. Even novice birdwatchers, though, worked more like human chess players, who from experience or instruction disregarded entire categories of moves at a glance, concentrating instead on the most likely ones in any situation. They decided whether what they saw was a hawk or a sparrow or asked what bird about as big as a crow would fly out of a marsh.

Birdwatchers had other methods, less systematic than the keys but reasonably effective, on which the next generation of guides would build. The guides assumed a general knowledge of form—the body shape and proportions that told people this was a hawk or a heron—and concentrated on plumage patterns, for novices usually focused on them, many were diagnostic, and they could be easily put into print or shown in even crude illustrations. In *Birds of Village and Field*, for example, Merriam pointed out that the "Yellow Warbler may be known by its uniformly yellow plumage, and the reddish brown streaks on its yellow breast; the Redstart by its salmon and black and its long fan-shaped tail; the Blackthroated Green by an inverted V of black underneath yellow cheeks, with white in its tail," and two pages of black-and-white wood engravings showing the head patterns of male warblers in the spring supplemented the descriptions.[30] Hoffman gave all sorts of information but clinched each case with distinguishing features in italics. The Bay-breasted Warbler was "the only warbler that has a *chestnut crown, throat, breast,* and *sides,*" while the "long [outer] feathers [of the tail] and the white in the tail distinguish the Barn Swallow from all other swallows." Where necessary, he made finer distinctions. The "reddish-brown crown and *unstreaked ashy breast* distinguish [the Chipping Sparrow] from most of the other sparrows; from its close relative the Field Sparrow it may be told in summer by its *black bill* and the *black line through the eye.*"[31]

In 1925 Ynez Mexia, a botanical collector and naturalist, offered her observations on methods in a two-part article in *Bird-Lore*, "Bird-Study for Beginners, by a Beginner."[32] She recommended, perhaps because her background made her familiar with keys, learning the ways taxonomists organized the families of birds; that allowed readers to quickly find the right section of the guide. She felt form was the first consideration, a point that guide writers believed but passed over with the casual injunction that beginners should learn the various families. People persisted in that casual attitude because they could tell sparrows from thrushes, ducks from gulls, and hawks from owls and with experience learned the rest. American readers can test Mexia's contention that form constituted an often unconscious first step to a name by birding in an area like Australia, where they will find identification of gulls no harder than at home but will have trouble even finding the right section of the book when confronted with a honey-eater, shrike-thrush, babbler, or whistler. After form, Mexia emphasized range and season (things Hoffman put at the front of his entries). Of the birds in your guide, she asked, which could you reasonably expect to see in your area at this time of year? She found color, the commonest character, less useful than the books believed. Many species, she pointed out, lacked distinctive colors, and in any case these did not always show up well in the field. Besides, many birds had several colors, so color keys—she cited Chapman's from *Color Key* and Bailey's from her western *Handbook*—produced as much confusion as clarity.[33] Size played an important role, and Mexia followed the early guides in telling readers to compare the unknown to a familiar bird like a robin or a sparrow. She went on to bill shape, which tied the bird to "its environment," tail shape, and flight, and she said mannerisms were "of great assistance" and song and call notes "once learned . . . are much more dependable than superficial markings." In the end, though, you could not learn the birds by having someone point them out to you or by "hunting them up in a 'bird guide' (useful as these sometimes are)." Guides, she warned, only gave an introduction to identification; people had to learn what to look for—the point Chapman made thirty years before when he said you learned birds as you did your friends, by experience.[34] The dream lives on, though, as novices still commonly begin with the idea that a book alone will let them put names on all they see.

· 55 ·

Mexia raised ideas and perspectives that still occupy birdwatchers. They almost always ignored her advice about learning the order of the families of birds. Some learned the order of the book, others paged frantically, and many made indexes and marked the edges of the pages, a solution popular enough to spawn a minor business in sheets and tabs. It declined as publishers indexed the edges of the pages. Despite her comments about indistinct colors in the field, color and plumage patterns remained the most popular technique until the 1960s, when growing knowledge of the fine points of birds' forms made form more prominent. Size became less important as experience showed how difficult it was to use in the field.[35] In the last twenty years, the downloading of songs and calls, as well as descriptions and pictures, to handheld electronics, have made these, which Mexia downplayed, more important.[36] Newer guides also followed her suggestions that they stress not technical characteristics but manner of flight and included outline drawings, but since birdwatchers used so many and such different clues, depending on their expertise and what they saw, including all the relevant information turned a guide into an encyclopedia.

Articles like Mexia's formed part of the communications binding together the developing community, a network in which *Bird-Lore* and its longtime editor and owner, Frank Chapman, played central roles. Though it published Audubon news and served as the society's national magazine, *Bird-Lore* was Chapman's private venture, part of his efforts to support bird study. A member of the last generation who learned

natural history by apprenticeship and collecting, he helped organize ornithology as a professional discipline, wrote several field guides,
arranged the first meeting of the New York Audubon Society (it took
place at the museum), sat on Audubon's national board, and started the
society's annual Christmas Bird Count. Born in 1864, the son of a New
York lawyer, he collected birds, eggs, and nests as a child but, seeing no
way to make bird study a career, took a job at a bank, spending his lunch
hours at a taxidermy shop and reading Coues's *Key* on his commuter
train. In 1884 he began contributing information on bird migration to
the newly established AOU, and on the strength of his first report was
invited to join the Linnaean Society of New York and become an associate member of the AOU. Four years later he happily abandoned
finance for a position at the American Museum of Natural History,
where he stayed until his retirement in 1942.[37]

In the first issue of *Bird-Lore,* he said that it aimed to meet the "widespread demand for a popular journal of ornithology which would be
addressed to observers rather than to collectors, or, in short, to those
who 'study birds through an opera-glass.'" The demand indeed proved
widespread. The initial printing of six thousand copies, projected to last
two months, almost sold out in two weeks.[38] Devoted to the "study and
protection of birds," the magazine had as its motto "A Bird in the Bush is
worth Two in the Hand." It had an "Audubon Department edited by
Mabel Osgood Wright and William Dutcher" (first head of National
Audubon) but also nature writing, stories, and pictures. An early ad
listed as contributors John Burroughs, Bradford Torrey, Ernest Thompson Seton, Olive Thorne Miller, Florence Merriam Bailey, Dr. Henry
Van Dyke, J. A. Allen, William Brewster, and Robert Ridgway. It promised "actual photographs of the birds in their haunts, showing them at
rest and in motion, brooding their eggs, or feeding their young," and "a
series of plates by Bruce Horsfall and Louis Agassiz Fuertes accurately
illustrating The Warblers in Color with figures of the male, female, and
the young (when their plumages differ) of every North American member of this fascinating family." Subscriptions cost a dollar a year.[39] This
attention to art and sentiment put off some readers; Coues, who edited
a short-lived competitor called *Osprey,* thought *Bird-Lore* ought to be
called *Bird-Love.*[40] For the birdwatcher Chapman printed lists of birds
seen in parks, towns, and counties, the results of local and state year-list
contests, and reports of unusual sightings and odd nest sites. He was
always on the lookout for new features, though he found Mabel Osgood
Wright's suggestion, in 1903, that he hire a "business manager to boom a
sort of ornithological *Ladies' Home Journal* . . . rather a damper" and

weakly suggested instead a "School Department with lesson outlines, question, compositions, etc."—which did find a place in the magazine.[41]

Guides and Lists as a Way to Nature

The Audubon movement spread quickly and within a generation attained most of its initial legislative goals; national legislation outlawed the feather trade, and many states passed laws to protect songbirds. Birdwatching, though originally pushed as a way to encourage conservation, did not decline but grew as a recreation, often defined by the making of lists. The practice, from natural history, was central to the hobby from the start. In her first book Merriam, urging her readers to get outdoors, pointed out that 57 species had been recorded from a backyard in Chicago in a year, 91 from another in Portland, Connecticut, and 142 from Central Park.[42] The Audubon movement built interest with competitions based on lists. While Bird-Lore did not, Chapman declared in an editorial, "believe that the making of a big list for the day or the season should be the one ambition of the field-glass student, yet an occasional effort of this kind, stimulated, perhaps, by friendly rivalry, may be a profitable as well as enjoyable pastime." He started the most popular of these rivalries by proposing a Christmas Bird Count as an alternative to the common Christmas hunt. Teams competed to find the most birds in a day afield (an annual event, still going strong). He also printed lists and reported on local competitions, in effect letting Bird-Lore's readers see what might be done.[43] Kate P. and E. W. Vietor found 93 species in Prospect Park during 135 visits in 1908, while E. Fleischer made 169 visits, found all but three of the Vietors' species, and brought the total up to 106. In 1913 Miss Annie W. Cobb had the highest total in the Massachusetts Audubon Society, 197 species, followed by Anna Kingman Barry at 169.[44] In 1914 Miss Barry led with 186 species, with Annie Cobb trailing at 181. Interest seemed general, for in 1915 Chapman reported that "the Audubon Society check lists have been in use by very many members." Only the occasional voice spoke against it; in the early 1920s Eugene Swope, managing the Audubon nature reserve at Oyster Bay, New York, grumbled that listers "were almost as a great a nuisance on the sanctuary as cats, and he hoped that their pastime was a fad that would soon run its course."[45]

Vain hope. The field guide's form, a catalog of species, invited checking them off, and that, joined to the normal human urge to collect, made listing an obvious thing to do. Besides, lists gave unambiguous measures of accomplishment and competition and offered the simplest way for novices to measure their progress. Birdwatching everywhere involved lists, but only in North America did they come to define the hobby. In Great Britain, Australia, and New Zealand, where the sport's roots lay more in amateur natural history than humane reform and conservation, bird study remained much more a matter of life-histories, field studies, and notes, and field guides contained much more information on migration, nesting, habitat, and food preferences than they did in the United States. Canada followed the American pattern, largely because they had the same birds and American publications.[46] Only after World War II did the American type of guide—text and illustrations arranged for rapid identification in the field, natural history information ruthlessly pruned—find a place in Britain, Australia, or New Zealand.[47]

Lists required rules. Birdwatching established the basic ones in its first generation, and magazines spread them, *Bird-Lore* taking the lead. Like magazines for sport hunters and fishermen, it printed stories of days afield, triumphs, insights, and disappointments, in the process pointing out appropriate behavior. Hunting and fishing journals kept their subscription prices low by selling ads for hunting and fishing gear. Birdwatching had less support from business, for birdwatchers needed far fewer gadgets, and bird-watching magazines led precarious, often short, lives. *Bird-Lore* lasted, in part, because of Chapman and because its Audubon connection gave it a reliable subscription base. It, too, preached a gospel of sport and, even more than the hunting journals, an ethic of conservation.

Birdwatching's first rule was that science made the rules. What counted was what ornithologists counted as a good species. Birdwatching as a recreation required a reasonably complete catalog of species, and by the 1880s the naturalists had compiled one and turned to arguing about the nature of subspecies and their distribution. Beginning birdwatchers could be sure that anything they saw was in the book and migration information was generally reliable. They could ignore the ornithologists' arguments about species and subspecies, except when they decided a species was really two distinct ones and "split" it, adding a new form to check off or, "lumping" previously "good" species into one, did away with a checkmark. Not only did birdwatchers count what the scientists counted, they made the AOU's study area, North America north of Mexico, their accepted field of play; used the naturalists' common lists—day, year, and area—as their own; and inherited some of their predecessors' favorite hunting grounds. Naturalists had haunted the Ramble in Central Park, and birdwatchers followed. They stayed. The first book about birdwatching on the Ramble appeared in 1894, the most recent in 2008.[48] They often compiled their lists on outings much like those of an earlier generation of amateur naturalists. The early Audubon clubs began excursions for instruction in a social setting appropriate for genteel ladies. They continued the practice because it was fun and more eyes meant more birds. As competition developed, companions verified lists and vouched for sightings.

Natural history's view gave birdwatching an unusual perspective. Unlike the growing movement for national parks, it made no distinction between the wild and the tame. Any free specimen of any wild species, seen anywhere, counted. The Peregrine Falcon hunting pigeons over Fifth Avenue had the same value on the checklist as the Peregrine Falcon on the Canadian tundra. Birdwatching had no necessary connections to the wilderness, the frontier, pioneers, rural America, or the strenuous life—the ties that gave recreations like sport hunting, hiking, and camping an orientation toward the wilderness— and its conservation programs seemed more the cultivation of a national garden than the preservation of a pioneer country. But while it did not seek the wilderness, it looked for the wild, the chance for contact with a world beyond human society. Only wild individuals of species breeding in the wild counted, and birds from overseas could be checked off only if they came under their own power or had established breeding populations here. More than devotees of other outdoor recreations, birdwatchers accepted the interpenetration of nature and culture, and they cultivated an awareness of the rhythms, processes, and events of the natural world even in cities and towns. At the same time, the hobby encouraged attention to realities beyond the sidewalk and the office. The Black-throated Green Warbler in the park during spring migration, the phoebe's nest under the eaves of a backyard shed, the geese calling overhead on autumn nights told of a world just beyond ours, touching it and enriching it.

Field guides included all the birds over a large area, usually the eastern or western half the United States and Canada or the entire continent north of Mexico. The AOU's definitions guided that approach, but so did economics. Readers might want guides that only showed the birds they would see, but publishers wanted to sell their books to as large a market as possible. Hoffman's guide to New England and eastern New York state suited many birdwatchers, but not the publishers. Language, culture, and the AOU's definition of its study area made the U.S.-Mexico border a definite southern boundary, but most Canadians spoke English. A rough biogeographical divide through the Great Plains led to eastern and western guides, with writers and publishers leaving it to readers to use range descriptions to eliminate the birds that were in the book but not their area. That encouraged novices, particularly enthusiastic children, to "find" birds far beyond their ranges, but it schooled all birdwatchers to see the species around home as part of the larger group and encouraged them to seek out new habitats close to home. Pages of ducks, herons, and rails pointed them toward the local swamps and pictures of meadowlarks and sparrows to weedy fields and pastures. Visions of larger lists led enthusiasts to dumps, landfills, and sewage farms.

Field guides organized birdwatchers' worlds in time as well as space. Ornithologists saw existing birds as the latest set in a line that stretched back to fossils, but the guides resolutely stuck to living birds. Only Reed among the early authors included even recently extinct species. While birdwatchers ignored deep time, they paid close attention to migration, those spectacular seasonal floods of life dictated by North American geography, biogeography, and climate. The early guides used naturalists' data on arrival and departure dates, and some included tables for the larger cities on the East Coast showing beginnings, peaks, and ends to the waves in spring and fall.[49] In the Northeast, where birdwatching began in America, each week through April and May brought new species of summer residents or transients on their way to breeding grounds further north, many in bright distinctive breeding plumage. September and October brought others. Like waterfowl hunters, who consulted the calendar and waited for opening day, birdwatchers patrolled the park for the first warblers.

Field guides not only gave birdwatching biological and geographical boundaries but also, even in the first generation, helped standardize birds' names. Field guide authors, facing a confusing and conflicting set of popular names, turned to the AOU's list of official English-language names, and over time made them the ones Americans knew and used. The European settlers had put European names on American species, borrowed names from Native Americans (particularly for unfamiliar species), and made up their own from calls, patterns, or behavior. A bird that walked head down on tree trunks became the "Devil-down Head" (White-breasted Nuthatch), and a particularly audacious scavenger around campsites, now the Gray Jay, was called the "Camp Robber." The Red-headed Woodpecker and the Great Horned Owl

2.4 · *Hoffman's Wren* · The page has an old-fashioned look and uses a standard wood engraving, but the layout arranged the information birdwatchers needed to answer their common questions. Ralph Hoffman, *A Guide to the Birds of New England and Eastern New York* (Boston: Houghton Mifflin, 1904).

CAROLINA WREN. *Thryothorus ludovicianus*

5.50

Ad. — Upper parts rich reddish-brown; *line over eye whitish;* throat white; breast and belly washed with buff.

Nest, bulky, of sticks, etc., in a hole in a tree or in some cavity about buildings. *Eggs*, whitish, speckled about the larger end with reddish-brown.

FIG. 7. Carolina Wren

The Carolina Wren is a very rare permanent resident of southern Rhode Island and southern Connecticut, and a rather common summer resident of the eastern slope of the Palisades; it occasionally wanders into Massachusetts. The bird's favorite haunts are brushy tangles. If a male is anywhere about he can hardly be overlooked; he is a constant singer, even in winter, and his song is so loud and clear that it can be heard easily a quarter of a mile away. It consists of short phrases of from two to four notes repeated again and again in a loud clear whistle. These phrases vary greatly; some of the common forms may be written *twip'pity, twip'pity; whiddy you', whiddy you' whiddy you'; thri'ou, thri'ou, thri'ou*. Certain phrases suggest notes both of the Cardinal and the Tufted Tit; a beginner should make a careful study of the notes of these three species. The alarm-note is a rather smooth *peurr*.

A Carolina Wren is easily recognized by its wren-like behavior, by the rich brown of its upper parts, and by the conspicuous *whitish line* over its eye.

THRASHERS AND MOCKINGBIRDS : FAMILY MIMIDÆ

The Catbird, Brown Thrasher, and Mockingbird form a small family characterized by their comparatively slender figure and length of tail.

· This looks like a nineteenth-century natural history text, with its species entry, short description in small type, and discursive text in a larger face.

· The wood engraving of the wren comes from a block Merriam used in *Birds of Village and Field*, the kind publishers kept for illustrating natural history texts and which Hoffman and Merriam used extensively.

· No AOU number here, but otherwise the standard, natural history description, species by species. The page-by-page arrangement made it easy to see all the information about one species but complicated comparisons in the field.

· The heading and arrangement follow natural history texts, but Hoffman put his information in a standard order addressing birdwatchers' questions—would you expect to find it here, at this time of year, in this habitat? It ended with a summary of key points for identification.

were named after their appearance, birds like the Bobwhite and the Whip-poor-will from their calls. Calls, though, were not uniform. New Englanders commonly spoke of the White-throated Sparrow as the Peabody bird, for it seemed to say, "Old Sam Peabody, Peabody, Peabody," but north of the border it sang "Oh Sweet Canada, Canada, Canada," except, *naturellement*, in Quebec, where it called *ou es-tu Frederic, Frederic, Frederic.*[50] Old names found new uses in the new country. What in Europe were called vultures became buzzards; the soaring raptors Europeans called buzzards (birds like the Red-tailed Hawk) became hawks. "Redbird" might mean the Cardinal (officially now Northern Cardinal) but also the Scarlet Tanager or the Summer Tanager. On the other hand, many birds had more than one name. At the extreme, Chapman reported more than a hundred names for the large brown ant-eating woodpecker commonly called "Flicker," and even the familiar thrush now officially the American Robin (in English) and *Turdus migratorius* (in Latin) was also called the American Fieldfare, after another European species.[51]

Authors used the AOU's English-language set as a fallback, adding two or three common names for popular species.[52] In *Birds through an Opera-Glass*, for example, Merriam labeled what the AOU now calls the Vesper Sparrow "Grass Finch; Vesper Sparrow; Bay-winged Bunting"; under "Baltimore Oriole" she gave as well the names "Fire-bird; Golden Robin; Hang-nest," and for the Chipping Sparrow, "Chip-Bird or Chippy; Hair-Bird; Chipping Sparrow; Social Sparrow" ("Hair-bird" came from its habit of using horsehair for its nests; the name's decline tracked the rise of Henry Ford's fortune).[53] As field guides became the common means of learning about the birds, popular names declined, and guides used only the "official" ones. That meant either less confusion or the fading of a rich heritage of American folk culture, possibly some of both, for ornithologists' names, even the Latin ones, could have the same sources. Linnaeus called the Eastern Kingbird, so named by the settlers for its aggressive defense of its nesting areas, *Tyrannus tyrannus*, which meant much the same thing, and the Cardinal was *Cardinalus cardinalus* for its red feathers and crest like a Roman Catholic ecclesiastic. The Snakebird, as it was then called, had the scientific name *Anhinga anhinga*, from a Native American language, and that eventually became the official English-language name as well. Changes in official names have, at times, aimed at making them descriptive, so "Audubon's Warbler" became the "Yellow-rumped Warbler," for the bird's most obvious field mark, though "Butter Butt," a now-fading folk name, did the job more vividly.

Twenty years after Merriam's first guide, birdwatching had grown into an established nature hobby, with a national infrastructure supporting programs of recreation, conservation, and childhood education. At first glance it seemed a hobby at odds with itself, for it deployed modern technology, science, and communications to get back to nature, but the paradox was only apparent. All outdoor recreations helped people not to escape society but to bring nature into their modern lives. Birdwatching opened a familiar kind of path into the now unfamiliar world of nature, presenting it as just another consumer good, something to be chosen to improve the quality of life, pursued by the familiar practice of making a list. Anyone could play and play as they wished—casually or obsessively, pursuing self-education, sentiment, insight, or the thrill of competition. In the interwar years a community of enthusiastic birdwatchers, loosely linked by clubs and friendships, largely succeeded in working out ways to identify all the birds, and one of the group, Roger Tory Peterson, put this knowledge into a book. That story occupies the next two chapters, the first centering on Ludlow Griscom, who played a crucial role in field identification and competitive birdwatching, the other on Peterson and his "Bird Book on a New Plan."

PART II

The Mature Guide
& the
Popular Hobby

THREE

Knowledge & Skills

It is *possible* to identify every species of
bird in the Eastern United
States in life in any of its plumages.

—LUDLOW GRISCOM (1922)

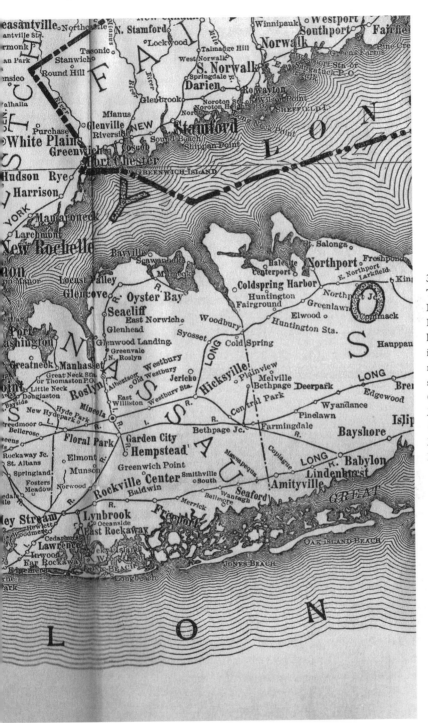

3.1. *Griscom's map* · The birdwatcher's New York City Region before the car left out highways but included all the railroads and their stops. From Ludlow Griscom, *Birds of the New York City Region* (New York: American Museum of Natural History, 1923).

In 1923 the American Museum of Natural History in New York brought out a yellow-brown volume, *Birds of the New York City Region.*[1] The cover had the embossed image of an Osprey with extended claws below the title, but otherwise it seemed more a scientific than a birdwatcher's book. The title page described the author, Ludlow Griscom, as "Assistant Curator of Ornithology," and said the book, number 9 in the museum's "Handbook Series," was published "with the cooperation of the Linnaean Society of New York." It was indeed a traditional scientific work, a local ornithology, an annotated list of species known in the area, with notes on their abundance, population, migration dates, and habitat, but it showed the changing face of the discipline, for it used data from birdwatchers as well as collectors. Sight records from the last two decades, Griscom said, made up half the data for the region. It also went beyond the local ornithology's usual task—making "existing information about local birds readily accessible"—to tell readers where to find them. "Its subtitle," Griscom said, "might well be: 'Our Local Birds, when and where to find them.'"[2] Here were several new things: an new kind of birdwatching book, the finding guide, a genre that would become almost as common as the field guide; the regional home range, a geographical tie among birdwatchers living in an area; and a new collaboration between scientists and hobbyists contributing to ornithology.

Birds of the New York City Region took a new middle ground of bird study, created as natural history split into the scientific field of ornithology—driven by research programs developed within the community of scientists—and the outdoor recreation of birdwatching. The alliance first appeared in New York partly because of Griscom's presence but more because the city's elite had for generations been interested in natural history. The American Museum of Natural History, established in 1869, was at once monument to the city's culture, research institution, site for public education, and gathering place for birdwatchers and amateur naturalists. With the blessings of Frank Chapman and his successors, the Linnaean Society of New York met there, giving enthusiasts a place to talk, argue, and exchange information. Besides the tradition of amateur natural history, birdwatching in New York had the advantages of geography and a modern transit system. On the shore, at the mouth of a river, along a major migration route, its habitats ranged from shore, beach, and swamp to meadow and forest, and trolleys and subways allowed rapid, inexpensive travel among them. Until cars became common, New York birdwatchers had better opportunities than their country cousins to run up long lists.

Griscom's career also reflected birdwatching's transformation from casual pursuit to an established hobby, preserving and teaching craft knowledge within a self-conscious community. The dean of field ornithologists, he was also the dean of birdwatchers. He led the campaign to make field identification a scientific tool, helped work out ways to identify all species by sight, trained people who went on to careers in birdwatching and ornithology, and spread along the East Coast his method of "instant identification," which took birdwatching expertise to a new level. His use of amateurs' observations pointed to a new relationship between them and professionals, grounded in the amateurs' increasing competence and the professionals' need for data on living birds in the field. In addition to exploring Griscom's career, this chapter examines his book as an aid to birdwatching and a reflection of birdwatchers' growing understanding of the land. Finding guides, organized by geography, placed birds on the land and traced their history back in time, giving birdwatchers a community map and a collective memory while tying their work to science. This chapter also takes up the passion that drove Griscom and his disciples and contributed so much to the development of field identification techniques and the changing nature of lists, listing, and competition. In the first generation, competition had centered on lists compiled over a year in a small area, often local parks. Cars gave new life to the day list, made by teams working at the height of spring migration, and extended birdwatchers' home ranges. Cars also changed birdwatchers' mental pictures of the land, as competitors went everywhere, including places genteel ladies avoided. They grew familiar with a wider area than the first generation, but their mental maps were less of connected territory than of hot spots connected by stretches of birdless highway, and memories centered more on special times set aside for birdwatching than events in daily life. Finally, this chapter considers the guides' effect on Americans' understanding of the world in this generation, a subject that comes back to lists and listing, but the wider context of the English-speaking countries shows how American

birdwatching got its unique focus.

Griscom: Refining Skills, Forming an Expert Community

Florence Merriam, a-birding on a bronco on Uncle Gustavus's ranch with Ridgway's *Manual*, testing whether it was possible to know all the birds without a gun, represented the pioneer birdwatcher. Ludlow Griscom, driving off with friends at 3:45 on a May morning, confident he could identify everything and intent on getting as long a list as possible, stood at the cutting edge of the second generation. Whereas Merriam rode her horse over a small area through a season, Griscom drove on day-long expeditions planned in advance with tide tables, weather reports, and news of rarities scouted earlier in the week or phoned in by friends. The men—competitive birding had become almost entirely male by the 1920s—went to the woods in the predawn dark for owls, to good feeding and resting areas for warblers at dawn, and marshes for ducks and shore birds in the middle of the day, fitting in side trips for rarities. Merriam drew on expert knowledge from a professional community, but not one concerned with field identification; Griscom had the help of people who made field identification their enthusiastic hobby.

Like Merriam, Griscom came from the same well-established part of society that supported the Audubon movement. Born in 1890 to a prominent New York family, educated at home and in private schools, he later estimated he had been to Europe fifteen times before he turned thirty.[3] Like most enthusiastic birdwatchers (or ornithologists for that matter) he began young, first with John Grant's book *Our Common Birds and How to Know Them* and then the Reed guides. In 1907 he discovered H. E. Parkhurst's *Birds' Calendar*, "an informal diary of a year's observations made, as business would permit, in Central Park, of New York City, in 1893," largely on the Ramble.[4] Parkhurst had a flowery style and dealt not so much with bird identification as with bird life, but something in the book struck Griscom, for after reading it he "started serious steady birding in Central Park, May 11 [1907], and never stop[ped]."[5] By the time he graduated from Columbia in 1912, he had a one-day record of ninety species. All he lacked was company; only when he joined the Linnaean Society of New York the same year did he find "blessed companionship for the first time in 15 years."[6] He could, more easily than an earlier generation, decide to make birds a career, for ornithology had become an academic field. He received a master's degree in ornithology from Cornell, the first student of Arthur A. Allen, the preeminent American ornithologist of his time. Two years later, in 1917, Griscom became an assistant in Chapman's office at the American Museum of Natural History, where he stayed until he moved to the Museum of Comparative Zoology at Harvard in 1927.

His master's thesis on field identification of ducks foreshadowed a life that mixed birdwatching and ornithology. He helped establish marks that identified all species and campaigned among his fellow ornithologists to have sight identification by a competent observer considered acceptable scientific data. In an article in the ornithological journal *Auk* in 1922 he said that his own experience and that of other field observers showed that, with rare exceptions, "it is *possible* to identify every species of bird in the Eastern United States in life in any of its plumages," a bold declaration at a time when scientific publications required identification along a shotgun barrel.[7] When species were unknown or little known, he argued, scientific skepticism had been justified, but now good observers could be trusted. A generation later he declared victory.

> [What] people are now able to do in the way of instantly recognizing a large number of birds by song, notes, tricks of flight, shape, etc, entirely apart from their colors, seems perfectly fabulous to the uninitiated and was flatly declared to be impossible a generation ago. . . . The battle for sight records and field identification of the living bird has been won, so far as I know, and there is no real quarrel left about what birds can be recognized alive and when this recognition can be used in scientific research.[8]

He did not mean that an expert could identify any specimen under any conditions, only that experts' judgments could be trusted. He had evidence, but the changing nature of ornithological research helped him. As scientists learned American birds and their ranges in detail, collecting became less necessary, and as public sentiment grew more opposed to it, less practical. Young men could still make their own collections, but museums and academic training meant they did not have to. Griscom spoke to a generation more familiar with watching birds and less accustomed to preparing them for the cabinet. They also had good professional reasons to consider his case. With almost all the species found, variations charted, and ranges reasonably well mapped out, field ornithologists turned to studies of population, diet, and behavior, which required research on living populations. If they had not been birdwatchers as children, they learned the methods in the course of their education.

Griscom affected ornithology but did more for birdwatching. He was, Peterson later said, "the high priest of the new cult of split-second identification. . . . My 'Field Guides' owe much to Ludlow," and commented that "the sharpest field experts can usually be traced either directly to Griscom's influence or indirectly. . . . He was indeed the dean of field ornithologists."[9] Peterson singled out "the Bronx boys" as Griscom's star pupils, a group that produced two ornithologists, Joseph J. Hickey and Alan Cruickshank, and served as a center for New York birdwatching. Outsiders, by which they meant those who did not live in the Bronx, could come on the club's trips if they were very good.[10] Hickey and two friends from parochial school formed the original nucleus, going out with a Reed guide Matty Mateszewski got from his older brother Charlie, who had it for a Boy Scout Merit Badge project. They found friends, and in late November 1924 they formed a club. Two months later they wrote to Ludlow Griscom, presenting themselves as six "younger folk who are interested in birds. . . . In fact, our aim is to try and make as thorough and as systematic a study of the [Bronx] County birds as is possible." They wanted to publish their own list, but "this does not now seem possible [due to] the lack of records," and they offered their information for him "to use . . . as you see fit."[11] They joined the Linnaean Society, which met at the Museum under Griscom's leadership, and became his disciples. They went with him in the field, soaked up his knowledge, and adopted his characteristic turns of speech. One even parted his hair in the middle in imitation of his idol. Griscom gave them encouragement and, for reports of unusual sightings, relentless skepticism.[12] Years later, Hickey thought Griscom's passion for field identification might have made it harder for his students to move beyond lists and identification to deeper aspects of bird study, but the heated competition within the club helped Griscom push fast and accurate identification to new heights. Earlier, Peterson said, it might have taken a lifetime to learn all the local birds, but "now it can be done in a crash program of a mere four of five years," a change that "Ludlow Griscom did much to make . . . possible, and in this way made one of his most significant contributions to ornithology."[13]

The relationship between master and disciples revealed a social shift as well as a methodological one. Hickey and his friends came from working-class, immigrant backgrounds, and without the common bond of birds would never have even met their mentor. Griscom's letter to the Guggenheim Foundation in 1944 enthusiastically recommending Hickey for a fellowship suggested the distance.[14] He described Hickey as "of a very low family background [and in the early days he] was a little Mick from the Bronx but early showed a natural aptitude and genius for field work in birds." In college Hickey had not thought of biology but had taken "some kind of a stereotyped arts course, after which he got a job as a bill collector with the Columbia Gas Company." He continued his interest in birds, though, and his "contacts with the members of the Linnaean Society and the New York Academy of Sciences developed and matured him along both social and intellectual lines to an astonishing degree." He became president of the Linnaean Society, and Griscom, back from Cambridge to address the group, watched him "preside at the meeting, lead in the discussion, comment or criticize the field notes submitted. . . . I rubbed my eyes with astonishment and admiration, as it seemed incredible that the unkempt little hoodlum had changed into the grown man I saw before me." Hickey, incidentally, was awarded the Guggenheim fellowship, which funded his Ph.D. work in ornithology.

Differences in background vanished in the field, where Griscom's disciples paid attention only to the birds and his methods, which moved the process of field identification from sorting through the possibilities by an abbreviated, mental key composed mainly of color and pattern and toward recognition based on integrating all the bits of information. Peterson compared the process to a "kaleidoscope. . . . All the fragments we know about birds—locality, season, habitat, voice, actions, field marks, and likelihood of occurrence—flash across the mirrors of the mind and fall into place—and we have the name of our bird."[15] That took the craft beyond early field guides, beyond even Peterson's work, which separated similar species by distinctive physical marks, and toward the process used by people who knew birds by long experience and close observation. A modern ornithologist, Jared Diamond, found that his informants in New Guinea among the Ketengban could pick out even small, closely related species living high in the treetops, birds he found difficult to identify with binoculars or even in the hand.[16] This uncanny skill came from having learned the birds as children, by "song, silhouette, posture, behavior, and general appearance, [rather than] fine details of plumage that are normally invisible to forest observers without binoculars anyway."[17] Having seen birds so often in so many situations, they easily picked out details of behavior that observers with less experience would never notice or could not use as diagnostic markers.

Naturalists knew that approach. In *A Natural History of Selbourne,* Gilbert White suggested that "a good ornithologist should be able to distinguish birds by their air as well as by their colours and shape. . . . For, though it must not be said that every species of birds [*sic*] has a manner peculiar to itself, yet there is somewhat in most genera at least that at first sight discriminates them, and enables a judicious observer to pronounce upon them with some certainty."[18] A century later Elliott Coues commented on the difference in form "and especially the discrepancy in their mode of flight" between the Turkey Vulture and the Black Vulture, which he described in language that would serve in a modern book on identifying large birds at a distance.[19] Connie Hagar, who spent much of the first half of the twentieth century watching birds around Rockport, Texas, could identify them even when her failing eyes could no longer make out plumage patterns, for she had "come to know the attitudes, behavior, and habits of the birds so well that lesser details were unnecessary."[20] What naturalists and birdwatchers lacked from White's day to Hagar's early years were the books that would simplify and shorten the learning process. Griscom's methods were the first step toward that.

As the hobby and the community grew, field guides, which had begun as introductions to the birds and the craft of identification, passed on new knowledge and the rules of the game to birders beyond the circle of the clubs. They became instruction manuals, catalogs, and reference books. They served as personal records and stores of memories, as owners put dates and places beside the entries and turned the indexes into life lists. Carried in the field they became, with binoculars, the badge of the fraternity. Each new generation of guides presented techniques worked out since the last appeared, told how the ornithologists had changed their lists, and described changes in birds' ranges.

Birdwatching Books beyond the Field Guide

Griscom's field experience and detailed understanding of plumage patterns and variations, gained by years of work with museum collections, allowed him to break new ground in recreation, and *Birds of the New*

3.2 · *Griscom's text* · A page from the Bronx County Bird Club's "Bible." They used it to find birds around New York but, as the discussion on separating immature Bald from Golden Eagles shows, tells us something about the state of field identification—and the range of birds now rarely seen in the city. From Ludlow Griscom, *Birds of the New York City Region* (New York: American Museum of Natural History, 1923).

on the larger marshes. Three records for Montclair (Howland); rare at Morristown (Thurber).

ENGLEWOOD REGION. Uncommon winter visitant, sometimes present all winter on the Overpeck Marshes, other years unrecorded. October 10, 1915 (J. M. Johnson and Rogers) to April 7, 1918 (J. M. Johnson).

GOLDEN EAGLE (*Aquila chrysaëtos*)

There is some evidence to show that in colonial times the Golden Eagle was less rare in the East than now, and it apparently bred in the Hudson Highlands. In our territory, however, it is purely casual. Only the most extraordinary luck would enable an observer to distinguish it in life from the Bald Eagle, as a *top view* would be essential. Immature birds could not possibly be told from an immature Bald Eagle.

Long Island. Three records, an old specimen from Canarsie; October 6, 1877; October 19, 1890.

New Jersey. Only two records, an adult female killed near Culver's Gap, Sussex County, November 23, 1918 (Miller, Auk, 1919, p. 293); another shot in the same locality September 22, 1922 (von Lengerke).

BALD EAGLE (*Haliæetus leucocephalus*)   Fig. 15

The experienced can recognize an Eagle at great distances by the enormous extent of the wings (often over seven feet) which is six or seven times the length of the tail. Country people, however, are likely to call any large bird flying at a great height an Eagle! These proportions are approached only by the Turkey Vulture, whose wings are much narrower, and whose flight and soaring characteristics are quite different. The Bald Eagle has a most irregular distribution in our area, which will be found in detail below. The bird nests very early; consequently its presence as a transient chiefly in late spring and early fall is hard to explain. Students can count on seeing it along the Palisades any winter just after a cold wave, when half a dozen or more birds can be seen sitting on ice cakes in the River during a short walk.

York City Region did the same across the boundaries between professionals and amateurs. It combined science and craft knowledge, but instead of using science to inform the hobby, as in the field guide, this book used birdwatchers' skills to inform science and gave birdwatchers information from ornithology. It offered accounts of the area's birds, defined a local range, and told where to find each species and at what time of year. It began when the Linnaean Society of New York decided to produce a new local ornithology. Finding it lacked the resources, it turned to the American Museum of Natural History, which assigned Griscom to update Frank Chapman's 1906 pamphlet *Birds of the Vicinity of New York City.*[21] Reviewing the literature, Griscom found it

· 78 ·

> difficult to conceive the change that has taken place in these seventeen years. For one person interested in birds then there are now hundreds, who cover almost every section of the area at every season of the year. When Dr. Chapman wrote, not only were many parts of his territory without a resident student, but many sections had never even been visited by anyone interested in birds, or had remained unvisited for many years. Twenty-five years ago an active field man went out collecting a few dozen times a year, or made two or three trips lasting a week or so apiece. Nowadays an active student will often be afield a hundred times in one year.[22]

Griscom's work seemed an ordinary scientific one, but in its omissions, organization, and emphases spoke of a new generation studying birds in a new way. Assuming that readers would identify birds on the wing and not in the hand, Griscom directed them to the "many inexpensive text-books, obtainable in any book store," though he gave "characters which I have found useful in recognizing many species of birds difficult to identify in life, wherever the subject has not been adequately treated." Where Chapman had defined the region as any land within fifty miles of City Hall, Griscom took into account New Yorkers' habits and interests and the recent scientific literature. He included all of Long Island ("for a century the favorite field of New York ornithologists") though it stretched well past the fifty-mile limit, and left out the slice of Connecticut cut by Chapman's circle ("adequately covered by a recent report on the birds of the state"), as well as areas along the Hudson with little data ("No bird student of any attainments has ever worked in Putnam County"). He took a similar approach to data, omitting "many matters ordinarily included in a scientific monograph or treatise," such as a complete bibliography of scientific literature, as well as any discussion of "life-zones, faunal areas, and migration," "habits, life histories . . . vanished species," and records of nesting dates. On the other hand, he went beyond the usual sources in using sight records. That imposed what he described as his "most difficult and ungracious task," weighing the reliability of sightings.[23] He eventually included only records he was sure of: his 1,250 field trips since 1907, which included "daily observations of twelve spring migrations, daily observations of two fall migrations, and daily observations of parts of eight others," and observations by people he knew or knew from other sources to be reliable observers, even though he admitted that this skeptical stand cut out some observations he was quite sure were accurate.[24]

Intended for ornithologists and serious naturalists, the book's wealth of detailed information told birdwatchers just when and where to go. The Mallard was an "uncommon transient, rare in winter" on Long Island, and the Clapper Rail a "common summer resident in our salt marshes, often heard but seldom seen," while the Saw-whet Owl was "a regular and often common winter visitant." He noted difficulties. Feral Mallards were so widespread through the Bronx that "truly wild birds cannot be satisfactorily differentiated." He offered tips on identification. The Broad-winged Hawk could "unquestionably claim the dubious distinction of being the most misidentified of our local birds" and must "not be identified by its size, its 'broad wings,' or the way it flaps its wings when soaring." He recommended a trip to the New Jersey hills, where the bird could be studied on its breeding grounds. Most important, the book told where to find species. "Perhaps the best place near New York city to see the Whistler [Common Goldeneye] is Prince's Bay, Staten Island, where a few birds occur every winter. . . . If the student could search church steeples, belfries, dove-cots in old farm buildings, and bars, as zealously as he did conifer groves and hollows in trees he would undoubtedly see more Barn Owls."[25]

The treatment fell squarely within amateur natural history's concern with a local, home ground studied through the year but, like its scientific predecessors, relied on a community, in this case birdwatchers, and served it. Showing where naturalists and now birdwatchers worked, and what they found, Griscom set out what was known and, by omission, what was not. Also like the scientific studies, this was a work in progress, to be revised as new knowledge accumulated and conditions changed. In 1942, updating Griscom's work, Allan Cruickshank used sight records without comment—evidence of Griscom's success in making them acceptable in ornithology—and omitted identification

(April 17–April 25)

Bittern	Blue-headed Vireo
Night Heron	Black and White Warbler
Clapper Rail	Myrtle Warbler
Virginia Rail	Black-throated Green Warbler
Towhee	Louisiana Water-thrush
Barn Swallow	Brown Thrasher

While it is most exceptional for one of these species not to arrive in April, they are the only ones which can be counted upon. In six years out of ten, however, there is a third movement between April 25th and 30th, bringing the majority of the following species:

(April 25–April 30)

Green Heron	Purple Martin
Greater Yellowlegs	Cliff Swallow
Spotted Sandpiper	Bank Swallow
Broad-winged Hawk	Rough-winged Swallow
Whippoorwill	Yellow Warbler
Chimney Swift	House Wren

May is the star month of the year for the bird-lover. The migration becomes more marked and continuous. A vast horde of birds flood the countryside and pour overhead at night, their calls coming to us from the sky. A rise in temperature and a light southerly wind is apt to bring a great "wave." As many as a dozen new species will arrive overnight. A drop in temperature, cold rain, or strong northerly or easterly winds are equally certain to bring a lull in migration. Five distinct groups of species can be distinguished during the month, but climatic factors will often bring about a totally different story for any given season. As a general rule the following species arrive between May 2nd and May 7th, and a "wave" usually occurs in this period bringing the majority of them with it. Those marked with an asterisk (*) occasionally arrive the last days of April. The balance are casual in April, but in the remarkable spring of 1914 the majority arrived on April 29th and 30th:

3.3 · *Griscom's migration information* · Putting numbers and dates on the importance of the spring migration, Griscom also called attention to one important way birdwatchers used their hobby to establish memories on the land and see the rhythms of life across the years. From Ludlow Griscom, *Birds of the New York City Region* (New York: American Museum of Natural History, 1923).

(May 2–May 7)

Solitary Sandpiper
*Pigeon Hawk
Hummingbird
Kingbird
Crested Flycatcher
*Least Flycatcher
Baltimore Oriole
Orchard Oriole
*Grasshopper Sparrow
Rose-breasted Grosbeak
Tanager
Warbling Vireo
Yellow-throated Vireo
White-eyed Vireo

Nashville Warbler
Blue-winged Warbler
Parula Warbler
Black-throated Blue Warbler
Chestnut-sided Warbler
*Prairie Warbler
*Northern Water-Thrush
Hooded Warbler
Northern Yellowthroat
*Ovenbird
*Redstart
*Catbird
*Wood Thrush
Veery

Between May 9th and May 12th there is often another well-marked "wave." During this period a few species arrive with great regularity. In backward seasons many of the species in the last list do not arrive until this "wave," which brings:

(May 9–May 12)

Acadian Flycatcher
Red-eyed Vireo
Worm-eating Warbler
Magnolia Warbler

Blackburnian Warbler
Chat
Canadian Warbler
Olive-backed Thrush

The third "wave" of the month usually takes place between May 10th and May 14th. It is eagerly awaited by the field student, as it is one of the two chief opportunities of finding the rarer species. The following commonly arrive at this time:

(May 10–May 14)

Nighthawk
Bobolink
White-crowned Sparrow
Lincoln's Sparrow
Golden-winged Warbler
Tennessee Warbler

Cape May Warbler
Bay-breasted Warbler
Blackpoll Warbler
Wilson's Warbler
Long-billed Marsh Wren
Gray-cheeked Thrush

tips, referring readers to Peterson's work. His book showed changes in the birds but also in birdwatching. Griscom's map of the region, tipped into the back, did not show roads but included all the rail lines and all their stops. Cruickshank spoke of a "network of motor parkways, bridges and causeways . . . [that] made places which two decades ago were considered remote, mere week end visits and, in some cases mere afternoon drives."[26]

Birds of the New York City Region put on paper birdwatchers' knowledge and extended it in time, for the notes on distribution and abundance spoke of now vanished bird landscapes. It still has this somewhat melancholy attraction. The Bald Eagle was "locally common in summer in the wilder sections" of Long Island, a "fairly common summer resident" at Mastic, and a "regular and often common winter visitant on the Hudson River in the section of the Palisades from December to late March, often seen from the 125th street Ferry." The "Duck Hawk or Peregrine is a permanent resident on the Palisades of the Hudson, at least two pairs nesting in our territory. These birds are not infrequently seen in various parts of New York City where they have learned that there is excellent pigeon hunting."[27] Birders may now use Chapman's 1906 pamphlet, Griscom's *Birds of the New York City Region*, Allan Cruickshank's *Birds around New York City: When and Where to Find Them* (1942), and John Bull's *Birds of the New York Area* (1964) to trace their birds through a century, seeing how species ebbed and flowed, left and returned as the land changed or conservation changed it or birds expanded their ranges—a form of birdwatching beyond the field guide.[28]

Besides recording changing bird landscapes, Griscom spoke of the growing concern about finding the wild. Urban birdwatchers depended on backyards and parks but also sought out swamps and fields, and as the city expanded and houses and factories replaced meadows and swamps, they became uneasy. He closed the introduction to *Birds in the New York City Region* with a plea for undeveloped areas. If it ever became too difficult or distant for city dwellers to reach wild land, he said, "our native birds, a priceless heritage, which it has taken mysterious forces and laws many ages to evolve, will have disappeared, never to return again."[29] Birdwatchers treasured those glimpses of "mysterious forces and laws," and the search for wild America and the campaign for its protection became conservation causes after birdwatchers won the feather wars and the campaign to end the shooting of songbirds.

Griscom's career tracked birdwatching's growth from an introduction to ornithology or the beauties of nature to a competitive hobby organized around the craft skill of field identification. His knowledge and methods made field identification a skill that could be taught—and Peterson gave everyone access to it with his guides. His systematic discussion of the local area in the context of natural history and birdwatching gave the local home range a clear definition, and helped make the combination of field guides, finding guides, checklists, and local ornithologies common tools of birdwatchers. The popularity of his methods within birdwatching clubs added to the community a group of intense competitors, focused on larger lists and better ways to distinguish species. That band was, in contrast to the original, largely female audience, mainly men, but it was still centered on the East Coast, and in the 1920s small enough and close enough to New York for Griscom to be the dominant or at least central figure.

New Lists for a New Generation

Birdwatchers took the practice of listing from natural history and, like their predecessors, made lists for every period from a day to a lifetime and areas from the backyard to the world, but in each generation the community, its knowledge, and the available transportation determined which lists set the competitive standard. The desire to excel remained constant. In 1899 Chapman couched his call for the Audubon Society Christmas Bird Count in competitive terms, and later said that "it was to the hunters' instinct and spirit of competition to which we appealed and, if we are not mistaken, it is these elemental traits, rather than interest in the science of ornithology, that still animates the census-taker."[30] The year list ruled in the early days of the Audubon movement, for it suited genteel women who could easily travel no further than the park. At first—a clear instance of culture affecting the perception of nature—birdwatchers ignored some species, most often the common pigeon and the House (at that time usually called the English) Sparrow, but within a generation consistency and the desire for another check-mark overcame snobbery.[31]

The units were species. Birdwatchers did not list "cormorant" but "Double-crested Cormorant" or "Neotropic Cormorant." Sex did not matter, even when it could easily be told in the field. A female Bay-breasted Warbler in her dull fall costume counted just as much, and in the same category, as her mate in his boldly patterned spring plumage, even though he stood out and it required some experience and expertise to identify her.[32] Lists changed as ornithologists made judgments about species. Early in the twentieth century they recognized the Lesser Snow Goose, Greater Snow Goose, and Blue Goose, but when it was found that a "Snow Goose," with pure white feathers with black wing-tips, might come from the same clutch as the "Blue Goose," a darker form, and that no biological criteria separated the "Lesser" and "Greater," they were declared to be color forms of a single species. Three check marks collapsed into one. Names, too, answered to the same standards. In the West, where fewer ornithologists than in the East worked for a shorter time among a more complex avifauna, enough confusion remained in the late 1930s that Peterson found the most difficult task in writing a western guide what to call the various subspecies. He included some established local names because birdwatchers were so familiar with them that leaving them out would have made his guide less useful, but he mainly attempted to enforce taxonomic orthodoxy. In the long run it took hold.

In the interwar years, the combination of Henry Ford and the campaign for good roads made the "Big Day" total, compiled by an all-day team effort, the competitive prize and the spring migration even more the height of the birdwatchers' year. In New York City, for instance, only thirty-seven species, about 10 percent of the total, stayed year-round; eighty-nine (24 percent) arrived in the spring to nest in the summer, and another seventy-eight (21 percent) passed through on their way to breeding grounds further north. The fall migration yielded thirty more (8 percent), but that was inconsequential.[33] Each week in April and May brought almost a dozen new species, some birds of passage that had to be seen then or not at all, and many in new, brightly colored breeding dress. The birdwatcher's Christmas came around Easter, and cars made the most of the precious time. The decline of genteel standards and recruitment of young boys to birdwatching, many through the Junior Audubon clubs, also changed the field. Birdwatchers had ignored some habitats, and therefore some birds, on social grounds. Merriam, recall, left out of Birds through an Opera-Glass "the divers, all kinds of swimmers, waders, herons, cranes, parrots, and others that most of us never see outside of museums."[34] They never saw them because respectable ladies did not visit swamps. The Bronx County Bird Club, with no genteel pretensions and access to New York's trolleys and subways, went everywhere. They soon made the Hunts' Point Dump one of their primary hunting grounds.

Social and technological changes meant much larger lists. In 1913 Chapman reported a record single-day count by "Prof Lynds Jones [and] two assistants of 144 species."[35] Then came the car. On May 17, 1931, Griscom and his friends set off at 3 a.m. and had 104 species by 7:30 a.m., 142 by the time they reached the coast, and at the end of the day, as his ornithological journal triumphantly recorded, "a *world record* list of 163."[36] Two years later Griscom and New Jersey expert Charles Urner drove three miles on May 14 to run up another record, 173 species.[37] Peterson recalled these trips from the early 1930s, when he and Griscom lived in Boston. The group met "before dawn at the cafeteria in Harvard Square. Like a commanding general, Ludlow took charge." They checked tide tables and weather maps, plotted each hour, and "invaded the realm of the birds with military thoroughness. . . . Fast travel between strategic areas with a tankful of gas and good brakes was part of our tactics." They relied as well on Griscom's "statewide grapevine the like of which has not been equaled anywhere else in North America," to keep them informed of conditions and rarities. Each hour must yield as many species as possible.[38]

Listing shaped birding as an activity, but not always what individual birdwatchers did. Novices often pursued new species, but as they exhausted the possibilities of their area, they found other goals or lost interest. They might compile more lists, for a day, a year, the state and country, or their backyard, or study a species' life history, feeding, behavior, or some other aspect of its life. A few became scientists. Listing ran like a fever through the Bronx County Bird Club. Peterson recalled that Joseph Hickey was losing interest as he ran out of new birds in the area, and then a non-Bronx birdwatcher, admitted to club outings for his expertise, took him in hand and introduced him to scientific studies.[39] Since the kind soul was Ernst Mayr, curator at the American Museum of Natural History and one of the founders of the neo-Darwinian synthesis, Hickey's was a rigorous introduction. A decade later, in his *Guide to Bird Watching*, Hickey condemned listing with the zeal of a reformed addict. Some, he said, measured "success in terms of the rarity, the first migrant, and the big list. At its best [listing] is a sport . . . At its worst it is a mad dash to the next oasis, with birds ticked off on the run, and a great reliance placed on both gasoline and brakes. Birds are *scanned*, but it scarcely can be said that they are *watched*—especially when one has an eye incessantly searching for a rarity in the next tree."[40]

Few birdwatchers took part in these marathons, but those who did had a key role in the hobby. Striving to outdo their friends, they found and tested what seemed reliable differences, and those that held up in the field became part of community knowledge. Incorporated into new guides, they helped less expert watchers sharpen their skills. The experts also defined what could be done. Ordinary birdwatchers bobbing around in a boat off the Massachusetts coast might not be able to distinguish Wilson's from Leach's Petrel, but they knew it could be done, and listening in the woods they knew that some of the *Empidonax* flycatchers could not safely be distinguished by plumage but only by song. More generally, listing organized not just birdwatchers' expeditions but the community, making the hobby less a solitary pursuit than a shared interest.

Even as Big Days led birdwatchers to closer studies of migration around home, scientific studies showed them the larger context of the birds they checked off in the park. Early in the twentieth century, naturalists began putting tags on the legs of individual birds, a practice called bird-banding in North America and "ringing" elsewhere, to follow their travels. When the United States and Canada agreed, under the Migratory Bird Treaty of 1916, to manage waterfowl populations, they set up a continental banding program coordinated by the Bureau of Biological Survey (predecessor of the Fish and Wildlife Service). Intended for migratory waterfowl, the Bureau soon took in almost all species. It enlisted thousands of volunteers who trapped, tagged, and released birds and sent the data to Washington. Bands from hunters and notes on retrapped birds soon outlined bird highways in the sky, which came to be called flyways, and then showed them in more detail. Just as the field guide used taxonomy to show birdwatchers the place an individual species had in the world's birds, migration returns put the warblers in the park and the ducks on the river in the context of continental geography and biogeography. They showed birdwatchers the importance of the Texas Gulf Coast, the line of the Appalachians, and California's Central Valley, observations that after World War II shaped bird tourism.

Competition turned birdwatchers inward, leading them to think about their own and other people's lists rather than nature, but it also forced a close attention to events in nature—that bird in the tree over there—and encouraged conservation. Record lists required detailed knowledge of the sort Griscom assembled for his comprehensive picture of birds in New York City, a fusion of amateur enthusiasm and quantitative science that set the model for later studies of larger areas and pointed birdwatchers toward the larger dimensions of their activity. At the extreme, people like Joseph Hickey turned their passion into academic careers, but many more banded birds, worked to preserve local wild areas, or studied some aspect of bird behavior.[41] More generally, competition increased consciousness about birds and about human threats to them. Listers, however focused on their totals and their friends' lists, could not ignore the toll development took on the meadows and swamps they quartered to build their lists.

346 WARBLERS

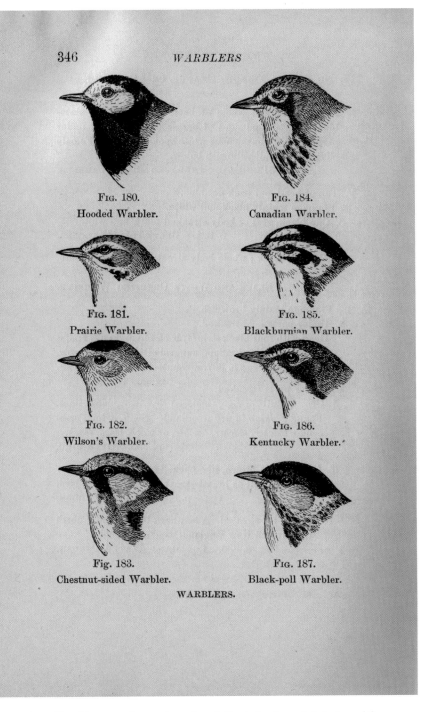

FIG. 180.
Hooded Warbler.

FIG. 184.
Canadian Warbler.

FIG. 181.
Prairie Warbler.

FIG. 185.
Blackburnian Warbler.

FIG. 182.
Wilson's Warbler.

FIG. 186.
Kentucky Warbler.

Fig. 183.
Chestnut-sided Warbler.

FIG. 187.
Black-poll Warbler.

WARBLERS.

Merriam's warblers · These wood engravings, the printing technology of 1898, showed the patterns of male warbler heads in spring plumage, arranged for easy comparison. From Florence Merriam, *Birds of Village and Field* (Boston: Houghton Mifflin, 1898).

WARBLERS (I)

1. KENTUCKY WARBLER, MALE
2. MOURNING WARBLER, *a.* MALE; *b.* FEMALE
3. CONNECTICUT WARBLER, *a.* MALE; *b.* FEMALE
4. NASHVILLE WARBLER
5. NORTHERN YELLOW-THROAT, *a.* MALE; *b.* FEMALE
6. HOODED WARBLER, *a.* MALE; *b.* FEMALE
7. WILSON'S WARBLER, *a.* MALE; *b.* FEMALE
8. BACHMAN'S WARBLER, *a.* MALE; *b.* FEMALE
9. BLUE-WINGED WARBLER, MALE
10. BREWSTER'S WARBLER
11. GOLDEN-WINGED WARBLER, MALE
12. LAWRENCE'S WARBLER
13. PROTHONOTARY WARBLER, *a.* MALE; *b.* FEMALE
14. YELLOW-BREASTED CHAT
15. YELLOW WARBLER, *a.* MALE; *b.* FEMALE
16. ORANGE-CROWNED WARBLER
17. WORM-EATING WARBLER
18. SWAINSON'S WARBLER
19. TENNESSEE WARBLER, MALE
20. PARULA WARBLER, *a.* MALE; *b.* FEMALE
21. BLACK-THROATED BLUE WARBLER, *a.* MALE; *b.* FEMALE
22. CERULEAN WARBLER, *a.* MALE; *b.* FEMALE

Peterson's warblers, 1934 · By 1934, printing costs and technologies allowed some color, which Peterson used for spring warblers. However, rather than names, the color plates had numbers keyed to a list on the facing page. The distinctive arrows, though, appeared in full bloom. From *A Field Guide to the Birds* by Roger Tory Peterson. Copyright © 1934, renewed 1961 by Roger Tory Peterson. Reprinted by permission of Houghton Mifflin Harcourt Publishing Company. All rights reserved.

MOURNING

CONNECTICUT

NASHVILLE

KENTUCKY

HOODED

WILSON'S

YELLOW-THROAT

LAWRENCE'S

BACHMAN'S

GOLDEN—WINGED

BREWSTER'S

BLUE—WINGED

PROTHONOTARY

YELLOW

Plate 50   187

SPRING WARBLERS
(Most of these have unstreaked breasts.)

MOURNING WARBLER   p. 206.
   Gray hood, black throat (male).

CONNECTICUT WARBLER   p. 205.
   Gray hood, white eye-ring.

NASHVILLE WARBLER   p. 191.
   Yellow throat, white eye-ring.

KENTUCKY WARBLER   p. 205.
   Black sideburns, yellow spectacles.

HOODED WARBLER   p. 207.
   Male: Black hood, yellow face.
   Female: See text.

WILSON'S WARBLER   p. 207.
   Male: Round black cap.
   Female: See text.

YELLOW-THROAT   p. 206.
   Male: Black mask.
   Female: Yellow throat, white belly.

BACHMAN'S WARBLER   p. 189.
   Male: Black cap, black bib; Southern, rare.
   Female: See text.

LAWRENCE'S WARBLER (Hybrid)   p. 189.
   Black bib, black cheek, yellow belly.

GOLDEN-WINGED WARBLER   p. 188.
   Black bib, black cheek, white belly.

BREWSTER'S WARBLER (Hybrid)   p. 188.
   Like Blue-wing with some white below.

BLUE-WINGED WARBLER   p. 188.
   Black eye-line, yellow under parts.

PROTHONOTARY WARBLER   p. 185.
   Golden head, bluish wings.

YELLOW WARBLER   p. 191.
   Yellowish back, yellow tail-spots.
   Reddish breast streaks (male).

CONFUSING FALL WARBLERS

(Most of these have streaks or wing-bars.)

* RUBY–CROWNED KINGLET   p. 175.
  Broken eye-ring, dark wing-bar.

CHESTNUT–SIDED WARBLER   p. 200.
  Immature: Yellow-green above, whitish below.

* YELLOW–THROATED VIREO   p. 180.
  Bright yellow breast, yellow spectacles.

BAY–BREASTED WARBLER   p. 200.
  Dark legs, buffy under tail (see text).

BLACK-POLL WARBLER   p. 201.
  Pale legs, white under tail (see text).

PINE WARBLER   p. 201.
  From preceding two by unstreaked back (see text).

PARULA WARBLER   p. 191.
  Immature: Bluish and yellow; wing bars.

MAGNOLIA WARBLER   p. 192.
  Immature: White band across tail.

PRAIRIE WARBLER   p. 203.
  Immature: Neck spot, side stripes; wags tail.

YELLOW WARBLER   p. 191.
  Yellow tail spots.

BLACKBURNIAN WARBLER   p. 197.
  Immature: Yellow throat, dark cheek, striped back.

BLACK–THROATED GREEN WARBLER   p. 196.
  Immature: Dusky streaks framing yellow cheek.

PALM WARBLER   p. 203.
  Brownish back; wags tail.

MYRTLE WARBLER   p. 193.
  Immature: Bright yellow rump.

CAPE MAY WARBLER   p. 192.
  Immature: Heavy streaks, neck spot (see text).

  * Not a Warbler, but often mistaken for one.

RUBY-CROWNED KINGLET

Immature
CHESTNUT-SIDED

YELLOW-THROATED
VIREO

♂
Adult

Immature

Immature

BLACKPOLL

Immature

♂ Adult

PINE

BAY-BREASTED

Immature

PARULA

Immature

MAGNOLIA

Immature

PRAIRIE

Immature
(Alaskan)

Immature

YELLOW

Immature

BLACKBURNIAN

Immature

BLACK-
THROATED
GREEN

PALM

Immature

MYRTLE

Immature

CAPE MAY

Peterson's fall warblers, 1947 · This moved beyond identification of the distinctive spring plumages to the more difficult fall ones, a look toward the birders' ultimate goal, identifying all the forms and plumages. The heading, "Confusing Fall Warblers," suggested these presented a challenge. From A Field Guide to the Birds by Roger Tory Peterson. Copyright © 1947, renewed 1974 by Roger Tory Peterson. Reprinted by permission of Houghton Mifflin Harcourt Publishing Company. All rights reserved.

WOOD WARBLERS (*Family* Parulidae) are small, very active, brightly colored songsters with slender, straight, pointed bills. Males in spring and early summer (through July) are fairly easy to recognize if you can get a good look at them. Since males do the singing, the great majority of birds seen in spring and summer are males in their breeding plumage. Look first for wingbars and characteristic head markings. Note the song patterns, which are diagnostic for most species.

Fall birds and spring females are difficult at first. Most female plumage patterns bear some resemblance to those of spring males, but are duller. For comparisons of fall plumages see pp. 276-277.

Our warblers are divided into 15 genera. Those in the same genus have some similarity in habits as well as in plumage and structure such as shape and size of bill. The genus *Seiurus* (Ovenbird and water thrushes), for example, includes birds that teeter like the Spotted Sandpiper and walk on the ground in search of food. The genus *Oporornis* is composed of relatively sluggish warblers that feed on the ground. Members of the genus *Wilsonia* catch insects on the wing.

During the nesting season, warblers remain in or close to their preferred habitats. During migration they gather in mixed flocks, frequently in company with chickadees or titmice. Then nearly all species occur in wood margins, hedgerows, orchards, and wooded swamps, along streams, or even in desert oases. Warblers migrate mainly a

WOOD WARBLERS WITHOUT WINGBARS - SPRING MALI

Worm-eating · Swainson's · Tennessee · Virginia's · Prothon

Ovenbird · Louisiana Waterthrush · Northern Waterthrush · Wilson's · Orange-cro

Yellow-breasted Chat · Yellowthroat · Kentucky · Canada · Nas

Bachman's · Hooded · Mourning · MacGillivray's · Conne

night, but watch for them flying within 500' of the treetops in early morning. Most winter in Mexico, Central America, or the West Indies.

The experienced observer can tell more than half the warblers just by their call notes. Learn the most distinctive chips first (such as those of Yellowthroat, Myrtle, Audubon's); then study the chips of the common birds in your area. Some will be impossible to recognize, but awareness of a chip that is different will aid you in fall by drawing attention to the less common species in a mixed flock.

Warblers are almost entirely insectivorous. Most warblers nest on or within 10' of the ground, but some, especially the Parula and some of the genus *Dendroica*, nest high in trees. Eggs, usually 4-5.

WOOD WARBLERS WITH WINGBARS - SPRING MALES

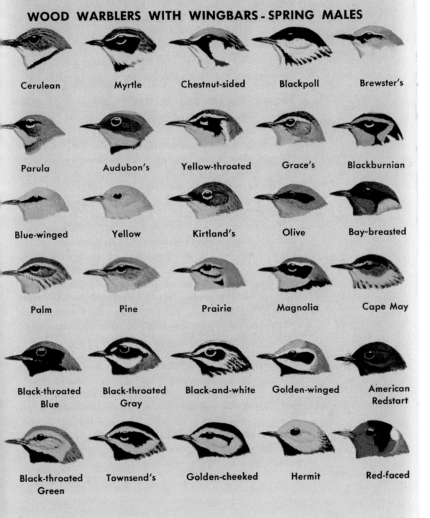

Cerulean	Myrtle	Chestnut-sided	Blackpoll	Brewster's
Parula	Audubon's	Yellow-throated	Grace's	Blackburnian
Blue-winged	Yellow	Kirtland's	Olive	Bay-breasted
Palm	Pine	Prairie	Magnolia	Cape May
Black-throated Blue	Black-throated Gray	Black-and-white	Golden-winged	American Redstart
Black-throated Green	Townsend's	Golden-cheeked	Hermit	Red-faced

Robbins's warbler heads · This modern version of Merriam's warbler heads has the birds in color. From *Birds of North America* by Chandler S. Robbins, Bertel Brun, and Herbert Zim. Illustrated by Arthur Singer. Copyright © Western Publishing Company, 1966. Used by permission of Chandler S. Robbins and Alan and Paul Singer, The Estate of Arthur Singer.

Wood-Warblers
Family: Parulidae

These are small active birds with short pointed bills. Many species are brilliantly colored in yellow, green, and blue and often have bold contrasting patterns. Wood-warblers are mainly solitary. They may form loose, mixed-species flocks in migration or winter (often with chickadees and other songbirds), but are never found in cohesive single-species flocks. All feed on small insects gleaned from leaves and twigs, as well as some berries and nectar. Songs are very useful in identification; most species sing two distinct song types in different situations, differing in rhythm and pattern. First-winter females are shown.

Genus *Dendroica*

YELLOW WARBLER, *page 334*

CHESTNUT-SIDED WARBLER, *page 335*

MAGNOLIA WARBLER, *page 335*

CAPE MAY WARBLER, *page 336*

BLACKBURNIAN WARBLER, *page 336*

BLACK-THROATED BLUE WARBLER, *page 337*

CERULEAN WARBLER, *page 337*

BLACK-THROATED GREEN WARBLER, *page 338*

GOLDEN-CHEEKED WARBLER, *page 338*

TOWNSEND'S WARBLER, *page 339*

HERMIT WARBLER, *page 339*

BLACK-THROATED GRAY WARBLER, *page 339*

YELLOW-RUMPED WARBLER, *page 340*

PALM WARBLER, *page 341*

PINE WARBLER, *page 342*

PRAIRIE WARBLER, *page 342*

BLACKPOLL WARBLER, *page 343*

BAY-BREASTED WARBLER, *page 343*

YELLOW-THROATED WARBLER, *page 344*

KIRTLAND'S WARBLER, *page 344*

night, but watch for them flying within 500' of the treetops in early morning. Most winter in Mexico, Central America, or the West Indies.

The experienced observer can tell more than half the warblers just by their call notes. Learn the most distinctive chips first (such as those of Yellowthroat, Myrtle, Audubon's); then study the chips of the common birds in your area. Some will be impossible to recognize, but awareness of a chip that is different will aid you in fall by drawing attention to the less common species in a mixed flock.

Warblers are almost entirely insectivorous. Most warblers nest on or within 10' of the ground, but some, especially the Parula and some of the genus *Dendroica*, nest high in trees. Eggs, usually 4-5.

WOOD WARBLERS WITH WINGBARS - SPRING MALES

Cerulean	Myrtle	Chestnut-sided	Blackpoll	Brewster's
Parula	Audubon's	Yellow-throated	Grace's	Blackburnian
Blue-winged	Yellow	Kirtland's	Olive	Bay-breasted
Palm	Pine	Prairie	Magnolia	Cape May
Black-throated Blue	Black-throated Gray	Black-and-white	Golden-winged	American Redstart
Black-throated Green	Townsend's	Golden-cheeked	Hermit	Red-faced

Robbins's warbler heads · This modern version of Merriam's warbler heads has the birds in color. From *Birds of North America* by Chandler S. Robbins, Bertel Brun, and Herbert Zim. Illustrated by Arthur Singer. Copyright © Western Publishing Company, 1966. Used by permission of Chandler S. Robbins and Alan and Paul Singer, The Estate of Arthur Singer.

Wood-Warblers

Family: Parulidae

These are small active birds with short pointed bills. Many species are brilliantly colored in yellow, green, and blue and often have bold contrasting patterns. Wood-warblers are mainly solitary. They may form loose, mixed-species flocks in migration or winter (often with chickadees and other songbirds), but are never found in cohesive single-species flocks. All feed on small insects gleaned from leaves and twigs, as well as some berries and nectar. Songs are very useful in identification; most species sing two distinct song types in different situations, differing in rhythm and pattern. First-winter females are shown.

Genus *Dendroica*

YELLOW WARBLER,
page 334

CHESTNUT-SIDED
WARBLER, *page 335*

MAGNOLIA
WARBLER,
page 335

CAPE MAY WARBLER,
page 336

BLACKBURNIAN
WARBLER,
page 336

BLACK-THROATED
BLUE WARBLER,
page 337

CERULEAN WARBLER,
page 337

BLACK-THROATED
GREEN WARBLER,
page 338

GOLDEN-CHEEKED
WARBLER,
page 338

TOWNSEND'S
WARBLER,
page 339

HERMIT WARBLER,
page 339

BLACK-THROATED
GRAY WARBLER,
page 339

YELLOW-RUMPED
WARBLER,
page 340

PALM WARBLER,
page 341

PINE WARBLER,
page 342

PRAIRIE WARBLER,
page 342

BLACKPOLL
WARBLER,
page 343

BAY-BREASTED
WARBLER, *page 343*

YELLOW-THROATED
WARBLER, *page 344*

KIRTLAND'S
WARBLER,
page 344

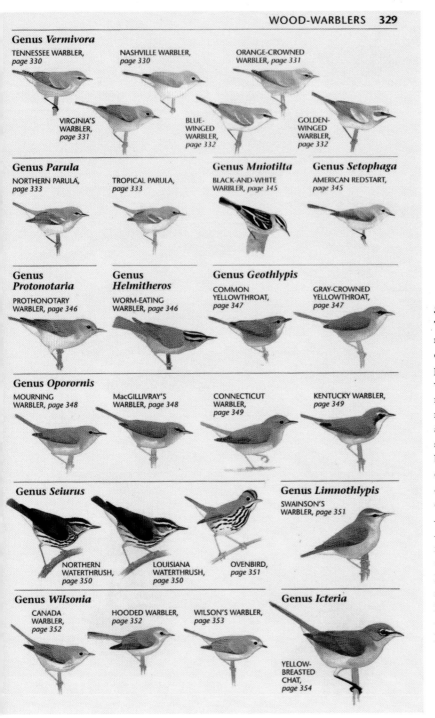

Genus *Vermivora*

TENNESSEE WARBLER, *page 330*

NASHVILLE WARBLER, *page 330*

ORANGE-CROWNED WARBLER, *page 331*

VIRGINIA'S WARBLER, *page 331*

BLUE-WINGED WARBLER, *page 332*

GOLDEN-WINGED WARBLER, *page 332*

Genus *Parula*

NORTHERN PARULA, *page 333*

TROPICAL PARULA, *page 333*

Genus *Mniotilta*

BLACK-AND-WHITE WARBLER, *page 345*

Genus *Setophaga*

AMERICAN REDSTART, *page 345*

Genus *Protonotaria*

PROTHONOTARY WARBLER, *page 346*

Genus *Helmitheros*

WORM-EATING WARBLER, *page 346*

Genus *Geothlypis*

COMMON YELLOWTHROAT, *page 347*

GRAY-CROWNED YELLOWTHROAT, *page 347*

Genus *Oporornis*

MOURNING WARBLER, *page 348*

MacGILLIVRAY'S WARBLER, *page 348*

CONNECTICUT WARBLER, *page 349*

KENTUCKY WARBLER, *page 349*

Genus *Seiurus*

NORTHERN WATERTHRUSH, *page 350*

LOUISIANA WATERTHRUSH, *page 350*

OVENBIRD, *page 351*

Genus *Limnothlypis*

SWAINSON'S WARBLER, *page 351*

Genus *Wilsonia*

CANADA WARBLER, *page 352*

HOODED WARBLER, *page 352*

WILSON'S WARBLER, *page 353*

Genus *Icteria*

YELLOW-BREASTED CHAT, *page 354*

Sibley's warblers · These pages, summarizing the family of warblers, had pictures of "First-winter females" rather than the more easily identifiable males, another sign of the modern birder's sophistication. From *The Sibley Guide to Birds of Eastern North America* by David Allen Sibley. Copyright © 2003 by Chanticleer Press, Inc. Used by Permission of Alfred A. Knopf, a division of Random House, Inc.

National Geographic's *warblers* · The extensive treatment of warblers in this very popular guide, with its plumages of the immature birds, showed how far the community of birders has come since Peterson had "Confusing Fall Warblers" on their own plate. From the National Geographic's *Field Guide to the Birds of North America.* Reprinted by arrangement with the National Geographic Society from *Field Guide to Birds of North America,* 5th edition. Copyright © 2006 National Geographic Society.

Birdwatching as an Approach to Nature in Industrial America

Many people saw Griscom and his friends as eccentrics, but birdwatchers stood in the mainstream of a major movement in industrial society—the search for individual contact with the world beyond society by playing in nature. To see where that led, place American birdwatching in the larger contexts of outdoor recreations and bird study in the other English-speaking countries. Outdoor recreations reflected national culture and conditions. From England to Australia people went hunting and fishing, but only in the United States and Canada did these hobbies become mixtures of pioneer woodcraft and English sporting ethics and tests of character and, in hunting, manliness. Hiking was common to all, but when Australians took the trolley out to the countryside on weekends they went "bushwalking," their gear packed like the "swagman," the legendary figure of the outback. American birdwatching had its patriotic appeals, the homage to Audubon and the search for the wild, a goal that became more visible as it became harder to reach the wild from the city. Birdwatching became a way of making contact with Nature's Nation and the wild that was its soul, and it made conservation the preservation of a national heritage.

Its origins in women's reform gave American birdwatching its focus on lists. Elsewhere the hobby grew out of amateur natural history, and bird students kept journals and compiled life-histories. They saw field identification, central to American study, as an essential skill, but only a precondition to worthwhile work. Well into the twentieth century lists and listing remained suspect. An Australian book, *Birdwatcher's Notebook* (1988), devoted three short paragraphs to the practice, labeled it "twitching," a term it handled with the tongs of parentheses, and began the next section: "At a more serious level . . ."[42] American birdwatching began with identification and found in competitive listing a way to encourage interest among an enthusiastic but inexperienced group of mainly women and children.

Population and population density encouraged listing by making collecting less desirable or useful. By the late nineteenth century, bulging museum drawers made collecting largely unnecessary, and it became apparent that a mass hobby that depended on killing birds would wipe them out. Besides, there were humane values to consider. In Australia and New Zealand—where people were few and professional ornithologists even fewer, unknown species remained, and little was known about variations and populations—collecting remained important. The Australian counterpart of the Junior Audubon Clubs, the Gould League of Bird Lovers, only condemned egg-collecting two decades after the Americans, and amateurs dominated the Royal Australian Ornithological Union into the 1960s, eighty years after its American counterpart had imposed professional qualifications on membership.[43] In Britain, general collecting passed as quickly as it did in the United States, but the strong tradition of local natural history studies and upper-class interest kept the hobby close to science.[44]

The differences appeared in the books. In the late 1930s Americans carried Peterson, who focused on identification, while British bird students had volumes with much more on migration, range, and breeding.[45] One British observer said that Richard Fitter's *Pocket Guide to British Birds* (1952) "moved the whole business of a bird-identification guide into the modern era," and two years later the Peterson series' *Field Guide to the Birds of Britain and Europe* "completely eclipsed the Englishman's achievement" and introduced Britons to a new world of watching.[46] The same was true in the antipodes, where Australians had Neville Cayley's work *What Bird is That?*, an ornithologically minded library volume, and New Zealanders had Perrine Moncrieff's *New Zealand Birds and How to Identify Them*, a pocket guide on the model of late nineteenth-century British amateur natural history studies.[47] Nature study remained amateur science, with readers sending in reports to newspaper nature columns (well after such features had dwindled and almost disappeared in American papers), which printed observations and detailed accounts of local abundance, migration, and nesting—even the mechanics of flight.[48] Outside the United States, only the Canadians followed the American lead, and that came from their reliance on American books, which continued into the twentieth century.[49]

Like all outdoor recreations, birdwatching depended on equipment, but it suffered less than others from the plague of consumer goods that overwhelmed hunting and fishing, largely because birdwatchers needed little more than binoculars.[50] In the first generation they made do with what was available, as indicated by Merriam's title *Birds through an Opera-Glass*. By the 1920s, they bought binoculars, for they let novices see patterns more clearly and allowed "experienced field observers like Griscom to sort out even the migrating fall warblers in their drab plumages."[51] Even Griscom's teenage disciples found the money for them. Peterson bought "a pair of four-power LeMaire glasses for seven dollars after seeing an ad for them in *Bird-Lore*." Binoculars, though, gave no decisive advantage—identifying birds depended more on knowing what to look for than seeing it with exquisite clarity. After World War II, optical firms began making binoculars and high-power scopes with birdwatchers in mind. Field guides, finding guides, and nature study books became profitable market niches, and in the 1970s bird tours and bird tourism began to develop. Now electronic guides and calls have become a new consumer category.

Through it all, American birdwatching retained at least something of natural history's wider vision. Alone among the ways that citizens of industrial societies went to nature, birdwatching organized the hobbyist's experiences in time and space and linked them to the larger world. Field guides—somewhat accidentally, to be sure—showed the birds around home as part of the birds of the region and the nation. Listing focused attention on migration and habitat, keeping people aware of the annual cycle of the seasons, the biotic ties running across North America, and species' dependence on the environment. Birdwatchers looked to ornithology, which extended their vision back in time, and found in the flyways patterns of life stretching from the Arctic to South America. Spotting hawks from a ridge in the Alleghenies or warblers in the park, they could relate what they saw to continental geography. They also built individual, local knowledge. Ludlow Griscom eventually looked back on a half century of observations that charted the movement of species into his area and out, the decline of some and the increase of others, the weather and its effects on migration. Few kept such meticulous notes, but all could construct from their years afield a knowledge of the life of the land and its changes through the years, recording the history of their involvement with the natural world.

In this second generation, birdwatching built an established community, still concentrated on the East Coast but represented across the country, improved field identification methods, and assembled a catalog of information. Rapid identification spread to the general birdwatching population; the life-list became a long-term goal and measure of competence, and the spring Big Day the standard of competition. *Birds of the New York City Region* set an example of a community local range and the form of the birdwatchers' second essential book, the finding guide. Although such a guide made the sport separate from science, this generation also tied their hobby more securely to the culture's formal knowledge by making field identification accurate enough for ornithologists to use, building a bridge between recreation and conservation that saw increased traffic as the years went by. This generation lacked, though, a guide that would make beginners' expeditions pleasant enough to attract many people to the hobby. The next chapter takes up that book, Roger Tory Peterson's *Field Guide to the Birds*, published in 1934.

FOUR

The Field Guide Comes of Age

*… and then somebody rang in this
skinny kid from upstate New York
who could identify anything.*

—JOSEPH HICKEY
(RECALLING EVENTS OF 1927)

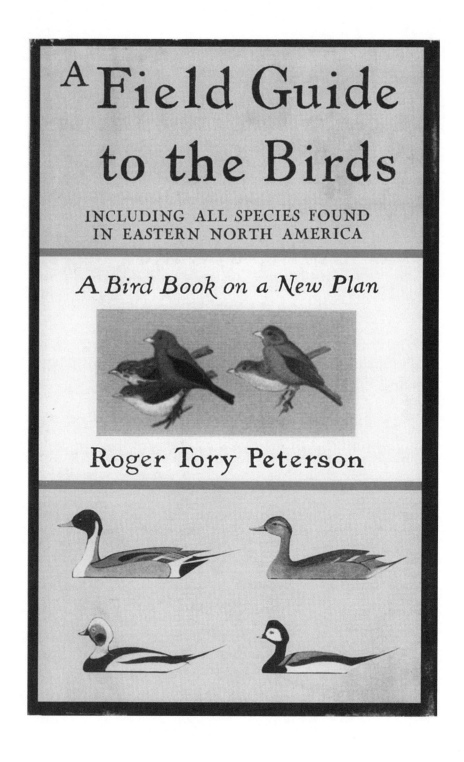

A Field Guide
to the Birds

INCLUDING ALL SPECIES FOUND
IN EASTERN NORTH AMERICA

A Bird Book on a New Plan

Roger Tory Peterson

One book captures the bird guides of the next generation, the one that revolutionized the genre and the hobby and became synonymous with birdwatching: Roger Tory Peterson's *Field Guide to the Birds*.[1] The first edition, published in 1934, seemed ordinary, a slim volume of 167 pages, half an inch thick, bound in green pebbled cloth, on the cover the title, the name Peterson, and the figure of a male Bufflehead Duck, picked out in silver. The dust jacket proclaimed it "A Bird Book on a New Plan," but casual bookstore browsers might have taken it for an abbreviated and simplified guide, with poor illustrations to boot. The descriptions were short, with little information on characteristic behavior and calls, and range descriptions were sketchy (Bell's Vireo—"Breeds east to Illinois and northwestern Indiana"). The plates, scattered through the book, showed birds in black and white (there were only four color plates), colored in blocks, against a neutral background.[2] On each, birds stood in the same pose, and the facing page gave key characteristics. Did that constitute a "new plan," worth $2.75, a good deal of money in the depths of the Depression? Even Houghton Mifflin had its doubts, for the contract gave Peterson no royalties on the first thousand copies. The first printing of two thousand copies, though, went quickly, later ones with gratifying speed, and in a few years it had swept the market.

It turned into Peterson's life-time project. Work on the eastern and western editions, and one for Texas, continued through his life. The fifth

4.1 · *Cover of first Peterson guide* · The cover to the first Peterson guide, with its declaration of a "new plan" and in the cover pictures a hint of its emphasis and arrangement. From *A Field Guide to the Birds* by Roger Tory Peterson. Copyright © 1934, renewed 1961 by Roger Tory Peterson. Reprinted by permission of Houghton Mifflin Harcourt Publishing Company. All rights reserved.

edition of the eastern guide, completed by others after his death, came out in 1996, and in 2008 Houghton Mifflin combined the eastern and western ones in a new *Peterson Field Guide to Birds of North America*.[3] The eastern guide dominated the market for three decades and remains a presence, and the first edition became a collector's item. An example from the first run, in almost any condition, would fetch over $1,000, and in good condition, with an intact dust jacket, up to $5,000. Examples of the later editions stand on bookshelves across America. Even birders who swear by "Sibley," the "Golden Guide," or "National Geographic" probably have "Peterson" on their shelves—if only to loan to a beginner.

Peterson and his career run through the rest of this book; this chapter traces his path from his youth in Jamestown, New York, in the 1920s through World War II, the years when he developed from bird-obsessed teenager and fledging writer to field guide author and illustrator, ready to make his living from bird art and birdwatching.[4] That he could turn this project into a career showed how far the hobby and the community had come since the days when Ludlow Griscom spent years alone before finding "blessed companionship" at the Linnaean Society of New York. The rest of this chapter considers changes in the hobby as it became truly national, something Peterson's western guide, published in 1939, encouraged. It also became a more competitive pursuit. All these changes took place against the backdrop of the Depression and the emergence of ecology and game management as academic and scientific disciplines, which had important implications for birdwatching after World War II. Finally, there was the state of the community on the eve of the postwar nature boom, the interest that fueled the environmental revolution in the 1960s and changed the basis of bird conservation and birdwatchers' perspective on wild America.

The Skinny Kid

The teenage Roger Peterson, out in the woods around Jamestown with Chapman's *Handbook* and a pair of four-power binoculars, had all the hallmarks of the birdwatcher but, like Joe Hickey and his friends in the Bronx County Bird Club, none of the social status that marked the first generation. Peterson grew up in a small industrial city, the son of an immigrant Swedish cabinetmaker, his only obvious career a factory job. Nothing marked him out but his passionate interest in nature. He spent his adolescence, he recalled, "in trouble up to my skinny neck," for he cared only for birds, and there was "nothing thoughtful or academic in my interest; it was so spontaneous I could not control it."[5] He found a direction in the school's Junior Audubon Club, where Miss Blanche Hornbeck, his seventh-grade teacher, gave each student a set of watercolors, a plate from *The Birds of New York State*, by the great bird painter Louis Agassiz Fuertes, to copy, and one of Reed's guides.[6] With that, and then Chapman's *Handbook*, which he began to use in high school, Peterson passed from "the thrill of discovery" to "the listing stage," when identifying species became a competitive sport, and on to a deeper interest in bird's habits and action. With Fuertes as his model he drew and painted, then began sending paintings to shows. Looking back, he saw his all-absorbing interest as a way to deal with the "strait jacket of a world which I did not comprehend" and make "some sort of peace with society. The birds, which started as an escape from the unreal, bridged the gap to reality and became a key whereby I might unlock eternal things."[7]

Birds did not reveal an obvious way to make a living, however. After graduating from high school in 1926, he worked for a year in a local furniture factory, decorating lacquered Chinese cabinets, saving his money to study commercial art in New York City. He went to the Art Student's League and then the National Academy of Design, where Winslow Homer, Frederic Remington, Howard Pyle, and Norman Rockwell had trained, supporting himself by refinishing and decorating furniture.[8] When he joined the Linnaean Society of New York he met Robert Porter Allen, along with what he later called the "legendary company . . . the seven young men of the Bronx County Bird Club," who nursed "the seemingly impossible hope of sighting 100 species on the [Audubon Society] Christmas Count."[9] They competed intensely among themselves and deferred to Ludlow Griscom, who was, Peterson recalled, "our God, and his *Birds of the New York City Region . . .* our bible." He joined them on outings, his expertise making up for the lack of a Bronx address.[10]

"It was because of my close friendship with Griscom and his young disciples in the Linnaean Society that I was able to prepare my own Field Guide." Birding with them, he learned all the methods and techniques and the "few key marks of each species. Being academically trained as an artist, I was able to put it all down and give it form."[11] In pictures, which people grasped more easily and quickly than text, he showed the "unique combinations of features which identify almost every species at a distance, whether afoot, abranch, or awing."[12] By the time he left New York in 1931 to teach natural science and art at a private school in Brookline, Massachusetts, he had "all the ingredients for my new synthesis." The term "field mark," which became identified with his system, he took from a paragraph heading in Edward Howe Forbush's *Birds of Massachusetts*, not directly but through Griscom, who changed its meaning from the usual one of all a bird's features to those that distinguished a species from the others. Pattern recognition came from Ernest Thompson Seton, to whom he paid tribute in the introduction to his first guide, and "Dr. John B. May, [who] in Forbush's *Birds of Massachusetts*, was the first to revive and popularize" Seton's practice.[13] Teaching nature study at Audubon summer camps showed him where in the process of identification novices had problems. When he showed his early sketches to William Vogt, another non-Bronx member of the Bronx County Bird Club, Vogt not only urged him to continue but took the manuscript to several New York publishers. When they turned it down, Peterson, believing Vogt had written to Houghton Mifflin, took it to the firm's Boston office. An editor who knew Griscom had him vouch for the drawings' accuracy as depictions of both the birds and what could be seen in the field with binoculars.[14]

At first glance Peterson's guide looked much like other bird guides. It had descriptions of all the species, arranged in taxonomic order, with what seemed to be simply colored plates of birds scattered through the book, almost all of them in black and white. The only obvious difference was the little lines that pointed to features on the birds. Peterson attributed the book's success to that innovation, the "schematic drawings and little arrows [that] taught people to look for those few diagnostic marks or patterns that would allow them to name almost every bird they saw. The very simplicity of the method, it has been suggested, was a major reason for the spectacular growth of birding."[15] The crucial innovation lay in making pictures rather than text primary. Written descriptions required readers to translate words into what they saw. Consider this account from Chapman's *Color Key*—"American Robin (*Merula migratoria*). L[ength]. 10; W[ing]. 4.9; T[ail]. 3.8. Outer tail-feathers with white tips. Ad[ult male] Breast and belly rich rust-brown; above dark slaty, head and spots in back black"—and compare it with Peterson's picture in the field guide.[16]

It is much easier to glance from bird to plate, and Peterson told readers to do just that: "In many instances the pictures tell the story

4.2 · *Herons and bitterns, 1934* · Modern readers may be dismayed at the relatively crude illustrations and the hand-lettered names, and, compared with the third edition shown in the next chapter, it was only a start, but look back at earlier guides. From *A Field Guide to the Birds* by Roger Tory Peterson. Copyright © 1934, renewed 1961 by Roger Tory Peterson. Reprinted by permission of Houghton Mifflin Harcourt Publishing Company. All rights reserved.

BLACK·CROWNED
NIGHT HERON

ADULT

IMMATURE

AMERICAN
BITTERN

LEAST BITTERN

YELLOW·CROWNED
NIGHT HERON
ADULT

GREEN HERON
ADULT

GREAT BLUE HERON

LITTLE BLUE HERON
ADULT

LITTLE BLUE HERON
IMMATURE

SNOWY EGRET

AMERICAN EGRET

LOUISIANA
HERON

HERONS
AND
BITTERNS

This shows the Peterson format: birds in ranks, colored in shadings that emphasized what you saw through binoculars.

Peterson's strength as a field guide artist lay in making plates that showed the birds as they appeared and that could be reproduced inexpensively enough to allow full illustrations in a popular guide.

Peterson liked simple, bold headings, something his emphasis on grouping similar species allowed.

In the 1947 edition, Peterson replaced these hand-lettered names with printed ones.

without help from the letterpress." He counted on their being able to find the right section, for while he urged them to become familiar, "in a general way, with the illustrations" and learn to tell a duck from a loon, a gull from a tern, and a warbler with its "needle-like bill" from a sparrow with its "stout seed-cracking" one, he focused on helping them separate similar species.[17] Birds that looked much alike stood together—all the spring warblers with solid yellow breasts on one plate, those with streaked breasts on another. All distractions were banished. Earlier artists showed petrels over the ocean, ducks in the marsh, and perching birds on twigs and branches, posed against shrubs and trees. Peterson stood quail and pheasant on the page without a blade of grass or a bit of ground under them; his ducks and geese floated on invisible ponds, their bodies ending at a ruler-straight waterline; woodpeckers perched on tree stumps of ectoplasm; and warblers curled their feet around the barest suggestion of a twig.

The paintings were a new, functional art, "not intended to be pictures or portraits" but to show "simple contour and pattern." Critics occasionally complained that he could not paint well, a charge he resented and countered with his fine art paintings, but judging field guide plates as fine art missed the point.[18] They existed not for aesthetics but to show, at a glance, the details that gave you "the clue you needed to identify [the bird] quickly," and the apparently crude pictures involved a sophisticated understanding of what lines and color on a page meant, an understanding well known in Western art but not in field guides.[19] In his popular *Elements of Drawing*, John Ruskin, the Victorian art critic and aesthete, had warned students against putting down on paper "not what you *see* but what you *know*." Sketch, he said, a bookcase and the books in it from three yards away, "from which distance the student would find that the appearance of lettering was exact but the actual titles were completely unreadable. . . . Everything that you can see in the world around you presents itself to your eyes only as an arrangement of patches of different colours variously shaded." The technical side of painting, therefore, consisted of recovering the ability to see the world as "flat stains of colour, merely as such, without consciousness of what they signify."[20] Audubon, showing his birds feather by feather, in the tradition of natural history illustration, served science but did not paint what people saw, masses of color they interpreted as feathers. Birdwatchers appreciated the point; Mabel Osgood Wright spoke of people seeing "shapes and general effects rather than detail," and Seton's diagrammatic paintings and Chapman's colored drawings in *Color Key* presented birds in that fashion.[21] Peterson knew which details to use, and his training in commercial art allowed him not just to put them on paper but to do it in a way that allowed inexpensive reproduction.

He arranged his text as well as illustrations for the birdwatcher rather than the ornithologist or amateur naturalist, concentrating on distinguishing features visible in the field. Except for the usual outline of a bird labeled with words like "primaries," "upper and lower tail coverts," "tarsus," and "superciliary line," he left out technical terms, ignored recently extinct species, and was silent about abundance unless it helped readers decide between species. He only hinted, for instance, at the impending fate of the Ivory-billed Woodpecker with the terse note "extremely rare." His accounts of the families or genera left out taxonomic niceties so as to zero in on distinctive differences. Ibises and Spoonbills were "long-legged Heron-like birds with long, slender, *decurved* bills. Similar to those of the Curlews. Unlike the Herons they fly with necks *outstretched*." Falcons were "hawks with long *pointed* wings and long tails. The wing strokes are rapid." Species descriptions emphasized diagnostic differences. The Northern Parula Warbler was "the only *bluish* Warbler with a *yellow* throat and breast," and the Ivory Gull "the only pure white gull with *black* legs." After the first edition, in which he passed over the Robin as "the one bird everybody knows," in the next edition he said it was "easily recognized by its gray back and *brick-red* breast. In the male, the head and tail are blackish; in the female, paler. The bill is *yellow*."[22]

He took this approach not just because people relied on sight and easily grasped patterns but because patterns were what could most easily be put on the page. Songs and calls, just as characteristic and even more useful in the woods, did not go well into print or diagrams. Musical notation conveyed only the general tenor of the song, and Peterson said that a description like "'sizzling trill' or a 'bubbling warble' conveys but a wretched idea of the real effect produced by the voice of any particular bird."[23] The Bobwhite said its name, and the Ovenbird called "Teacher, teacher, teacher," but few species had such good enunciation. Peterson's description of the calls of the Alder Flycatcher, for instance, seemed more suggestive than clear. In New York State, he said, it "gave a call that might be rendered *way-be-o* with the accent on the *middle* syllable. . . . [while] the Ohio birds gave utterance to a sneezy *fitz-bew*."[24] Later guides tried sonograms, which displayed sounds as lines plotted on grid (time in seconds against pitch in kilocycles/second), and birdwatchers tried records, then tapes and CD-ROMs. Now they download apps giving calls for all the birds.[25] Printed guides did some things well, other things poorly, and birdwatchers necessarily relied on what the guides could best tell them.

The Field Guide Comes of Age

Birdwatchers immediately recognized Peterson's guide as a major step forward. Connie Hagar, a South Texas birding legend, spoke for many when she told nature writer Edwin Way Teale that she began bird-watching on the Texas coast in the early 1930s with only "a small Reed's pocket guide with colored illustrations, 'some good, some terrible,' and Arthur Cleveland Bent's *Life Histories of North American Waterfowl*, published by the Smithsonian Institution in Washington. 'I tell you, it was rough,' she commented. 'When Roger Peterson's field guide appeared, I felt let out the cage.'"[26] Others used more measured language, but to the same end. Frank Chapman declared it "unique," for its virtues went beyond "keen discrimination and sympathetic observation, field-experience with birds and birdmen, and exceptional skill as a draughtsman." It blazed a "new trail in bird-lore." Only those who had begun bird study with a gun could "fully realize the significance to field ornithology of the appearance of Mr. Peterson's 'Field Guide.'"[27] Sales continued strong, and Houghton Mifflin brought out a revised edition in 1939 and Peterson's western guide two years later.[28] The nature writer Donald Culross Peattie, trying out the new western volume in the field, could by then refer to "the famed Peterson rapid-identification system" and report that it worked "in the West with the same *Blitzkrieg* efficiency as in the East."[29]

Peterson revolutionized birdwatching, but the popular legend that he ended the era of the shotgun and ushered in the time of binoculars gave him too much credit.[30] Collecting was already declining.[31] What Peterson did do was boost a shift Chapman noted when he said "the 'life-list' has taken the place of the collection, and the census has replaced the bag, and with this change in objective has come a change in method." Instead of the solitary collector contributing to science, many people now played a fascinating game, and if the activity had no value for science, did that matter? Was it "essential that our relations with birds be scientific in order that we may reap in large measure their value to man?" Can we not "go a-birding without feeling that we must make some contribution to the science of ornithology?"[32] Peterson agreed, though he was somewhat apologetic about simple enjoyment. "Field birding as most of us engage in it is a game—a most absorbing game." Old-timers, he went on, "minimize the scientific value of this type of

4.3 · *Thrushes* · This plate of plump, posed thrushes showed the hallmark of the "Peterson system," the "little arrows" pointing to identifying characteristics. From *A Field Guide to the Birds* by Roger Tory Peterson. Copyright © 1934, renewed 1961 by Roger Tory Peterson. Reprinted by permission of Houghton Mifflin Harcourt Publishing Company. All rights reserved.

REDDISH HEAD

REDDISH TAIL

LARGE
ROUND SPOTS

WOOD

HERMIT

UNIFORMLY REDDISH
UPPERPARTS

VERY LITTLE
SPOTTING

VEERY

GRAY CHEEKS

EYE-RING
BUFFY CHEEKS

UNIFORMLY GRAY-BROWN
UPPERPARTS

GRAY-CHEEKED

OLIVE-BACKED

THRUSHES

One of Peterson's subtle trademarks was this instantly recognizable layout. Compare his with other guides.

Black and white shading conveys not only the breast spots but the subtle color differences on the back that birders use to identify these birds.

For this group Peterson could use a simple title. He divided larger families by such characteristics as wing bars and streaks on the breast.

A classic use of his little arrows, reinforced by the text beside it. Later editions used a legend page, leaving the plates uncluttered.

bird work. Truly, it has little. Recognition is not the end and aim of or-nithology, but is certainly a most fascinating diversion—and a stage through which the person who desires to contribute to our knowledge of ornithology might profitably pass."[33] For most birdwatchers, though, it was simply a most absorbing game.

Peterson set the form of the modern guide—a pocket-sized catalog using pictures to emphasize distinguishing marks, arranged for easy comparison of similar species. He took information from science and recreation, using museum collections and consulting ornithologists (becoming expert enough to serve on scientific committees), while for field marks he relied heavily on expert but amateur observers. He consulted Griscom and the Bronx boys, people he met as a staff mem-ber for the National Audubon Society, and once he established him-self, his enthusiastic fans. In the 1947 edition of the eastern guide he included a half-page list of those who made "anywhere from one or two suggestions to a hundred or more," tips that filled "between 1000 and 1500 filing cards." Besides these, he went on, "scores of other users of the guide have given me their verbal comments. So I can truly say that this book is written not only for the bird students of America, but by them."[34]

Birdwatchers' knowledge made Peterson's guide possible, and their numbers let him think about a career as a field guide author and illus-trator, but it took a decade of work to turn possibilities into reality. Even as the first edition appeared, he had improvements in mind. In Septem-ber 1934 he wrote to Frank Chapman that the book needed, at a min-imum, two plates of "shore-birds at rest—as they are on the beach. After all, that is the way we learn them. This is the most evident gap in the il-lustrative material."[35] Two months later he joined the staff of the Na-tional Audubon Society, where he stayed until he was drafted during World War II. He revised the eastern guide (second edition, 1939) and wrote a western one (1941), an astonishing productivity, given his work at Audubon, which included illustrations for *Bird-Lore*, writing new nature pamphlets for the school program, even revising the require-ments for the Boy Scouts' merit badge in ornithology. He gained expe-rience with birds, birdwatchers, and their problems, but by the time the war put his career on hold, he was restless.

Stationed near Washington, D.C., where he illustrated technical publications and aircraft identification manuals, he stayed in touch

4.4 · *Peterson's hawks* · From *A Field Guide to the Birds* by Roger Tory Peterson. Copy-right © 1934, renewed 1961 by Roger Tory Peterson. Reprinted by permission of Houghton Mifflin Harcourt Publishing Company. All rights reserved.

COOPER'S HAWK

GOSHAWK

SHARP-SHINNED HAWK

LIGHT PHASE

ROUGH-LEGGED HAWK

ABOVE

DARK PHASE

BROAD-WINGED HAWK

RED-SHOULDERED HAWK

RED-TAILED HAWK

SWAINSON'S HAWK

DARK PHASE

SHORT-TAILED HAWK

LIGHT PHASE

This plate shows Seton's influence, both in arrangement and emphasis on the birds' "uniforms." Compare with the second plate in chapter two.

An ideal use of black-and-white. It is often difficult to see colors on birds against the sky, and these emphasize what you do see—distinctive patterns like the breast band on Swainson's Hawk or the Rough-legged's dark belly.

This certainly needs no title.

Here Peterson emphasized a characteristic of some hawks—distinctive differently colored forms of the same species.

with birdwatching. He accepted an invitation to speak at the annual meeting of the Washington Audubon Society, unless, he said gloomily, he had "guard duty that night."[36] He wrote Audubon president John Baker that if he worked only six months a year for Audubon he would have "much more time to work effectively on my Field Guide series and on my paintings."[37] By painting he meant fine art. He wrote his editor at Houghton Mifflin, Paul Brooks, that he had to "do some tall stepping to bring my bird painting up to the high standard I hope it will eventually reach," and again to Baker that while working for the society he had been "unable to pursue my chief aim—that of developing myself into a first-rate bird artist."[38] Two weeks later he wrote Baker another letter saying his "chief hope for the next ten years is to make myself into a first-rate bird painter," but even as he complained about needing time to improve his art, he asked Brooks if the firm was still "as anxious as ever to get on with the [planned field guide] series." He still was, and he also wanted to "completely revamp the Eastern Field Guide and make it a really bang-up job. The plates have to be done over again anyway [and] instead of four color plates I would like six, as in the Western book." That would "include a page of difficult fall warblers, a point that will sell a good many copies to more advanced students who already own the book. In addition, I want to include a series of common silhouettes." All the drawings, as well as the plates, should be redone, and "the captions set in type, instead of the present poor hand lettering."[39]

He faced the same technical problems as his predecessors and had much the same complaints, down to the quality of the reproductions, but he worked in a very different context. Rather than giving tips and encouragement to people beginning a new kind of outdoor activity, he addressed an audience of novices who knew what birdwatching was and more expert watchers who wanted to improve their skills. Instead of inventing a genre, he gave it its mature form. At the heart of his work lay this distinct kind of nature art, illustrations aimed solely at field identification, and as much as Audubon, his job was not simply to make the images but to oversee their translation from individual copy to mass-produced image. He brought to that job a unique set of skills: extensive field experience, an up-to-date knowledge of field identification, a good understanding of where in the process of identification novices needed help, and experience painting what printers and presses could put on the page. He also appreciated field guides as a business. Finally, he had a strong work ethic, an even stronger competitive streak, and a relentless perfectionism.

Two items in *Bird-Lore* in the late 1930s highlighted birdwatchers' growing interest in listing as a competitive hobby and personal pursuit, a development Peterson's guide catered to and encouraged. Early in 1937, under the title "Unprecedented in Bird Annals," *Bird-Lore* reported that for "several weeks bird-lovers have been traveling to Gorham, Maine, to see a songbird that never before has been recorded as found east of the Mississippi River, a Rosy Finch (*Luecosticte tephrocotis littoralis*)." A grayish bird with a blackish crown and a tinge of pink on rump and wings, it normally lived near the snow line in western mountains, but it had appeared "some time before Christmas" in Maine, where it "was first identified by Mrs. William Roberts and the writer (Jesse L. Keene, Gorham Normal School)," then "identified and banded by Dr. Alfred O. Gross of Bowdoin College."[40] Two years later, in "The Lure of the List," Guy Emerson, a banker and longtime Audubon director, told of his quest for a new record for species and subspecies in North America seen during a single year.[41] Listing as a goal of birdwatching visibly moved from personal records and competitions among friends and toward a competitive activity within a national community. The pilgrimage to Gorham, Maine, showed the fever for the life-list spreading from experts to ordinary birders. In 1929, Ludlow Griscom wrote to Joseph Grinnell about his continuing contest "to see who can see the greatest number of A.O.U. birds in life. Bent and Townsend are over 700 and I am just below, but if I can get in a good lick in California I will put them both to sleep." Grinnell, though an objective scientist to his core and the very model of a museum ornithologist, assured him the trip would indeed give him a good chance "to grow a record 'life list,'" and offered to guide him to some of the rarities he was looking for.[42] The year-list became the yardstick for competition and the life-list a long-term measure of competence or accomplishment.

Emerson's article foreshadowed the North American year-list as a competitive standard and public contest. Like the "Big Day," it relied on modern travel. His work for the Bankers Trust Company involved travel to banks around the country, and he tried to match his business trips with the birds' calendar, visiting banks near wintering grounds in January and those near migration hot spots in May, and using the friendships formed through years as an Audubon director to get local information. In 1939 birds and banks came together, and he checked off the astounding total of 674 species and subspecies. "The Lure of the List" took competition to a new level, but Emerson did not put the list in these terms and was even mildly apologetic about his preeminence. The pursuit of birds provided exercise, kept him from focusing all his energies on business, and got him off the beaten track, to places where he met "people who are close to the soil, to the woods, to the waters— quiet people with different ways of living and simpler tastes than those of city dwellers; people with long vistas in their eyes, strong, unworried people close to the heart of America."[43] The total had no real importance, though it was "of some interest to know how many varieties of birds can be seen in this country in a year." In any event, the record was the result of "a cooperative venture," for some twenty people had generously guided him around land they knew well. Without them, he could not have made his list.[44] Modesty and his interest in the heart of America did not stop him from speculating that it would be possible with good timing and help from local experts to notch up some 700 or 750 of America's 1,088 species and subspecies.[45]

Even as cars and trains allowed birdwatchers to seek wider horizons, wildlife research gave them a new perspective on the need to save nature and how it should be done. In the late nineteenth century, state legislatures began trying to save game by cutting the human toll with season and bag limits and the natural toll by killing predators. The interwar years saw some visible, sometimes spectacular failures as the ecological consequences of these policies worked themselves out on the land. As Aldo Leopold put it in his classic essay "Thinking Like a Mountain," fewer wolves did not mean more game, and no wolves did not bring a sportsman's paradise.[46] To the contrary, some of the most vigorously protected species suffered the worst fates. Deer populations from Arizona to Pennsylvania went through population booms and busts, with the herd in the Kaibab National Forest, on the North Rim of the Grand Canyon, becoming a national issue.[47] Despite the 1916 Migratory Bird Treaty, ducks and geese continued to decline, so much so that by the early 1930s there were suggestions of a one-year suspension of all waterfowl shooting. Quail, the most popular upland bird, became scarcer, even in states where they were protected and encouraged on land managed for them.[48] A few, Leopold among them, borrowed ideas and research programs from the still-developing discipline of animal ecology to make a new applied science, game management. Audubon kept members abreast of new ideas. In 1931, *Bird-Lore* published "A Little Essay on Vermin," by a Bureau of Biological Survey biologist, Waldo L. McAtee, arguing that all species were admirable and all should be saved. The journal reported on Paul Errington's research on Bobwhite Quail in Wisconsin, showing that habitat, rather than predators, kept that population in check, and reprinted Leopold's remarks to the American Game Conference about the futility of most predator control.[49] More to the point, the Audubon Society stopped shooting bird-eating hawks on its reserves.[50]

Bird-Lore had to educate readers, for the connections between birds and their habitat were not as obvious as those between birds and market or sport hunters. It seemed logical to protect rookeries to save egrets and stop the shooting of songbirds to have more robins on the lawn, but ecological research often told counterintuitive tales that were hard to explain to a general public. In Georgia, Herbert Stoddard traced the decline of quail not to predators but to farming practices and road improvements. The dirt roads and snake fences of the late nineteenth century gave quail gravel for their crops and dust for baths to kill mites in their feathers. The zigzag fences made nesting places safe from farm equipment and harbored weed seeds that they ate. Straight fences and paved roads did not. In Wisconsin, Errington found the limit on winter survival of quail was the number, frequency, and severity of winter storms, not the presence or even the population of predators.[51]

Hunters, arms and ammunition manufacturers, and government agencies supported research on these species, but few took up the cause of nongame birds. The disappearance of the Passenger Pigeon in the early 1900s and the slow dwindling of the Carolina Paraquot in the next decade made the public aware that humans could wipe out entire species but did not suggest what might be done. In 1922, when the Whooping Cranes abandoned their last known nesting site, in Saskatchewan, a few papers printed (premature) obituaries, but no one took action, not from indifference but because no one knew what had to be done, or even how many cranes remained.[52] The hope that birds were only scarce, not gone, possibly still abundant in some back-country refuge, kept them in guides long after they vanished from the field. Reed described the range of the Carolina Paroquet as "formerly the southern states, but now confined to the interior of Florida and, possibly, Indian Territory."[53] Peterson did not mention the Carolina Paraquot in his 1934 edition of the eastern guide but in 1939 said there was "still a bare chance that a stray individual or a flock might turn up." In 1947 that dwindled to "naturalists still hope that a stray individual" might turn up.[54] Chapman included the Passenger Pigeon in *Color Key*, though by 1903 it was "so rare that the observation of a single individual is noteworthy."[55] In the entry for the Mourning Dove in his 1934 guide, Peterson said that while the Passenger Pigeon was "now pretty definitely known to be extinct . . . still reports of individuals *seen* are frequently brought to our attention."[56]

The Field Guide Comes of Age

As it became harder to find the wild near home, birdwatchers defended areas as well as species. In 1923 Griscom recorded the loss of habitat around the city in *Birds of the New York City Region* and hoped that woods and fields would never become so distant that most city people could not reach them.[57] A decade later, birdwatchers organized a campaign to protect Hawk Mountain, a passage-point in Pennsylvania that saw an annual slaughter of migrating hawks. Audubon did not lead, but it joined the cause, printed articles about the value of predators in what would soon be called ecosystems, and argued for saving the bird-eating accipiters as parts of the beauty of the world and Nature's nation.

Under John T. Baker, who became Audubon's national president in 1934, the society began not only to advocate for endangered species but to do research to save them, which took it into new territory. Field biology, like game management, was moving toward sophisticated research methods. Ludlow Griscom, for example, had a master's degree, but he urged Hickey to get the "graduate work in biology and zoology that were, of course, essential for a professional career." Hickey did, using "a virtually unexploited gold mine of bird-banding data . . . [and] the then-new technique of life-table analysis" (data gathered mainly by enthusiastic birders) for a dissertation titled "Survival Studies of Banded Birds."[58] The new work left Griscom far behind.[59]

Before they could employ sophisticated techniques, though, scientists needed basic life-history studies. Audubon began with the California Condor and the Roseate Spoonbill (disappearing from Florida but not in danger of extinction). The condor had been in peril for decades. Its wingspan, eight or nine feet, made it a tempting target, and its low reproductive rate made even small losses significant. Even in the 1890s many believed it would vanish, but it still hung on in the 1930s, and Baker was determined to see if it could be saved. He found a kindred spirit in Joseph Grinnell, director of the Museum of Vertebrate Zoology at the University of California, Berkeley, and in 1939 Audubon funded a fellowship for Carl Koford to study the species' life-history and current population under the direction of Grinnell and his assistant, Alden Miller. The birds were scarce, and Koford came to know a large part of the population well enough to observe individual differences, but watching them at the nest he had to keep his distance and his patience, for they did the things he wanted to see, like feeding their young, infrequently, and when they left the nest he spent much of his time just finding them. Over the next two years he spent four hundred days observing condors in the wild, then eighty more when he returned from navy service in World War II. His report, a complete life-history of the species and an assessment of its status, appeared in 1953, as Audubon Research Report No. 4, and by then a UNESCO conference (which led to the formation of the International Union for the Conservation of Nature) listed the condor as one of thirteen bird species in need of emergency protection.[60] Though scientific, this report included the birdwatchers' passions as well. "The beauty of a California condor," Koford wrote, "is in the magnificence of its soaring flight. A condor in a cage is uninspiring, pitiful, and ugly to one who has seen them soaring over the mountains."[61]

To study the Roseate Spoonbill, Baker sent Robert Porter Allen—a bird enthusiast who was working in the society's library because the Depression had forced him out of college—to Florida. Allen lacked basic academic credentials, but that hardly mattered, for this sort of life-history was so new that enthusiasm and shrewdness served at least as well as degrees and course work.[62] Herbert Stoddard, who did the first modern work on the Bobwhite Quail in Georgia in the late 1920s, was a self-educated naturalist, and Paul Errington was at the beginning of his career, working on his doctorate, when he duplicated Stoddard's work at the other end of the quail's range, in Wisconsin. Their research consisted of measuring anything affecting population size, from nesting success and clutch size to predation and disease, a line of research first clearly set out in Charles Elton's *Animal Ecology* in 1927 (though Stoddard only read Elton's work when his own was done). Since he could hardly shoot specimens to study their stomach contents, Allen watched where they fed, then sieved the water and mud for organisms. Like Koford's, his project proved labor-intensive and took far more time than originally planned. He published his findings as an Audubon research report in 1942.[63]

The Ivory-billed Woodpecker presented an even more difficult problem, for it was hard to find birds to study. The species declined as old-growth southern forests were logged, a process that accelerated in the early twentieth century, and collectors pursued the few that remained. In 1924 the Cornell ornithologist Arthur A. Allen spent a week observing the last known nesting pair, in Florida. Shortly after he left the area collectors shot the birds. The next report—and another dead specimen—came from northeastern Louisiana in 1935. Allen found living birds on a tract owned by the Singer Sewing Machine Company, and with George Sutton (who began bird study with a copy of Chapman's *Bird-Lore*), a graduate student, and a sound technician, recorded the birds' calls and knocks and made the only motion pictures of the bird ever taken. The graduate student, James Tanner, returned in 1937,

supported in part by Audubon research funds, and published his doc-
toral research as *The Ivory-billed Woodpecker*. By then the Singer Company had sold the logging rights to the area, and by 1944 the timber and
birds were gone.[64]

Studying the Whooping Crane proved just as difficult. Its numbers
were unknown and its breeding ground a mystery. A spectacular white
bird, five feet tall with a wingspread of seven feet and a call that carried
a mile or more across the swamps, it had never been abundant, and by
the early twentieth century it was so scarce that conservationists included a ten-year closed season in the 1916 Migratory Bird Treaty. For
the next twenty years, its preservation remained the passion and cause
of a few dedicated people, particularly Fred Bradshaw, director of the
Saskatchewan Museum of Natural History, who raised awareness across
the province and sent letters from the Arctic to northern South America seeking information.[65] Audubon joined the cause in the late 1930s,
when Baker sent Robert Porter Allen to Regina to go over Bradshaw's
records for clues to the mysterious breeding grounds, then sent Olin
Pettingill the next year. Finally Baker hired Fred Bard, who had been
Bradshaw's assistant. The first breakthrough came in 1938, when the
crane's wintering grounds on the Blackjack Peninsula on the south coast
of Texas were set aside as Aransas National Wildlife Refuge. That
allowed counts every winter, the first continuing study ever done on the
birds. The numbers revealed the depth of the crisis: there were fewer
than two dozen Whooping Cranes in the world. In 1945 Audubon
reached an agreement with the Fish and Wildlife Service that Baker
grandly described as the "Cooperative Whooping Crane Project." It
amounted to little more than letting Audubon researchers study the
crane at Aransas in the winter and tag along on waterfowl census flights
in Canada during the summer to look for nesting grounds. In the short
run Audubon's efforts seemed futile, but work between the wars laid
foundations for campaigns after World War II that had the Whooping
Crane as their symbol and led to the first federal endangered species
legislation.

Saving endangered species required new programs and a new approach, for the problems were very different from those Audubon had
faced in its earlier conservation work. Work had to begin with scientific
studies, for they were often needed to define the crisis and always
needed to say what must be done. Only then could Audubon rally the
public, a more difficult task than it had been. In the 1890s Audubon
could speak of slaughtered parent birds and deserted rookeries, appealing to humane sentiments. Now it had to show the public how

swamps and fields were essential for birds through the cycle of their lives or at particular points, and a call for reserves and habitat restoration lacked the simplicity of passing a law to outlaw bird slaughters. Many Audubon members had made the necessary mental leap but not all, and for the same reason it took wildlife managers a generation to convince hunters to take this view. Cooper's Hawks killed Bobwhite Quail, so killing hawks should mean more and larger coveys, and by the same logic, fewer wolves meant more deer. It took a different eye to see the value of gravel roads and snake fences. Seeing the value of these new measures meant breaking old habits, ceasing to think in terms of individual organisms and events and looking instead at populations, processes, and relationships, the pressure of human change across the whole country, and the importance of small areas or seemingly insignificant events. It would be another generation before public policies recognized humans as major influences on wild nature across wild America.

Second-Generation Birdwatching

World War II put conservation, recreation, and careers on hold. Peterson left for the army, while Griscom counted gasoline ration coupons and explained to Coast Guard patrols what he was doing out on the beach with binoculars.[66] By then birdwatching, though still centered on the East Coast, had outposts across the country, drew many more men, and had a core group self-consciously devoted to improving techniques and knowledge of field identification. Identification had become its own activity, a skill cultivated without any necessary connection to nature study or conservation. Recreation had a new and more complex relation to science. Ornithology drew on birdwatchers' data, and conservationists depended on ornithologists to guide them. Guides helped make birdwatching an "engaging game" while they also relied—even more than earlier ones—on science, taught scientific categories, and used only the names scientists approved.

Competition reached new heights. The Christmas Bird Count, once a matter of individuals and small groups working informally, close to home, became a matter of organized teams scouring the country. In 1931 Chapman noted that these reports, which had told what people saw out the window, now told what they saw through the windshield.[67] People planned their expeditions and divided responsibilities among a team to make sure they covered their territories. The Big Day became popular enough that in 1945 *Audubon* printed an article titled "Ludlow Griscom: Virtuoso of Field Identification," by the popular nature writer Edwin

Way Teale. It described a day with Griscom as a cross between a military expedition and an athletic event. "From the time the car rolled out of his Cambridge driveway a little after four-thirty in the morning until it rolled back in again sometime after ten o'clock that night, the trip ran like a subway schedule," as the group traveled 140 miles and logged seventy-six species. After a day afield with Griscom, people would "be ready to elevate this robust, he-man activity to a place beside mountain climbing and the cross-country marathon."[68] Aggressive competition, though, existed alongside the genteel expedition to the park, so familiar even to non-birdwatchers that the *New Yorker* could print a cartoon of people peering up into a tree with binoculars over the deadpan caption "The Audubon Bird Walkers Add a Scarlet Tanager to Their List."[69]

While lists dominated, birdwatchers often pursued as well a personal version of natural history's project of putting in order and understanding the life of the land, taking on specialized studies that might use science but did not necessarily contribute to it. These endeavors lacked the scope, organization, and rigor of ornithological research but had the advantage of opening a path to nature that people could follow without leaving their jobs or their ordinary rounds, a way for them to map their experience on the land through time, creating a personal emotional geography of nature organized by science's authoritative understanding. That kind of curiosity went back to Gilbert White's study of his parish, *A Natural History of Selborne*, natural history's first literary classic (published in 1787 and still in print), in which White said it had been "more than forty years that I have paid some attention to the ornithology of the district, without being able to exhaust the subject: new occurrences still arise as long as any inquiries are kept alive."[70] And, like birdwatchers thumbing through Peterson, he related his observations to authoritative accounts. The hen of a honey buzzard (the female of a species that in the United States would be called a hawk) answered "exactly to Mr. Ray's [John Ray, a seventeenth-century founder of natural history] description of that species; [it] had a black cere, short thick legs, and a long tail." White went on to say that "on the wing this species may be readily distinguished from the common buzzard by its hawk-like appearance, small head, wings not so blunt, and longer tail."[71] Advanced birdwatchers in Griscom's generation knew species by the length of wing or bulk of body, the next generation would move toward checking off each species by, as White put it, "a manner peculiar to itself," and a few years later all birdwatchers had books tutoring them in this kind of discrimination.[72] Casual birdwatchers had fewer notes but, often, a well-marked-up field guide to nudge their memories.[73]

Even as birdwatching became separate from bird study, changes in the discipline and the hobby brought field ornithology and birdwatching closer. Griscom compiled *Birds of the New York City Region* when most ornithologists had abandoned the field for the laboratory and sight records had little standing. As more ornithologists took to the field to study living populations, they needed birdwatchers' skills, and they also enlisted the growing corps of increasingly expert amateurs. Allan D. Cruickshank's 1942 revision of Griscom's work showed the extent of the change. A member of the Bronx County Bird Club, Cruickshank followed Chapman and Griscom as a curator at the American Museum of Natural History. Drawing on "nineteen additional years of intensive birding by scores of keen field ornithologists," Cruickshank's *Birds around New York City: Where and When to Find Them* relied on "numerous valuable local lists . . . a wealth of analyzed [and published] data . . . [and] [a]bove all an unbelievable mountain of field notes by local observers . . . that allowed a local picture of bird life that would have been considered well nigh impossible two decades ago." The region could now be treated as a whole, for a "network of motor parkways, bridges and causeways has . . . made places which two decades ago were considered remote, mere weekend visits and in some cases, mere afternoon drives. Moreover, interest in birds has been steadily increasing, and for every competent observer twenty years ago there are now a dozen."[74] The local ornithology continued as a scientific production, but observations replaced collections as the primary source of up-to-date information.

Even as birdwatchers contributed to ornithologists' books, the scientists returned the favor. Authors had used taxonomy to arrange their entries (though they did not always strictly follow it) but in his western guide Peterson took that to a new level. In naming western birds, he had to contend with popular names bequeathed to the amateurs by nineteenth-century ornithologists, a nomenclature that now clashed with modern thought. Ornithologists cataloged and classified the West's birds at a time when they were fascinated by the problems and possibilities of subspecies. Seeing variation within a species as an expression of, and possibly a key to, evolution, museum directors made extensive collections of each species across its range in order to chart variations.[75] To take account of this phenomenon, they erected a new taxonomic category, the subspecies, by tacking a third name onto the canonical Linnaean binomial, producing the "trinomial nomenclature" that Coues referred to as "peculiar to the 'American school.'"[76] The next generation found too many cases of continuous variation, which suggested that the divisions reflected the classifiers' ideas rather than biological realities, and that too many names had been attached to populations that differed very little from the norm. By then, though, western birdwatchers were happily checking off birds that ornithologists no longer considered "good" species or, for that matter, anything but minor variations.

The problem lay not simply in the many forms but in the differences and the kinds of differences. In some cases, the geographic "races" (the biological term then current for variant populations within a species) could be identified in the field. That is, birdwatchers could confidently give birds they saw in the field names on the basis of their external characteristics. In others, the differences could only be seen in the hand; a taxonomist with a good eye could assign individual specimens to a particular race by comparing them against museum collections. In still other cases, the existence of a race could only be inferred by a taxonomist comparing the average of a set of specimens from one area with the averages of sets from other parts of the species' range and deciding that the differences were large enough to warrant giving each population its own name.

Peterson consulted some two dozen eastern and western ornithologists and birdwatchers to work out a nomenclature that recognized current popular practice but pushed toward the modern scientific one. Alden Miller, then director of the Museum of Vertebrate Zoology in Berkeley, urged him "to establish simple specific names used widely over the continent," but Peterson protested that he could not simply throw overboard this "poor system of common names now in vogue." The "name Lutescent Warbler [for a race of the Orange-crowned Warbler] is so thoroughly established through usage that if it were left out and the species name Orange-crowned substituted, it would not be received very kindly by most California birders."[77] He wound up putting a new section on subspecies in the western guide to explain the problems and his position. He included the subspecies that were "readily identifiable in the field" and "when there were no apparent field differences [gave only] the range *for the species* as a whole," asserting that "it is necessary to include at least the *names* of subspecies, however."[78] That done, he declared that the term "subspecies" had no good definition, "other than it is a geographical race that often blends with others of the same species" in a way that makes it impossible clearly to mark off one from another. Steller's Jay, for example, "could just as easily be [divided into] ten races ... as five, depending on where the lines are to be drawn or how fine the splitting is to be."[79] His solution recognized both the authority of ornithology and the reality of common practice and steered between the guide's need to sell and the hobby's need for names everyone recognized. He had to explain himself because he faced not an audience of novices ready to accept the ornithologists' judgments but an established group with its own standards.[80] However scientifically outdated the names they used, they had to be taken into account.

He recognized the importance of names in other ways. In a 1942 article in *Audubon*, "A Bird by Any Other Name," he called for the revival of Old World names for raptors, generally all called "hawks" in the United States. Rural people saw all "hawks" as bad and commonly shot them on sight. Changing the names, he thought, would help break that connection and encourage hawk conservation.[81] Under this scheme the Duck Hawk became the Peregrine, the Pigeon Hawk the Merlin, the Sparrow Hawk the Kestrel, and the Marsh Hawk the Harrier. Walter Spofford's campaign in Tennessee for these names, Peterson said, had already shown results, and the AOU should help. In the next issue of *Audubon*, Donald Culross Peattie appealed to "tidy-minded Roger" to respect local names as "part of the rich regional variety of America."[82] That brought out a question that was implied in the first guides: what's in a name? Every generation dealt with it, for there were no good, simple answers. In the appendix to his 1947 eastern guide, Peterson defended Americans' inconsistent use of English bird names, and in 1974, again appealing to patriotism, he told Chandler Robbins that he preferred the name "Anhinga" for the species *Anhinga anhinga*, because "it is a name with flavor and does refer strictly to our North American species."[83]

Peterson's views took into account a central truth: as the culture and science changed, so did birds' names. The popular regionalism of Depression America lay behind Peattie's appeal; elsewhere, other considerations determined what birds were called. The early white settlers of Australia and New Zealand gave birds familiar names, ones taken from "home," and then in the first wave of nationalism in the early twentieth century looked for names associated with the new land. The educator and nature study advocate John A. Leach, from Victoria, Australia, lamented that "so many of our popular names come from America" and called for more "good descriptive names for our varied and beautiful birds—more children's and poets' names, and less of the deadly formal" ones.[84] New Zealanders, coming to celebrate their unique bird life as the nation's heritage, scorned the exotics that twenty years before had been hailed as reminders of "home" and moved toward popular names for native species. A second wave of nationalism, after World War II, led Australians to turn to Aboriginal names and New Zealanders to Maori ones, and bird guides and schoolbooks presented them to a new generation as part of their country's native heritage.[85] The trend everywhere ran toward a national set of names, shaped by history and filtered through scientific organizations. Emphasizing the AOU's official set but accepting, even embracing, changes that served bird conservation and local associations, Peterson gave a clear direction to the trend in the United States, and the names in modern guides and ornithologies alike reflect his commitment to science and American nature.

Birdwatching's growth in the interwar years foreshadowed its expansion during the postwar nature boom, but it changed in more than numbers. Enthusiasts like Griscom set the hobby on a solid base by working out ways to identify all the birds in all their forms—male, female, young, breeding plumage, and the more sober uniforms that came with the next molt—an achievement that set the field of play for recreational birding and gave ornithology a field tool. As more watchers took to the field and became more expert, the community spread across a spectrum from expert to novice, obsessive lister to backyard birder, held together by a common practice, a network of clubs and friendships, and a common text. Peterson, putting the hobby's accumulated knowledge into a book that made it easy to have fun afield, did more than anyone else to transform birdwatching from the hobby of a few to the recreation of many. Like recreation, conservation changed, moving from the defense of a few species on the basis of humane ideals or aesthetic considerations to defending all for their roles in the systems of nature, and from episodic campaigns for small areas and toward a continuing national program. Through it all, the Audubon Society kept its central place, serving conservation through public education, lobbying, and land preservation and recreation through articles and lectures.

This first half century established the hobby; the second, from the 1940s to the present, reshaped it. The next chapter takes up that first part of that shift: birdwatching during the long economic boom that followed World War II and the field guide that reigned over it, Peterson's 1947 edition of his eastern book. It made birdwatching popular and served, as well, as the flagship of a field guide series that now includes some four dozen books, "flashguides" (laminated sheets with illustrations of common species), and audio or video guides. The biologist Paul Ehrlich called Peterson "the inventor of the modern field guide," whose "greatest contribution to the preservation of biological diversity has been in getting tens of millions of people outdoors with Peterson field guides in their pockets."[86] That seems a reasonable assessment.

FIVE

Birds over America

with Roger Tory Peterson's
Field Guide to the Birds and binoculars in hand,
as all true naturalists in America must...

—E. O. WILSON, *NATURALIST* (1994)

GREEN HERON

Adult

Adult

Immature

Adult

YELLOW-
NIGHT

CROWNED
HERON

LEAST
BITTERN

BLACK-CROWNED
NIGHT HERON

AMERICAN
BITTERN

Immature

Immature

YELLOW-CROWNED
NIGHT HERON

BLACK-CROWNED
NIGHT HERON

WHITE IBIS

GLOSSY   IBIS

LIMPKIN

Immature

Adult

WOOD IBIS

WHITE IBIS

Plate 24   37

LONG-LEGGED WADERS

YELLOW–CROWNED NIGHT HERON   p. 24.
Adult: Gray body, black head, light crown.
Immature: Like Black-crown but slatier, more finely
          speckled, legs longer.

BLACK–CROWNED NIGHT HERON   p. 24.
Adult: White breast, black back, black crown.
Immature: Brown, large spots on back.

GREEN HERON   p. 24.
Small dark Heron, short legs.

LEAST BITTERN   p. 25.
Tiny; back and crown black, wings buff.

AMERICAN BITTERN   p. 25.
Tawny; black neck-mark; bill pointed up.

WHITE IBIS   p. 29.
Adult: Red face, decurved bill.
Immature: Decurved bill, white belly, white rump.

GLOSSY IBIS   p. 28.
Dark body, decurved bill.

LIMPKIN   p. 79.
Spotted; decurved bill.

WOOD IBIS   p. 28.
Naked gray head, large black wing areas.

Herons and Bitterns fly with
necks folded; Ibises and Limp-
kins with necks extended.

5.1 · *Peterson's waders, 1947* · Peterson felt that this was the mature form of his guide, and this plate showed Houghton Mifflin's dedication to this revision. Compare with the second plate in the previous chapter. From *A Field Guide to the Birds* by Roger Tory Peterson. Copyright © 1947, renewed 1974 by Roger Tory Peterson. Reprinted by permission of Houghton Mifflin Harcourt Publishing Company. All rights reserved.

Four books tell the tale of birdwatching during the postwar nature boom—two field guides, a finding guide, and a story of two naturalists touring America. They speak of a new generation of guides reaching birdwatchers with wider horizons and the search for wonder in the world beyond the sidewalks. First, a small volume bound in green, the figure of a male bobolink in spring plumage on the cover, the title *A Field Guide to the Birds,* and a name, "Peterson."[1] It claimed to be the "second edition, revised," but since the next one, in 1981, called itself the fourth, it was, effectively, the third. This was the book that transformed birdwatching into a recreation for the masses and made "Peterson" a common noun, as in "What does Peterson say?" Next, a small paperback, six by four inches and less than half an inch thick, on the cover two robins on a dogwood branch in full bloom, the title *Birds: A Guide to the Most Familiar American Birds,* the promise of "112 Birds in Full Color," and the declaration "A Golden Nature Guide."[2] Here was another aspect of the expanding empire of the field guide, the colonization of the children's book market. Olin Pettingill's *Guide to Bird Finding East of the Mississippi* and its companion volume for the area west of the river signaled birdwatchers' expanding horizons.[3] Enough birdwatchers were exploring beyond their homes and local ranges to create a demand for a book giving exact directions to birding hot spots in every state and the best times of the year to visit them.

The fourth book, Roger Tory Peterson and James Fisher's *Wild America,* spoke of the search for wonder in nature, part of birdwatching from the beginning but in the postwar years a public enthusiasm.[4] It told the story of the two naturalists' explorations in American nature in the summer of 1953. They set a new record for birds seen in a single year in North America north of Mexico, but they had a larger purpose, exploring Nature's nation, making a connection to the world of which we were a part and yet apart, and seeing its value for all of us. The concern for a tie to nature ran through the postwar years, most memorably in Rachel Carson's 1956 article for *Woman's Home Companion* urging parents to give their children a "sense of wonder" that would sustain them all their lives, but also in what, from an environmental perspective, seemed the neglected stepchild: conservation. Endangered species became a concern, if not a public issue, and the Whooping Crane a symbol of a vanishing wild America. Even before *Silent Spring*, activists and scientists worried about DDT and, more generally, the dark side of progress; and a few asked about the contradictions in searching for nature on modern highways in a shiny station wagon.

Like their predecessors at the turn of the century, these books drew on the idea of America as Nature's nation, but they were also the products of postwar prosperity. Millions took advantage of well-paid jobs and vacations to, as the slogan had it, "see America first."[5] The summer tour of the western national parks with the kids became almost a patriotic pilgrimage. At home the parents watched birds in the backyards of their new suburban homes while their children explored vacant lots, finding out about birds, frogs, and poison ivy. The field guide business boomed. Adults used Peterson's bird guides and other volumes—on plants, butterflies, or mammals. Children carried Zim and Gabrielson's little book. Birdwatchers among them found directions in Pettingill's finding guides and inspiration in *Wild America*. For a time they paid little attention to conservation, for fifteen years of economic depression and war made it easy to dismiss paved-over fields, cut-over forests, rivers reeking with pulp-mill waste, and air you could see as the price of progress. As the years went on and technology produced problems as well as miracles, concern grew. The environmental enthusiasm that rose so quickly in the wake of Rachel Carson's *Silent Spring* had its origin in the vague worries of these quiet years.

The Field Guide Revolution

Peterson said the 1947 edition marked the field guide's coming of age, and that proved true in intellectual and commercial ways. He made the improvements he had planned since the first edition, and Houghton Mifflin, realizing it had a winner, made it a handsome production.[6] Sales of the earlier editions justified the effort, but so did Peterson's discovery that people made the book their own. It came with a waterproof cover, but he found "many copies with home-made oilcloth jackets; I have seen copies torn apart, reorganized and rebound to suit the owner's taste; others have been tabbed with index tabs, or fitted with flaps or envelopes to hold daily check lists." He included in the new edition "a life list, so that the owner will not need to mark up the index for this purpose."[7] Houghton Mifflin, he wrote Griscom, had gone "the limit on publication costs in trying to make my new book a first-rate job." It paid more for the plates, with the understanding that there would be corrections, and made two or three proofs for each, each of which Peterson checked. The plates were printed on a heavier, more expensive paper that allowed finer detail, the text on a lightweight but opaque paper "so as to cut down on the bulk of the book." Peterson insisted on dispersing the plates throughout rather than grouping them, though it cost more, for he wanted a legend page with names and prominent field marks opposite each sheet. Another firm was hired to bind the books by hand, with frequent inspections, to ensure correct placement.[8]

Peterson held up his end by redoing the existing plates and painting others, bringing their number from thirty-six to sixty, with seventeen (up from four) in color. He included many more plumages and poses. Three plates showed warblers in the spring and two more showed "Confusing Fall Warblers." Two plates of shorebirds on the ground plugged what he said in 1934 was "the most evident gap in the illustrative material."[9] To aid readers, he grouped members of large families by obvious characteristics—sparrows with streaked breasts went together, and so did the unstreaked; one plate showed vireos with wing bars, another without. In earlier editions, the plates had been printed on one side and the birds' names hand-lettered below, or, for the color plates, numbered to correspond with a list on the facing page. Here the plates were printed on both sides, the names set in type beside each image, and a facing page gave important field marks and a page number for the full description. Across from the picture of the Cape May Warbler, for example, the reader found: "*Male*: Chestnut cheek" and "*Female*: Yellow neck spot."[10] Remedying another deficiency of the first edition, this one had twenty "Roadside Silhouettes" on the front endpapers—black against a white background, birds perched on wires, trees, a fence, or on the ground—twenty-six "Flight Silhouettes" in the back, with the Goldfinch and Flicker showing undulating dotted lines behind them to suggest their distinctive flight patterns, and twenty-three "shore silhouettes" on two pages just before the appendices. There was a ten-page list of "accidentals," birds seen fewer than twenty times in the region, and following the example of his western guide, a seventeen-page appendix on subspecies with a list of recognized eastern ones.[11]

Peterson still had complaints. With "the best color reproduction I have yet enjoyed," the "two sparrow plates are too dark. They were the first ones the engraver shot, and even though I sent them back twice for correction, there was not much that could be done to bring them around. I will probably have them done over at my expense." He fretted that the book's high price, $3.50, might put off new readers. He worried in vain; experts and the public alike greeted it with enthusiasm.[12] Chandler Robbins, who twenty years later wrote the first guide that gave "Peterson" serious competition, thanked him for "a copy of the new Bible"; Edwin Way Teale declared that Peterson had "*done* it"; and Connie Hagar said it "passes the second edition so far it hardly seems possible." She went on to tell Peterson "you don't realize how completely people follow your marks, till you hear them say 'Peterson doesn't mention it.'"[13] The new edition did all that Peterson and his editor, Paul Brooks, had hoped for, and somewhat more. Not only did it become the birdwatchers' standard for a generation, it made field guides so popular that other publishers began working on their own competing products.

Peterson's improvements and Houghton Mifflin's care helped the new edition sell, but so did its timing. The first edition came out during the worst of the Great Depression, the second on the eve of World War II, and this one as the postwar economic boom was raising millions into the middle class. Suburban women, almost as cut off from the world of work as Neltje Blanchan's generation, put up bird feeders, campaigned for neighborhood parks, and protested to City Hall when they found dead robins on their lawns after the DDT trucks went through. Nature study in elementary school had a modest revival, and Zim and Gabrielson's book carried that interest outside the classroom. New cars and new roads made it easier to see the country. Just after World War II, the Pennsylvania Turnpike proclaimed itself the "road of the twenty first century," and with its 130 miles of limited-access, dual-lane highway, no stoplights, and seven tunnels, it seemed indeed the marvel of the age. A decade later, it looked like a secondary highway. Cars became longer, wider, faster, and more reliable. The V-8 engine became common and air conditioning an affordable luxury. Families toured the western national parks and camped in the national forests; the committed birdwatchers among them took Pettingill along to make the best use of their time on the road.

Peterson's bird guides sold well, but now not as an independent production but as the flagships of a series that began in conversations during World War II between Peterson and his editor at Houghton Mifflin, Paul Brooks. Each volume, Peterson wrote, would have "an identity of its own . . . [but the whole] built around the bird guides," holding, "in a general way, to the basic ideas developed in them, comparative marks and distinctions between similar species."[14] That strategy dated to the 1890s, when publishers brought out nature books in uniform series, each covering a popular topic, which they kept in print for years. Some authors made that their business. Between 1895 and 1910, for instance, Edward Knobel turned out a dozen guides, most for Bradlee Whidden Company in Boston, and his 1899 book on grasses, sedges, and rushes lived on in a revised reprint edition a century later.[15] Chester Reed and his father, Charles, built a business around pocket-sized guides illustrated with the younger Reed's paintings and photographs.[16] Commercial publishers picked up the most popular ones, and they lived on through the Depression.[17] G. P. Putnam had an eighteen-volume series in the interwar years, to which it added a new bird book for the eastern United States in 1946. By then Houghton Mifflin had in process volumes on seashells and mammals, and Brooks told Peterson he definitely had "the green light from us to approach potential authors for new books in the series."[18] In 1947 the new eastern bird guide and one on Atlantic and Gulf coast seashells appeared. A volume on butterflies was published in 1951, mammals and Pacific Coast shells in 1952, then rocks and minerals, and in 1954 a guide to British and European birds, with an accompanying British edition by a well-known nature publisher, Collins.[19] Murie's volume on animal tracks appeared that year, and one on ferns in 1956.

The next, A *Field Guide to the Birds of Texas*, responded directly to the postwar nature boom and the rising interest in bird tourism. In the 1930s, Connie Hagar's reports from the south Texas coast attracted a federal ornithologist, Harry Oberholzer, who arrived to correct an over-enthusiastic amateur and left praising a well-qualified observer. The vanguard of the listers, Ludlow Griscom and Guy Emerson, followed, and by the early 1940s serious birdwatchers were making winter pilgrimages to Hagar's tourist cottages. In 1949 *Audubon* spread the word with an article on the "Lady with Binoculars."[20] The Texas Game and Fish Commission (now the Texas Parks and Wildlife Department) took note of the annual pilgrimage, for while the state was not a haven for naturalists or deeply committed to conservation, it welcomed tourist dollars and saw a field guide to Texas birds as a way to draw more. It supported the new book in exchange for exclusive sales rights for the first year, and to raise interest sold it for $3.00 rather than Houghton-Mifflin's $4.95.[21] Peterson's introduction was titled, naturally, "Texas, the No. 1 Bird State."

Peterson's name stood for those "schematic drawings and little arrows," but he found it impossible to replicate the method throughout the series, for it depended in part on the characteristics of the class of birds.[22] The eight hundred species his guides covered came in some three dozen families that most people knew or at least knew something about. They could tell a hawk from a heron and a thrush from a sparrow. Many species had distinctive plumage patterns or calls, and birds could usually be seen. Mammals, on the other hand, were mostly small, often secretive, and difficult to distinguish even when seen. Frogs were small, were slimy, lived in bogs and swamps, and commonly squatted in water up to their eyes. Many plant families had so many species (250 penstemons, 90 monkeyflowers) that identification at the species level was impractical. Butterflies—visible, colorful, and often distinctly patterned—could be identified in the field, and butterfly watching grew. People bought and used guides to all these forms but rarely made identifying them a serious hobby.

Peterson admitted to Brooks that "each subject must be treated a little differently," but, commenting on the proposed Rocky Mountain wildflower guide, said he wanted "two things which will give our books distinction: include where possible a section on similar species, and . . . have a legend page opposite every plate [with] a line or two of distinguishing marks."[23] In the volume on minerals, he asked "for the sake of consistency in the series . . . a little color, even though it is not important for identification," and for a line of descriptive text, even if impressionistic, opposite the illustration.[24] That proved to be all the uniformity he could enforce. In *Field Guide to Trees and Shrubs*, George Petrides used natural history's standard tool, the dichotomous key, and in *Field Guide to Wildflowers*, Peterson and McKenny used "A Visual Approach Arranged by Color, Form, and Detail," a modified key system that sent readers first to the color of the blossom, then to the form ("umbrella-like clusters" or "rayless or near-rayless composites"). Hal H. Harrison's *Birds' Nests* put nests in the taxonomic order of the birds that built them, which had little relation to what the nests looked like.[25] Adolph Murie's guide to animal tracks resembled a woodcraft manual from an earlier generation, with its sketches of tracks, descriptions of claw marks and scat, and instructions on making plaster casts of tracks in the field.[26]

Peterson edited all the books, but the bird guides remained his passion, and he kept a close eye on "the competition." Arguing for more color for the 1947 edition, he said that "one of the chief selling points or novel features in the Hausman Guide [*Field Book of Eastern Birds*, Putnam, 1946] is a color plate of half a dozen Hawks on the wing," and the

"Doubleday Doran book [Richard Pough, *Eastern Land Birds*, 1946, the first of the Audubon guides] has two pages of Owls in color and if we have our Owls in color we will have shown all the birds treated in their first volume in color."[27] The urgency came only from within. Hausman's field book had color plates, but they were not well done, and the book lacked Peterson's systematic approach, careful organization, and diagrammatic paintings. It showed a modern form only in the descriptions, which consistently told what could be seen at a distance, and the line drawings of each species. The series in which it appeared fell far short of Peterson's, with much older books by less expert authors and only scattered coverage of natural history. Five books in the series were by F. Schuyler Matthews (author of the early guide on birdsong), three of them written before 1915. The series had some broad treatments of poorly defined topics, such as the book on ponds and streams and another on animals in winter, and Herbert Durand's *My Wild Flower Garden: A New Departure in Floriculture*, stood at the margins of the genre.

The Audubon guides, published by Doubleday, began to appear as Peterson and Houghton Mifflin launched their series. The first volume, *Eastern Land Birds*, written by one Audubon staffer, Richard Pough, and illustrated by another, Don Eckelberry, came out in 1946, and the others over the next decade.[28] The Peterson and Audubon guides had different audiences, though. Peterson aimed at novice but not completely inexperienced birdwatchers and emphasized identification; the Audubon books catered more to the amateur naturalist and included much information not related to identification. They said, for example, that the spread of the introduced Chukar Partridge could be related to another introduced species, cheatgrass, and that habitat changes caused by cattle grazing might have led to the extirpation of the Masked Bobwhite.[29] They had color plates, which worried Peterson, and the descriptions showed his influence, but they were not organized for the field. Separate volumes for land and water birds did not serve birdwatchers well, and the western volumes omitted descriptions of birds found in the East, referring readers to those volumes.[30] Rather than putting plates near the description, they were in a single section, and they showed birds in different poses, grouped in ways that did not help

5.2 · *Greater Yellowlegs from the Hausman guide* · Peterson thought this book, published in 1946, presented no real competition, and this page shows why. Compare it with the illustrations from his third edition, which appeared the next year. From *Field Book of Eastern Birds* by Leon Augustus Hausman, copyright 1946 by Leon Augustus Hausman, © renewed 1973 by Ethel Hinckley Hausman. Used by permission of G.P. Putnam's Sons, a division of Penguin Group (USA) Inc.

GREATER YELLOWLEGS *Totanus melanoleucus*— 14.00 inches

OTHER NAMES—Winter Yellowlegs, Big Yellowlegs, Big Tattler, Telltale Snipe, Stone Snipe, Big Telltale, Horse Yellowlegs, Cucu, Yelper.

FIELD MARKS—Long bright-lemon-yellow legs, and in flight a whitish rump and tail.

FIELD DESCRIPTION—Upper parts dark gray speckled with white, the head lighter. Underparts white, lightly marked on the neck and sides of the body with black. Upper tail coverts and tail white barred with black. Legs long and a bright lemon yellow.

CHARACTERISTIC HABITS—After alighting it stretches its wings up over its body before folding them down, then bobs and bows several times before beginning to feed. A very alert bird, very clamorous, hence the name Yelper. Sometimes wades into a pool up to its belly.

NOTES—Clear, loud, incisive, cheerful whistles or pipes, *kew, kew, kew, kew,* or *te-whee, te-whee, te-whee;* also clucks and other henlike utterances.

HABITAT—Marshes and flooded tidal meadows, tidal creeks, muddy banks, swamps, and shallow ponds, only rarely on the beaches.

RANGE—In our area, from Newfoundland, Labrador, and the Hudson Bay region southward to the Gulf of St. Lawrence and southern Ontario. In winter from North Carolina (casually) southward.

Layout and information reflect an earlier generation, when names were less standard, but it was also an arrangement for field use, with each category given its own bold heading.

The line drawing showed pattern and pose in a characteristic habitat.

Hausman labeled the bird in the common fashion, putting the English-language name in large, bold capitals, the scientist's Latin one in smaller, italic type.

This includes one of Peterson's favorite phrases, "Field Marks," and the entry, arranged under headings, speaks to field identification. However, there is little attention to the comparison of similar species, Peterson's great interest.

comparison of similar species. One plate in the western guide, for example, showed two warblers, a nuthatch, a gnatcatcher, the Mountain Accentor, and the Wryneck.[31]

Peterson, worried about distinguishing his book from theirs, for they, too, covered the country, gave detailed descriptions of species, had many illustrations, and would, he warned Brooks, be close "to the dimensions of my own field guide and sell for the same price—$2.75." They had considered the title "Audubon Field Guide to the Birds, but inasmuch as this would create such a confusion of name with my own Guide, I insisted that they leave the word Field out."[32] With evident relief, he told Brooks the "illustrations will not be of the comparative, diagrammatic nature such as those in my own book . . . [and] Pough [did] not intend to make it essentially a field guide stressing field characteristics but rather to stress the ecology, environment, nest, eggs, habits. etc." He hoped Pough would stick to that, otherwise the Audubon guide would duplicate his book and "perhaps be more attractive to many field students because of the large volume of color."[33] When the first one appeared, he praised the illustrations and noted the differences in method. It showed six to eight birds on a plate, "each plumage shown to good advantage and all the rarities included." Eckelberry's work was "beautiful . . . straight bird portraiture instead of color diagrams." To counter the attraction of those forty-eight plates, he told Brooks he wanted "at least 12 plates to cover the land birds" in the forthcoming 1947 edition, and argued that higher sales—he estimated fifty thousand in eight to ten years—would justify the cost.[34] Two years later, in a letter declining to do line drawings for the second volume of the Audubon series, he wrote Pough that he and his publisher had no "objection to some line drawings scattered through the text, provided they were portraits. . . . I would be unhappy only if you presented your drawings in the same comparative patternistic way to which my guide is dedicated."[35]

Peterson used persuasion and friendship but relied mainly on hard work and a relentless attention to detail, including production details. Writing to Guy Montfort, his collaborator on the guide to European birds, he warned of a possible problem with

the trim or chopping of the stitched books just before binding. . . . In measuring and ripping apart several copies of my Eastern Field Guide I found that there was an inconsistency in the different printings. Some were cut precisely so that the over-all double page spread would come to exactly 9 inches. . . . On others . . . the double spread came to an average of 8 7/8 inches which meant that the single page was a six-teenth of an inch shorter [and] plates that wrapped around signatures would have the benefit of the full width but those which were within signatures would be cropped a bit shorter by the machine. [The plate on] the outside of a signature . . . usually comes out OK. If it is on the inside a letter or two is sometimes chopped.[36]

A decade later, discussing revisions, he opposed putting the plates in a single section, for that meant either sacrificing the legend pages or using twice the color press (for the legend pages would have to be printed on that as well). He was not sure if they could be "interleaved sheet by sheet. This again is a costly process as compared with the usual cutting and folding of signatures."[37] A year later he wrote to complain of color reproductions; the "lack of brownness in the olivaceous warbler and the lack of warmth in the garden warbler were not due to my original draw-ings as much as to reproduction—also the weakness of the yellow on the icterine and melodious warblers."[38]

While Peterson served the adult market, others extended the genre to children's books. Gabrielson and Zim's paperback *Birds*, published in 1949, dropped the conventional mixture of facts and stories in favor of a children's version of the modern guide. It was the start of a children's nature series, Golden Nature Guides, which by the 1970s had two dozen titles, part of a larger enterprise that included Science Guides, Hand-books, Handbook Guides, Regional Guides, Travel Guides, Art Guides, and just plain Guides.[39] Each, according to the blurb on the back, had been written by "an outstanding authority on science education" to give young readers "an introduction to the world of nature, presenting those things which are most common and most easily seen." The driving force behind this publishing empire was Herbert S. Zim, who had a Ph.D. in education and a "doctorate of science" (credentials his books usually mentioned), twenty years of experience teaching elementary school science classes, and a shrewd sense of what would sell. He founded the Golden Guides in 1945 and edited them for twenty-five years, serving as author or coauthor of roughly a hundred, on topics ranging from birds to secret codes.

Changes in book production and distribution made possible these inexpensive, colorful texts. Less than twenty years after Peterson's muddy black-and-white plates, printed on separate stock, and two years after his new edition had more, but still separate, color plates, Zim put color paintings and a colored map on the same paper and the

This shows a set of small tree dwellers in characteristic poses arrayed across two pages in "ganged" section.

Rather than Peterson's diagrammatic paintings, Don Eckelberry produced bird portraits.

Golden-crowned Kinglet
.p.126

♂ Ruby-crowned Kin
p.127

♀

♀

White-breasted Nuthatch
p.94

Brown-headed Nuthat
p.

Red-breas
Nuthat
p.

PLATE 14

5.3 · *Chickadees and such, Pough guide* · A plate from the Audubon Society post-war guides, which Peterson did not consider direct competitors. From *Audubon Land Bird Field Guide* by Richard Pough. Used with permission of Tristram H. Pough, executor of the estate of Richard H. Pough, and (for the artwork) Woodson Art Museum, Wausau, WI.

Black-crested
Titmouse
p.93

Tufted Titmouse
p.92

Black-capped Chickadee
p.89

Carolina
Chickadee
p.90

Brown-capped
Chickadee
p.91

Brown
Creeper
p.97

PLATE 15

Blue-gray
Gnatcatcher
p.125

Like all the plates in this book, there was no title, only a plate number.

Like early Peterson, this had script names on the plate but also page numbers, necessary as the plates did not stand close to the text, as they did in Peterson.

same pages as printed text—not nearly the same quality, but adequate for a child's paperback. Paperbacks and new channels of distribution let him reach a wide audience. Although paperbacks dated to the mid-nineteenth century, only in the 1930s did it became possible to print respectable-looking, reasonably durable ones. What began as genre fiction sold in bus stations and drugstores, then Armed Forces editions during World War II, became a flood after the war that carried books out of bookstores. Racks at the drugstore carried novels by Leo Tolstoy and Mickey Spillane, explanations of modern physics, and instructions on fixing leaky faucets. Golden Guides, which before the war would have had few outlets, could easily reach parents and children in cities and in suburbs.

Birds had all the marks of a guide, and, except for adding topics like feeding birds and putting up nest boxes, it hewed to the genre. It proclaimed itself a "field book made to fit your pocket when you go looking for birds," and at six by four inches, with 160 pages, and plastic-coated covers, it did. It had pictures and descriptions of 112 "of the most familiar American birds" (later editions included 129). These, with the "additional and related species" described in the text, helped "the reader identify over 260 birds in all."[40] Just like "Peterson," it included a page with "Parts of a Bird," three more with a "simplified list of the main bird groups," a section titled "How to Use This Book," and all the standard advice to beginners, down to the injunction to use the range maps to find what birds were in your area and the migration tables in the back to find out when they appeared or left. "Mark each bird you are likely to see, and when you have seen it enter the place and date on the 'Record' pages."[41] On each page, a painting of a male in characteristic habitat stood at the top; below that appeared the name, a description, and an outline of the United States colored red for summer, blue for winter, and purple where the bird was a year-round resident—a method adult guides would not use for another twenty years. The descriptions concentrated on what you could see. The Red-tailed Hawk was "a large, soaring hawk. Its wings are broad but its tail, fan-shaped and chestnut-red above, is not always visible. This hawk is light underneath with dark streaks across the belly." The Flicker was "large, distinctly brown woodpecker." The Tree Swallow's "unbroken blue-black above and unbroken white below" made it stand out. "Spot the Pintail by its long, pointed

5.4 · *Gabrielson and Zim's Red-tail* · This adapted the field guide form for children, with the pictures emphasizing distinctive characteristics, the text identification. From Herbert S. Zim and Ira N. Gabrielson, *Birds: A Guide to the Most Familiar American Birds* (New York: Simon and Schuster, 1949).

RED-TAILED HAWK The Red-tailed is a large, soaring hawk. Its wings are broad but its tail, fan-shaped and chestnut-red above, is not always visible. This hawk is light underneath with dark streaks across the belly. Red-shouldered Hawk is similar with a distinctly banded tail. Other soaring hawks include the small Broad-winged Hawk (16 in.) of the East with its prominently barred tail; and Swainson's Hawk (21 in.) of the West with its broad, dark breast band.—*Length: 19-22 in. Female larger, but similar. Young with dark, faintly barred tail.*

· The picture nicely showed off the hawk's diagnostic red tail.

· Changes in printing made color inexpensive enough to use in a children's guide, and it could even be done on the same page with the letterpress. The quality, of course, was not up to that of the adult guides.

· The children learned only the English-language name, a feature that spoke to the decline of amateur natural history.

· The distinctive feature of this book, not used in adult guides for a generation, is the colored map showing range. Red stood for the summer range, blue (absent here) the winter, and purple for year-round residence.

tail, slender neck, and in flight by the white stripe on the trailing edge of its wing."[42]

Like its adult counterparts, the Golden Guides became a series covering natural history and, in the 1970s, ecology. *Flowers* appeared in 1950, *Insects* and *Stars* in 1951, *Trees* in 1952, *Reptiles and Amphibians* in 1953, *Seashores* and *Mammals* in 1955, *Fishes* in 1956, *Rocks and Minerals* and *Weather* in 1957, each in hardcover and paperback, all with the same format—a large colored picture at the top of the page, text below, and (where appropriate) a range map. Also like the Peterson series, these guides treated each subject a bit differently. For organisms like flowers, not easily identified at the species level, guides showed families or genera; the range map for "Yellow Coneflowers," for instance, had the note "90 species," and the one for Goldenrods "125 species."[43] *Stars* explained the types of stars and star clusters and described meteors and comets, then gave pages to the individual constellations. To locate the constellations, though, there were only small star charts of the seasons, which probably confused as many children as they enlightened.[44] Still, like Reed's books fifty years before, they offered an inexpensive, portable introduction to things in nature, and the Golden Nature Guides proved a durable brand.

Both adult and children's guides benefited from the rising interest in nature. Emphasizing names and using science in an unstructured fashion, field guides allowed people to learn about nature at their own pace and encouraged open-ended study, the approach that Anna Comstock had set out in that bible of Progressive nature study the *Handbook of Nature-Study*, and that ran through amateur natural history. City dwellers and suburbanites found field guides ideal. At home they could identify a familiar bird (or mouse or snake); on vacation they could find in the national park gift shop a book that told them about the mountain flowers or ground squirrels they saw on the trails.

Enough people moved beyond field guides that in 1964 Peterson wrote Paul Brooks about a trend "in modern nature book publishing that will be interesting to watch," the growing popularity of local studies. The American Museum of Natural History had published Griscom's volume on birds in the New York City area, and Cruickshank's revision, but there was enough interest by the 1960s that Harper and Row, an established trade publisher, brought out John Bull's *Birds of the New York Area*. Morrow, Peterson said, was about to publish Norman Hill's *Birds of Cape Cod*, written from Ludlow Griscom's notes.[45] "Here again is a formal annotated checklist type of book . . . [a]nd now Dover [specializing in out-of-copyright reprints] is reissuing the two large volumes, *Bird Studies of Old Cape May*, by Witmer Stone, just adding a long foreword about changes since that time. If commercial publishers can now put out books of this sort—all of a highly local and formal nature—[it] indicates a growth of the general audience beyond anything we dreamed of a few years ago."[46]

Commercial interest in Bull's *Birds of the New York Area* pointed out the growing number of people with a serious interest in nature, and the book itself showed changes not just in the birds but in birdwatching. Bull came from a second generation of the Bronx County Bird Club, younger than the storied group around Griscom, and had, like Chapman and Griscom, an association with the American Museum of Natural History—though as "research assistant" rather than "curator" and as a field rather than a museum ornithologist. More birdwatchers meant more complete coverage. In 1906 Chapman recorded 337 species in the region; Griscom had 363 in his 1923 study, Cruickshank 375 in 1942, and Bull 412. Recognizing birders' increasing range, Bull included parts of Connecticut, New York state (including Putnam County, which Griscom had ignored because "[n]o bird student of any attainments has ever worked" there), and New Jersey. Besides the scientific literature, museum collections, and his own observations, Bull relied, without extended comment, on "a voluminous mass of unpublished notes by many field workers."[47] The mapping of life onto the land, the province of natural history in the nineteenth century and field ornithology in the early twentieth, had become a shared domain, with amateurs collecting much of the information the experts collated and analyzed.

Touring Nature's Nation

Even as birdwatchers plowed local ground they looked to far horizons. Vacations, cars, and roads made seeing all the birds in the guide a plausible if daunting project and the nation a range to explore. Bird-watchers turned to Pettingill's national finding guide to plan their travels and Peterson and Fisher's *Wild America* for inspiration. Pettingill's book was as much a necessity for the touring birdwatcher as the guide for the beginner. Griscom's disciples used his local ornithology as a guide, but it was arranged for the ornithologist, not the birdwatcher. Pettingill turned the local ornithology inside out, listing places rather than species.

Peterson considered writing a book like this in the 1930s as a complement to his field guide but abandoned the project, and in 1946 Olin Sewall Pettingill, Jr., birdwatcher turned ornithologist, picked it up. He compiled and arranged "precise locations of ornithological interest and specific directions for reaching them," consulting first his friends and people he met through his work with the Audubon Society, then the expanding network his inquiries built. He had correspondents across the country and received information from over three hundred. "Time and again, I was deeply impressed by their willingness to meet requests and in many instances, to go out of their way to gather data not readily available to them. (Some of the persons who helped immeasurably I have never met.)"[48] The eastern volume appeared in 1951, the western one two years later. Birdwatchers could now plan continental equivalents of Griscom's Big Days. There was something for every birdwatcher: spots where listers could find particular species or rarities, breeding or wintering ground where many species or many of a single kind could be seen, and habitats near cities so the business traveler could see a few new birds.

Locations were organized by states, for "the average bird finder . . . like most other Americans, pictures his country in terms of states," with an overview, followed by detailed descriptions of places and how to reach them. Griscom had presumed, in *Birds of the New York City Region*, a general familiarity with the area and was, in any case, concerned with the bird's range, not the best spot to stand and look for it. Pettingill told how to get to the right spot. Under the entry for Montclair, New Jersey, for example, he said that one

of the best spots for watching the hawk flights in northeastern New Jersey is a clearing on the Crest of FIRST WATCHUNG MOUN-TAIN above an abandoned traprock quarry. To approach it from the center of Montclair, drive approximately 2½ miles north on Upper Mountain Avenue and turn left onto Bradford Avenue, which crosses the ridge. At the top of the ridge, turn right on Quarry Road, which runs into the quarry. The clearing above the quarry can be reached only on foot. Use the lookout clearing above the south side of the quarry in the fall and the clearing opposite in the spring.[49]

In this print analog of Guy Emerson's network of friends and colleagues, the consumer economy found another service to sell to birdwatchers.

Peterson and Fisher's *Wild America* served very different purposes. Telling the tale of the two naturalists' summer of traveling across America, it gave an example—the more powerful for being implicit—of the search for the country's wild heart. Just as Pettingill presented a recreational map for birdwatching, Peterson and Fisher laid out the hobby's

moral geography on the ground of American history. The title came from Stephen Vincent Benet's poem "Daniel Boone," a fragment that spoke of the ghosts of the deer arising as Boone went about by night, deer with "all lost, wild America . . . burning in their eyes." Chapter titles harked back to history and popular culture—"Rude Bridge," "On Top of Old Smoky," "Deep South," and "Golden Coast." The authors mixed history with natural wonders, celebrated America's natural variety, visited bird-rich spots, and looked for the Ivory-billed Woodpecker. As Peterson told the tale, the trip began as a way to repay Fisher, all in one lump, for guiding him around Europe, but as the species list grew, it "occurred to me that we might as well do things up brown and try for a record." For thirteen years Guy Emerson's "497 species (no subspecies included) . . . stood unchallenged." Though they wanted to see "everything that walked, hopped, swam, or flew, and the plants and rocks too, nevertheless we had the ideal chance to top Emerson's score . . . [for] we would, in the next few weeks, be breasting the full tide of the advancing stream of the spring migration."[50] From Nova Scotia in early April they flew to New England, then drove to Washington, D.C., down the Blue Ridge Parkway to the Great Smokies National Park, on to the Florida Keys, and then inland to search for the Ivory-bill. After stopping at McIlhenny's refuge at Avery Island, Louisiana, they scoured the Texas coast for the last spring migrants, took a side trip into Mexico, covered California from the coast to the Sierras, and then flew to Alaska. The "crucial bird—Number 498—came shortly after we reached Anchorage. Flying overhead near the airport was a short-billed gull. We sent Guy Emerson a telegram informing him that he had lost his throne as champ of the bird-listers." By the end of the year, Peterson had "572 species (not counting an additional 65 Mexican birds)" and Fisher "536, plus the 65 Mexican species, plus 117 others seen in Europe, a total of 718." Because Peterson remained in the hotel to work on a drawing while Fisher took a side trip, "for a month, an Englishman held the record list of birds seen in one year in North America. It was not until I returned across the continent in August that I caught up."[51]

The route sprawled across the map, but Fisher suspected their "apparently casual stop in these pinelands of northern Arizona had . . . been contrived, quite deliberately, at Roger's desk in Maryland the previous winter," and Peterson had arranged one rendezvous during the Christmas holidays. And while he wrote that the idea of a record "occurred" to him on the trip, he had in February written to Frank Pitelka at the Museum of Vertebrate Zoology that "one of the primary objectives of our trip will be to see as many species of American sea birds as possible," and he certainly set their schedule to meet the spring migration head on.[52] They also seized every chance that came along. In Miami, they "had intelligence of a rarity . . . a tropical bird new to the United States, the spot-breasted oriole. . . . We had the oriole's address—street, block, and house number—so, with an hour to kill while a tire was being repaired, we set forth" and soon located the male "in a grove of banana trees."[53]

The quest for the record gave the book a structure, but the naturalists had a more important, though more diffuse, theme: celebrating the nation's natural wonders and encouraging work to preserve wild America. They had less interest in the wilderness than the wild, the wild in Thoreau's sense, that quality in nature that is essential to our lives. Thoreau found it in Concord, Peterson in New York City. "Divorced as it is," Peterson said, "from the wilderness, wild America is to be found here in strong distilled form—in the museum, at the zoo, the botanical gardens, and at the National Audubon Society." It might appear whole, if only for a moment. "If a lad in the Bronx cannot travel to the northern tundra, he may yet see a rough-legged hawk at Clason Point on the East River. If he cannot go to the West Indies to see sooty terns, there is a chance that a hurricane may strand one at Gravesend Bay, in Brooklyn, only a subway fare away." He told how as a teenager Joseph Hickey climbed into the treetops near his Bronx home to see migrating warblers.[54] The naturalists found the wild but also saw it dwindling. Birding hot spots Peterson had haunted in the 1930s were filled with houses, and Fisher found in the Northeast little that could "be called *wild* America . . . tucked away here and there are small remnants of wilderness that have withstood three centuries of ever-expanding civilization." In the end, though, he said he had never "seen such wonders or met landlords so worthy of their land. They have had, and still have, the power to ravage it; and instead have made it a garden." That judgment had in it flattery and something of a sales pitch but also birdwatching's vision of a country that embraced progress but retained the wild, of people living modern lives in touch with pioneer America, working to defend this national heritage that enriched their lives.[55]

Although Peterson and Fisher did fly, for the most part they drove, relying on Peterson's new Ford Country Wagon—a station wagon, the automotive badge of suburban prosperity—crammed with gear, and their narrative fit the story of discovering America on the road, the same form Edwin Way Teale used in his most popular work, his four books on the seasons. Between 1951, when *North with the Spring* appeared, and 1965, when he closed the series with *Wandering through*

Winter, he wrote about traveling with his wife, Nellie, on journeys that ran from the equinox or solstice that began a season to the one that ended it.[56] In travelogues organized around natural history's wide-ranging interest in the world, he celebrated America's wild heritage and its rural roots, gave travel information, and told stories about the people they met and the history of the land, all embedded in accounts of wild animals, birds, plants, and the weather. Birds and birdwatching ran through the books, from the flocks of Tree Swallows he and Nellie found in the Everglades at the start of spring through Scissor-tailed Flycatchers on fence posts in *Journeying through Summer* (the occasion for a meditation on the mysteries of birds' ranges and distributions) to the several species of hummingbirds they found feeding together in Arizona in *Wandering through Winter*—where he told of visiting the legendary Texas birder Connie Hagar, seeing the Whooping Cranes at Aransas National Wildlife Refuge, and passing through the hometown of ornithologist Robert Ridgway.

Teale brought up a troubling issue at the heart of these modern nature journeys, one that ran through *Wild America*. Cars and roads made it possible to see all the varied aspects of a single season across the country but were "part of a present paradox: the more the land is traversed, the less it is seen." The dilemma, he observed, had a respectable ancestry; in the nineteenth century John Muir protested that nothing could be seen from a stagecoach traveling at forty miles a day.[57] It also, though he did not mention it, infected birdwatching. Recall Hickey's condemnation of the "mad dash to the next oasis, with birds ticked off on the run, and a great reliance placed on both gasoline and brakes."[58] *Wild America* had both close observation of nature and marathon drives. The car promised to take us to Nature's nation, to Wilson, Nuttall, and Audubon's America, on trips where we might find all the birds in the field guide, but it had something of the lure of fairy gold. Teale met the problem by balancing the charms of place against the lure of the road, using the road to reach the land where he found the sort of people of whom Guy Emerson spoke, people in touch with "the heart of America." Teale mapped the local onto the national, with words and then on the endpapers of his books. That met the dilemma, at least in a literary sense, but did not solve it.[59] Peterson and Fisher did not address it.

The *Wild America* trip quickly became part of birdwatching's lore and literature, a touchstone whose changing significance pointed to changes in birdwatching. The record list first held birdwatchers' attention. A year after the book appeared, Stuart Keith and his brother Anthony retraced the route, and Stuart set a new record for species seen north of Mexico, 598—though Peterson and Fisher still had, with their Mexican detour, a higher year-total for the continent, 701.[60] Kenn Kaufman, who left school at sixteen to hitchhike around the country in pursuit of birds and in 1973 made his own run at the record (described in *Kingbird Highway: The Story of a Natural Obsession That Got a Little Out of Hand*) said that in his early teens his "'bible' had been *Wild America*. Coauthored by my hero, Roger Tory Peterson," it showed that lists "could turn birdwatching into birding, an active game, even a competitive sport."[61] A Canadian naturalist led a group in Peterson and Fisher's (metaphorical) footsteps to see what had happened "to wild America in the last thirty years." They were less concerned with a species count than assessing the state of the planet's gains and losses. Along with the losses, they experienced "wild places and magic moments in the wilderness." In 2003, Scot Weidensaul used the route as a "broad framework" for a journey to "see how the continent's natural soul—and ours—was faring at the dawn of the twenty-first century."[62] He found wild America still there, "its tenacity and strength surprising," the result of "nature's resiliency" and "the more enlightened policies of the last half century."[63]

Wild America looked at the nation as home range and the source of an essential element for our own lives, sentiments widespread in the culture and common among birdwatchers. Griscom called on readers to save wild areas near cites, lest they lose that priceless heritage of native birds, and in his *Guide to Bird Watching* Joseph Hickey, by then a tough-minded scientist, spoke of "the riches offered by a life-long hobby . . . reflected in health, in recreation, and in a peace of mind beyond the price of money." Peterson said: "birds, which started as an escape from the unreal, bridged the gap to reality and became a key whereby I might unlock eternal things." That concern with a world beyond lay at the center of Henry Beston's *Outermost House*, an interwar nature classic, one of Rachel Carson's favorites, and in the 1960s a Ballantine "Style of Life" book. In it, Beston set down "the core of what I continue to believe. Nature is a part of humanity, and without some awareness and experience of that divine mystery man ceases to be man. . . . The world today is sick to its thin blood for lack of elemental things, for fire before the hands, for water welling from the earth, for air, for the dear earth itself underfoot."[64] But even people not seeking the wild had *Wild America's* perspective. The Trappist monk Thomas Merton wrote of "this world of birds, which is not concerned with us or our problems," a world he approached, like everyone else, with "binoculars and a bird book."[65]

The most popular postwar declaration in this vein, Carson's 1956 article "Help Your Child to Wonder" in *Woman's Home Companion*, became a trade book in 1965, titled *A Sense of Wonder* (a Book-of-the-Month Club selection). It remained popular enough to be reprinted with a new introduction in 1999.[66] Few now associate Carson with simple awe at nature's wonders, but she made a career as a nature writer by invoking the wonders of the sea in popular accounts based in science. Under the Sea Wind appeared at the beginning of World War II and got lost in the rush of public events, but *The Sea around Us*, a decade later, brought her public acclaim, a National Book Award, and enough money to allow her to abandon government biology for full-time writing. She spoke of nature in secular but mystical terms. *The Sea around Us* ended with an invocation: "For all at last return to the sea—to Oceanus, the ocean river, like the ever-flowing stream of time, the beginning and the end," and the preface to *The Edge of the Sea* began: "Like the sea itself, the shore fascinates us who return to it, the place of our dim ancestral beginnings." There were in its rhythms and life "the obvious attraction of movement and change and beauty. There is also, I am convinced, a deeper fascination born of inner meaning and significance."[67]

In "Help Your Child to Wonder," Carson urged parents to give their children a love of nature by keeping alive their view of a world "fresh and new and beautiful, full of wonder and excitement. It is our misfortune that for most of us that clear-eyed vision, that true instinct for what is beautiful and awe-inspiring, is dimmed and even lost before we reach adulthood." Parents should use example and teaching to foster "a sense of wonder so indestructible that it would last throughout life, as an unfailing antidote against the boredom and disenchantments of later years, the sterile preoccupation with things that are artificial, the alienation from the sources of our strength." Nature's joys stood open to all who would place themselves

under the influence of earth, sea and sky and their amazing life. Those who dwell, as scientists or laymen, among the beauties and mysteries of the earth are never alone or weary of life [and will] find reserves of strength that will endure as long as life lasts. There is symbolic as well as actual beauty in the migration of the birds, the ebb and flow of the tides . . . something infinitely healing in the repeated refrains of nature—the assurance that dawn comes after night, and spring after the winter.[68]

Birdwatching began with that sense of wonder, and even the relentless focus on the list served it. Blanchan spoke of awe and beauty in *Bird*

Neighbors; these themes filled John Burroughs's popular essays; and most ornithologists, scientists though they were, could have echoed Peterson's comment about there being "nothing thoughtful or academic in my interest [in birds].[69] A. A. Allen polled his fellow AOU members and found all had been hooked on birds by the time they were out of their teens and 90 percent by the age of ten.[70] A modern California birder told Kenn Kaufman that birds were "magical" and searching for them "a Great Adventure," with the list "just a frivolous incentive for birding. . . . The journey is what counts."[71] The list had the unacknowledged but vital function of framing the search. Carson spoke of a child's unfocused interest, and Edwin Way Teale lamented the pressure to "do something" and rejoiced that more people were "realizing that just to stop, just to enjoy nature, has its own significance."[72] But people did not simply "appreciate" nature for the same reason they did not sit around appreciating their families at reunions. They ate, played games, and gossiped about the relatives, pursuing by indirection an activity that allowed no direct approach. Birdwatching provided something to do. It might lead to awe, wonder, or insight into the world, but if enlightenment did not appear, there was at least a list.

The Dark Side of the Postwar Dream

The postwar nature boom built on the economic one, as millions took advantage of their new middle-class status to tour the national parks on their summer vacations, visit woods and nature reserves near home on weekends, and explore the still undeveloped land near their suburban homes. Even as they studied nature, though, they watched it disappear. Concern was evident not only in Teale's mixed emotions about the modern roads that made his travels possible and in Peterson and Fisher's search for the wild in developed America but also in suburbia. The gradual occupation of empty lots caused regret, but the use of new pesticides brought something stronger. Campaigns against the gypsy moth in the Northeast and the beetles carrying Dutch elm disease across the Midwest left towns blanketed with residues. Homeowners, organic farmers, and scientists protested spraying on Long Island in 1958, and when letters to the newspapers brought no relief, they went to court. Another newspaper debate stirred Carson to expand a projected series of articles for the *New Yorker* into a book, *Silent Spring*.[73] Others worked and worried without publicity. Lorrie Otto, a doctor's wife raising her family in the Milwaukee suburbs, noticed dead robins around her home and fewer salamanders and frogs each year in the local creek where she

· 142 ·

took Girl Scouts on nature trips. When the suburbs around her began using DDT to combat Dutch elm disease, she went to town council meetings with a stack of scientific papers and, as visual aid, a shoebox of dead robins from her freezer. When *Silent Spring* appeared, she found it a familiar story.[74]

Carson's charges came as news because the postwar prosperity, coming after fifteen years of depression and war, made it easy to dismiss pollution as the price of progress, and wartime scientific miracles like DDT and penicillin encouraged the belief that the new pesticides were dangerous only to their intended targets. Lacking hard evidence about the effects of these substances, Audubon could only urge caution in their use and campaign for conservation. It published articles on conservation, distributed booklets on nature and nature study to schools, sent out touring lecturers with slides and films, and gave Houghton Mifflin the right to print on the Peterson field guide of 1947 the words "Sponsored by National Audubon Society." Saving endangered species became its cause, with the Whooping Crane the primary concern and a dramatic example of the perils to wild America.[75] After the war, Robert Allen resumed his life-history research for the society, and in 1952 Audubon published *The Whooping Crane* as Research Report No. 3. With the help of Fred Bard, who succeeded Fred Bradshaw at the Saskatchewan Museum of Natural History, it publicized the bird's plight along the central flyway, and by the late 1950s the spring and fall migrations made news across the plains.[76]

In 1954, the discovery of the cranes' long-sought nesting grounds, in Wood Buffalo National Park in northern Alberta, made it possible to take action to save them. (After the last survivor of a nonmigratory flock died after being chased down by Fish and Wildlife Service personnel in 1940, no one wanted to try capturing one of the adults.) The news, as John Lynch, a biologist with the Fish and Wildlife Service, pointed out to his superiors, presented political problems. The agency was in "an unenviable public relations position." If the whooper recovered, "the Audible boy Bird-Watchers [the National Audubon Society] would grab the credit. If, as is more likely to happen, the species soon becomes extinct, the USFWS might be handed the blame." At times, he said, he wondered if Audubon was "operating on the unbeatable principle of 'Heads they win, tails we lose.'"[77] Lynch did not take that stand because he opposed saving the crane. He wrote to Joseph Hickey that wildlife managers had for too long seen nongame species as "the sole responsibility of the birdwatchers and similar amateur groups." That was wrong. "The endangered species is NOT beneath our professional dignity. It is a moral, professional, and in some cases a legal responsibility."[78]

Plans to save the birds quickly brought out disagreements about what was to be saved. Lynch pressed for what amounted to an emergency program of large poultry management. Eggs would be taken and a flock raised in captivity. The birds might grow up tame, but they could be reintroduced into the wild. Audubon scientists worried that taking the eggs would disturb the birds but found the idea of captivity even more disturbing. In 1953, writing to Fred Bard, Robert Allen called captive breeding impractical. "And in addition, I for one don't relish the idea of those great birds ending their days with clipped wings inside a pen. It makes me burn with shame to even contemplate it."[79] Karl Koford had said much the same thing the year before about the California Condor. Citing Aldo Leopold, he said its recreational value was "in inverse proportion to its artificiality."[80]

The American and Canadian governments eventually agreed on a cooperative captive breeding program, and the cranes recovered, but the issue remained, and the same arguments, sometimes offered by the same groups, came up twenty years later when it was suggested that all the remaining California Condors be removed from the wild for a breeding program. The passion came from the birdwatchers' attachment to the wild. They wanted the wilderness somewhere "out there," but even more they wanted the wild to touch their lives. Peterson found it, strong and concentrated, in the drawers and cabinets of New York's Museum of Natural History only because it lived outside the museum, and the thrill of seeing warblers in Central Park in April came in part from their connection to the tropics they had left and the boreal forests where they would nest. Previous generations took the wild for granted. Griscom fretted about feral mallards in the Bronx and the loss of undeveloped land near the city, but his were worries in a minor key, about access to the wild, not about its survival. The millions Peterson brought outdoors with his guides in their pockets worried about more than access as it became apparent that DDT, the wartime "miracle" that became the pesticide of choice for farms, forests, and suburbs, was contaminating the world.[81] Conservation became a cause, saving the planet, which made recreation, the engaging and competitive game of toting up species, seem trivial. These elements diverged under the pressure of the environmental crisis.[82] Only after a decade of confusion would these poles of birdwatching find a new balance.

PART III

Environmental Birding

Birding in a Silent Spring

We were not birdwatching. We were *birding,*
and that made all the difference.
We became a *community* of birders.

—KENN KAUFMAN (1997)

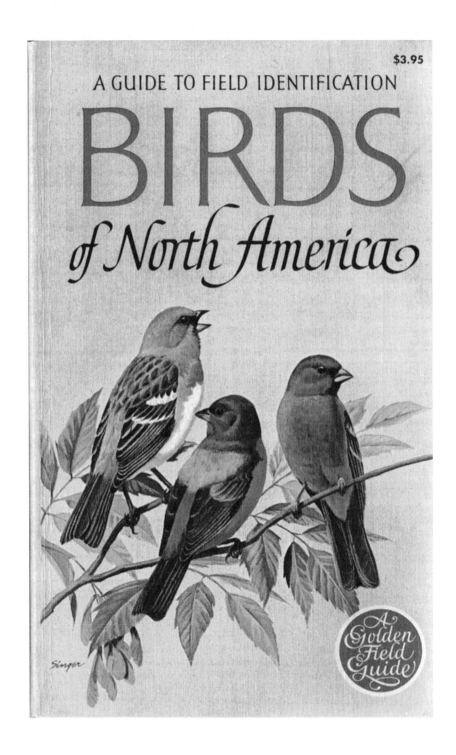

$3.95

A GUIDE TO FIELD IDENTIFICATION

BIRDS
of North America

Singer

A Golden Field Guide

SIX

T hree books represent the early environmental years: Rachel Carson's *Silent Spring*, Chandler Robbins and Arthur Singer's *Birds of North America*, and Kenn Kaufman's *Kingbird Highway*.[1] The first edition of Carson's famous work, with its nicely printed text and line drawings heading each chapter, had a respectable, even sedate look. Later ones, such as a 1970s paperback with a bird's skeleton and the blurb "The World-famous Bestseller about our Ravaged Environment and the Man-made Pollution that is Imperiling All Life on Earth" on the cover and quotations from an incongruous pair, Margaret Mead and Richard Nixon, on the back showed the effects of fame.[2] The other two books spoke of the growing interest in field identification, the sophistication of its methods, and the intensity of the competition. *Birds of North America*, by Chandler S. Robbins, Bertel Brunn, and Herbert S. Zim, illustrated by Arthur Singer, published in 1966, looked like a "bird book," with its sturdy, water-resistant cover decorated with a picture of three buntings, the declaration that this was "A Guide to Field Identification," and the logo "A Golden Field Guide." It was just the size of Peterson's 1947 edition, but the browser in the bookstore would have noted some important differences. All the plates were in color, and the silhouettes not an afterthought on the endpapers and in the limbo of the back matter. They marched in ranks across the plates, inviting birdwatchers to use body shape as well as field marks. Rather than describing birds' ranges in words, this guide had maps, color coded for

6.1 · *Cover of Robbins-Singer guide* · This "guide to field identification" incorporated knowledge gathered since Peterson's 1947 edition and new ways of presenting information. From *Birds of North America* by Chandler S. Robbins, Bertel Brun, and Herbert Zim, illustrated by Arthur Singer, © Western Publishing Company, 1966. Used by permission of Chandler S. Robbins and of Alan and Paul Singer, The Estate of Arthur Singer.

season, and (most striking to those frustrated by having to flip from plate to full description) all the information about each species on the page facing the picture. Finally, Kaufman's memoir of growing up birding, organized around his quest for a new record list from North America, spoke of a larger, and younger, national community of expert birders. Taken together, the books recorded a time when conservation became a vital, even a moral, matter and recreation became a more intense and competitive activity.

Conservation became an urgent matter as the public became alarmed about the residues of chemicals returning from fields and forests to their bodies, accumulating in the tissues with results no one could predict. Nature protection became more than a matter of saving the world beyond society for aesthetic enjoyment. It meant protecting human health and the future of life on earth. New crowds swelled the ranks of established conservation groups and formed many new ones. And while they read *Silent Spring* for its account of residues in our bodies, cancer, and birds' failure to reproduce, they made it a core environmental text for Carson's analysis of the problems produced by industrial society and her vision of a new relation between humans and the rest of nature. They found in it a compelling way to think about their relation, as a species and as individuals, to the world.

This chapter traces birdwatching in the early environmental years, as a new tension developed between conservation and recreation. The first part takes up conservation's transformation from a genteel concern with birds as something good in our lives to a vigorous defense of the ecosystems on which both birds and humans depend. It looks at Rachel Carson's ideas and in particular the battle over DDT, in which birders from Lorrie Otto to Joseph Hickey played key roles. The story of their concern, particularly Hickey's movement from indifference toward DDT to active opposition to it, followed a common trajectory, but Hickey was more than ordinarily conscious of how and when his ideas changed and had an important role in the battle. The next section considers recreational birding, represented by a new generation of field guides and the growing national competition for a record list, a quest few undertook but many watched. Like many of its predecessors, *Birds of North America* grew out of ornithologists' interest in recreation. Chandler Robbins, like Frank Chapman sixty years before him, wrote his guide to serve his hobby, for he began as a bird-struck teenager writing to Ludlow Griscom, then became an ornithologist with the U.S. Fish and Wildlife Service. His guide built on Peterson's work, adding new knowledge about identification and refining its presentation on the page. It had more poses and plumages, treated subspecies more thoroughly, and had a simpler format, but it also moved beyond plumage patterns, relying more heavily on form. It gave "Peterson" its first serious competition and marked the start of a new era of competition in the general field guide market. Kaufman's *Kingbird Highway*, with its tale of a teenager hitchhiking around the country in the early 1970s in search of a record list, showed the competitive edge of this larger and more expert community, the people who needed or appreciated the new guide. Like the boys of the Bronx County Bird Club, Kaufman had friends and mentors, an audience and a cheering section, but his were spread across the country.

A New Foundation for Conservation

By the time she died, Rachel Carson had become a nature saint, though the iconic photographs—standing against a wooded background with a pair of binoculars around her neck or on her hands and knees peering under a sea-side boulder—showed only a small, serious, middle-aged woman. They suggested her love of nature but said nothing about her fierce commitment to the sense of wonder and joy she found there or the radical path she came to espouse.[3] She found the common cause of our apparently disconnected problems of dwindling wildlife, contaminated air and water, and new threats to human health in our our arrogant belief that we could and should conquer nature. Her eloquence and evidence converted a growing public unease into a political cause. In 1960 only scientists used the word "environment," and "ecology" meant a subfield of biology; in 1970 a quarter of a million people gathered for the first Earth Day in Washington, where they heard speeches by members of Congress, politicians, and activists calling for environmental legislation and ecological responsibility. By then, two states had banned most uses of DDT, and two years later the federal government ended all but emergency use of the chemical that in 1945 had been the wonder of the age and evidence of the Progress of Mankind.

Silent Spring had two careers, a short but turbulent one as best-selling exposé, then a continuing role as an environmental text, a guide to how we should live with nature in our modern society. Accident and publicity made it a cause célèbre. In the summer of 1962, as the *New Yorker* printed excerpts from the forthcoming manuscript, it was found that an apparently safe drug, thalidomide, used as a sleeping pill, caused horrifying birth defects if taken at a certain point in pregnancy. Several thousand children were born, mostly in Europe, without arms, their hands attached to their shoulders; without legs, with feet directly attached to hips; or with other characteristic deformities. The news stories all noted that an American manufacturer had been pressing for approval to sell the drug in the United States, against the opposition of an FDA staff physician, Dr. Frances Kelsey, who felt its safety had not been established. In the face of that vivid evidence of the hidden dangers in chemicals, the National Agricultural Chemicals Association, representing the pesticide manufacturers, campaigned against *Silent Spring*, not only disputing Carson's science but calling her a hysterical woman opposed to science, progress, and the greatest accomplishment of Western civilization—as the group saw it: the conquest of nature. She wanted us, the association said, to go back to living in caves, eating nuts and berries, and dying young of preventable diseases.[4]

Silent Spring looked like earlier muckraking books, exposés like Kallett and Schlink's Depression-era sensation *100,000,000 Guinea Pigs* (to which it was compared), but whereas that book looked at chemicals deliberately added to foods, drugs, and cosmetics, saw them in the context of public health, and looked for solutions in legislation, Carson's book made a larger case. The central problem of the modern age, she charged, aside from the prospect of "nuclear war [was] the contamination of man's total environment with such substances of incredible potential for harm—substances that accumulate in the tissues . . . and even penetrate the germ cells to shatter or alter the very material of heredity upon which the shape of the future depends." We had put

> poisonous and biologically potent chemicals indiscriminately into the hands of persons largely or wholly ignorant of their potential for harm [and] allowed them to be used with little or no advance investigation of their effects on soil, water, wildlife, and man himself. Future generations are unlikely to condone our lack of prudent concern for the integrity of the natural world that supports all life.

The way out lay not in banning chemicals but in abandoning the "smooth superhighway of chemical controls" that led on to disaster. We should turn to the vast array of biological solutions, some now in use, others being tested, still others only yet ideas, all "based on an understanding of the living organism they seek to control, and of the whole fabric of life to which these organisms belong." They offered "our only chance to reach a destination that assures the preservation of our earth."[5]

Critics and defenders argued vigorously about Carson's use of science but fiercely about her call to learn to live with nature. Her supporters saw in it a guide that would save us and the wild world, her opponents an "end of all human progress, reversion to a passive social state devoid of technology, scientific medicine, agriculture, sanitation. It means disease, epidemics, starvation, misery, and suffering."[6] Both sides appealed to science, but to different sciences and for different ends. Her defenders relied on ecology, which described the processes and relationships that bound organisms together, and made Aldo Leopold's dictum from *A Sand County Almanac* an environmental Golden Rule. "A thing is right when it tends to preserve the integrity, stability, and beauty of the biotic community. It is wrong when it tends otherwise."[7] Critics used mainly the biological and physical sciences, but more fundamentally they saw the conquest of nature as the first requirement of civilization. Further progress, they believed, depended on ignoring environmentalists' fears.

Carson's view had deep roots in Western intellectual history, going back to visions of Eden, but it grew more from her life. As a child she explored the woods around home with her mother, identified birds, made a life-list, and read nature literature.[8] In college she majored in English but also studied biology, went on to a master's of science in that field, and took a job with the Fish and Wildlife Service, where she divided her time between marine research and editing agency publications. She wrote nature articles on the side, and in 1952 the success of *The Sea around Us* allowed her to leave the agency. She wrote mainly of her first love, the sea, but followed the pesticide question. She wrote an unpublished manuscript in the late 1940s, using the results of the Service's wartime studies of forest sprays. A decade later, when she returned to the topic, virtually everyone had DDT residues in their body fat, DDT production was at its peak, and the public was becoming worried about suburban sprays for gypsy moths and the bark beetles that carried Dutch elm disease.

In 1958, protests in the letters column of a Boston paper inspired her to write *Silent Spring*.[9] She used examples from the headlines but built her case on research and concerns that went back to the wartime tests. In the summer of 1944, for example, one of Ludlow Griscom's friends wrote to him about a story in *Time* about the Fish and Wildlife Service's forest spraying of DDT. It had virtually wiped out leaf-eating insects and flies. Nothing in the report, he said, answered or even raised "some of the questions that occur to a moderately ignorant layman." What would this do to plants or birds? Griscom replied that he had no information but "commonsense biology proves that the wholesale elimination of any living creatures is always certain to have an [sic] backfire somewhere, sometime, somehow."[10] The next year, Chandler Robbins wrote to Griscom that he would be spending his summer at the Fish and Wildlife Service's Patuxent Research Center assessing the effects of DDT on breeding bird populations. A year later, the president of the National Audubon Society, John Baker, warned that DDT might have unexpected and disastrous side-effects, and two years later the Society issued a press release calling for restraint in its use. The dangers were clear enough that two Fish and Wildlife Service officers wrote an article warning economic entomologists of the dangers of careless spraying and of any spraying around water.[11] The combination of new kinds of problems and greater threats to wild areas from expanding suburbs and factories led Audubon's leaders to move beyond programs that directly protected birds to those that saved essential habitat, a change in policy so marked that in 1949 Peterson wrote to Griscom that "one of the criticisms I hear most about the Society these days, and it is a danger too, is that it is becoming less and less of a bird organization and is losing its identity as a rather nebulous, thinly spread, conservation society [sic]."[12]

Audubon needed new policies, though, to meet a new threat to wildlife, even more diffuse than the habitat changes that spurred interwar game management work. The new chemical pesticides spread from the farm to the world. Farmers applied DDT to fruits, vegetables, row crops, cow barns, and dairy cows; timber companies sprayed entire forests; towns sent spray trucks down tree-lined streets to keep suburban yards mosquito-free; and housewives bought "bug bombs" to kill insects around the house. In the desperate days before the Salk vaccine, a few communities sprayed schoolchildren, hoping the miracle chemical would protect them against polio. The materials did not remain where they were applied, though, and they were persistent. When DDT was applied to cow barns, even when the cows were in the field, its residues appeared in the milk. By 1950, residues were so ubiquitous that baby-food manufacturers abandoned their rule of allowing no residues in their products. Only five years after the chemical had been approved for civilian use, the Centers for Disease Control reported that virtually everyone in the United States had DDT in their body fat. Insects developed resistance with alarming speed; in 1950 military entomologists found that body lice on American, Korean, and Chinese troops survived treatments that in World War II had easily killed them. Soon birders and amateur naturalists saw troubling signs. Charles Broley, a retired banker who took up banding and studying Bald Eagles near his home in Florida, found in the mid-1950s that the birds were failing to raise young. Extrapolating from Fish and Wildlife research, he suggested that DDT might be to blame.[13]

Lorrie Otto traveled from Milwaukee to see Joseph Hickey, now professor of Wildlife Management at the University of Wisconsin in Madison. He gave her a skeptical hearing. Observations by housewives, he thought, were not science. Then, in the summer of 1958, a mulberry tree in an Illinois town roused his suspicions. It was loaded with berries, and there was not a bird in sight.[14] Finding robins outside town, he wondered if reports in the *Bulletin of the Illinois Audubon Society* about birds vanishing from small towns—reports he had dismissed because the bulletin was not a scientific publication—might be true. Back in Madison, his graduate students worked out how much DDT it took to poison robins and then looked at the breeding populations in sprayed and unsprayed towns. While they counted robins in the suburbs, Hickey saw the situation close up as authorities sprayed the campus in Madison to ward off Dutch elm disease. He was appalled, for "they literally used tons of DDT on the campus and birds were dying all over the place— robins, Yellow Warblers, and so on. We lost our Screech Owls, which never came back . . . [and] all the Yellow Warblers in front of the Ag. School building . . . and it took them years and years to come back." Collecting dead robins and counting nesting pairs, he estimated that 89 percent had been killed. The graduate students reported that the longer a town sprayed, the fewer robins it had. Wauwatosa, which sprayed for three years in a row, lost 98 percent of its breeding population. It had, he said, "experienced *Silent Spring*."[15]

His colleagues' work added to his concern. George Wallace found that spraying on the campus of Michigan State University decimated songbirds, and Roy Barker at the University of Illinois's Urbana campus told an even more disturbing tale. Spraying left residues on elm leaves, which fell to the ground in the fall and were eaten by earthworms; robins returning the next spring ate the worms and died of the accumulated residues. Hickey learned that scientists in California had traced the die-off of Western Grebes at Clear Lake to the buildup of DDD, a chemical closely related to DDT, in the lake water. Applied to the lake in very low concentrations to kill midges, it built up in the lake's food chains; the grebes, at the top end, had levels in their body fat eighty thousand times those in the water. Those were local problems. Then in 1962 he heard, but dismissed as rumor, that "the Peregrine Falcons in the eastern part of the United States . . . had not raised a single young." An article by the British ornithologist Derek Ratcliffe made him reconsider. It found "that the Peregrine Falcon population in Britain had collapsed and that it possibly could be due to insecticides." That caused Hickey to warn Carl Buchheister, president of the National Audubon Society, that if the same thing was going on in North America, "then we indeed were in trouble."[16] The next spring he sent "two young historical naturalists named D. D. Berger and Charles Sindelar on a 14,000 [mile] trip around the eastern part of the United States" to check eyries. He went to Europe, where he learned that many populations were "gone . . . [for] not a single bird was fledged." When he returned, Berger and Sindelar told him they had not found a single fledging from Georgia to Nova Scotia.[17] But while their report and the European's story "fit right together like a beautiful mesh . . . we did not understand what had happened to the American birds." To find out, he organized a conference on Peregrine Falcon populations.

At this point he felt caught between his friends and his scientific convictions. He felt it was all right for conservationists, like Roger Tory Peterson or Carl Buchheister, to take a stand, but as a scientist he had to be more cautious, for science meant testing hypotheses, and they might be wrong. Until he had convincing evidence, he was not willing to come out against DDT. In a letter to Buchheister he said that "perhaps to Roger's distress, I approach this peregrine problem less directly than he would. . . . I view this crash cautiously and allude to [the upcoming] conference as one 'on the biology of *Falco peregrinus*' (population biology would be a better term)." The conference would document the species' decline, but Peregrine Falcons and Bald Eagles "just don't lend themselves to uncomplicated research projects on pesticides hypotheses. The more conclusive evidence is apt to come from work on pelicans, cormorants, herons, and the like."[18] He had reason to speak of "Roger's distress," for a year earlier Peterson had written to Olin Pettingill that he was "becoming almost frantic about [the problem of pesticides]—particularly in relation to the birds" at the end of long food chains. "And have you noticed the drastic decline of butterflies: We did not have a single large Saturnid moth at my studio lights all spring and only two or three Polyphemus last year."[19]

Hickey wanted the conference funded by nonpartisan sources, but when the federal agencies turned him down he took a substantial grant from the Audubon Society. In Madison, the ornithologists' reports showed that on two continents and in habitats as different as the Arctic tundra and the East Coast of the United States, Peregrine Falcons had failed to raise young. They laid no eggs, the eggs broke or did not hatch, or the chicks died. Some blamed pesticides, and a few suggested an experimental ban on DDT on the East Coast, but others, including Hickey, wanted more research. After learning that museum and private collections in Great Britain had shown a thinning of eggshells in 1947, he set a graduate student to check American collections. In California and Massachusetts, average shell thickness dropped just after DDT came into common use. Meanwhile, analytical chemists tested Herring Gull eggs from the East Coast and the Great Lakes for "residue levels . . . [and] for eggshell thickness," and, Hickey said, "we found a perfectly inverse correlation—the higher the residue levels in the eggs the thinner the eggshell. And analyzed statistically the indications were that this could have occurred by chance were one in a thousand times. And *that* convinced me [in] I believe . . . June of '68, that DDT," in the form of a breakdown product called DDE, was responsible for the birds' plight.

Around this time, Lorrie Otto came back, urging action, and Hickey suggested she get in touch with a new group he had heard about on Long Island, a dozen people calling themselves the Environmental Defense Fund. It seemed an unlikely force for change: a pugnacious workmen's compensation lawyer, Victor Yannacone (his motto was "Sue the Bastards"), a young biologist, Charles Wurster, a small group of enthusiasts, and no money. Its attempts, in Michigan, failed, as did its first one in Wisconsin, an action against the city of Milwaukee.[20] It turned out that Milwaukee and the spraying company had not signed a contract to spray, as alleged in the complaint, and the hearing examiner promptly ended the hearing. Lorrie Otto, according to the examiner, began to cry (she later did not remember that detail). Curious, he asked Yannacone what was going on. There would be no spraying and this woman was crying? After Yannacone explained they wanted a forum to present a case against DDT, the examiner told them to request a declaratory ruling, a provision that allowed businesses to discover whether their proposed operations would comply with state law. The Environmental Defense Fund promptly asked the state Department of Natural Resources to rule on whether DDT was or was not a water pollutant. At the hearing, Hickey not only testified but organized a scientific research service (staffed by graduate students) to help Yannacone prepare for cross-examination. By the time the hearing ended, Michigan had already banned DDT, the Environmental Defense Fund had many requests to bring suits, and the movement to ban DDT had become national. Within a few years, a coalition of conservation organizations petitioned the new Environmental Protection Agency to ban DDT. By 1974 its use and manufacture in the United States were at an end.

The campaign, which depended on amateur-expert cooperation, justified the first generation's belief that watching birds would rally people for bird conservation, but also showed the shrinking role ordinary birders had. Otto saw dead robins on the lawn, Broley eagles in Florida failing to raise young, Peterson the Ospreys disappearing from around his home in Connecticut, but it took the concerted efforts of ornithologists on two continents to discover the connections among these phenomena, to trace such things as thin eggshells back to the resides of chemicals applied miles away. Protecting birds now required expertise, planning, and coordination among groups, agencies, even governments. It was not enough for citizens to lobby for laws. In saving endangered species, for example, amateurs had important roles only if the scientists allowed them to. The Whooping Crane project, for example, became almost entirely an agency program. In 1967, following passage of the first federal Endangered Species Act, the Fish and Wildlife Service began captive breeding of cranes at a special facility in Maryland, using eggs from the nests in Wood Buffalo National Park in Alberta, and for years it refused amateurs access to eggs.[21] Restoring Peregrine Falcons in the eastern United States, on the other hand, involved much more teamwork across scientific borders. That the species was not, worldwide, in immediate danger and the falcon not a national symbol of the wild may have allowed this, but the decisions reflected as well the willingness of people like Tom Cade, a Cornell ornithologist who helped organize the work, to enlist falconers in breeding birds for release into the wild. By 1975, birds were being hatched and raised in captivity. Fields ranging from ethology to veterinary medicine helped define the birds' requirements, but hatching and rearing depended on patience and insight, qualities not always well correlated with degrees and research skills.[22] Experience helped, and here the amateurs, used to raising their own birds, were the experts. It took more work and several trials to find ways of releasing the captives into the wild with a good chance of survival (Great Horned Owls often killed the birds released in the early days), but soon the falcon was reoccupying its old range.[23]

Audubon found new roles in these new campaigns but defended old values, for these had become part of the environmental movement, in part through *Silent Spring*. The text relentlessly footnoted scientific studies, but Carson set the argument in the context of the first chapter, "A Fable for Tomorrow," which presented a dystopian vision of a world destroyed by chemical residues in an American small town where nature was part of humans' lives. Neither Carson nor her readers saw any contradiction in that mixture. Nature literature relied on science to induce awe and wonder, amateur nature study harked back to natural history's roots in natural theology, mixing piety and self-improvement, and conservation used science to guide action, while seeking support with appeals to wildlife as symbols of the precious natural heritage that was wild America. Environmentalism did not discard older values and commitments but gave them a new, ecological context.

Conventional Birding Refined, Perhaps Redefined

The environmental crusade swept up an established, somewhat staid conservation movement in an aggressive crusade to save the planet, but recycling newspapers and turning down the thermostat did not interfere with watching birds. Often enough, the watchers had in their pocket not "Peterson" but the Robbins-Singer volume, often called just the Golden Guide. Unlike Pough and Eckelberry's Audubon series, which was aimed at amateur naturalists, or Hausman's, catering to beginners, Robbins-Singer competed for Peterson's audience, people with some experience who wanted to learn to identify all they saw, while also serving the more expert group trained on and ready to go beyond "Peterson." It built on his crucial innovation of making pictures rather than words central, offering a greater array of plumages and poses, making body shape a key criterion, and completing the shift in the book's form from text pages interrupted by plates to a set of plates accompanied by text. The bookstore browser found paintings on the right, shown in color against a neutral background, and all the information about each species on the facing page, arranged so as to answer common questions. Rather than field marks, descriptions began by indicating abundance—"common," "uncommon," or a phrase like "common (but quiet, retiring, and easily overlooked)" (Yellow-bellied Sapsucker)—and included behavior: "Rides on the water in tight flocks; flies on loose flocks over short distances, in long lines when migrating" (White-winged Scoter). Peterson used words for the ranges. (For the Louisiana Water-thrush, for instance: "Breeds from w. New England, s. Ontario, se. Minnesota and e. Nebraska to cent. South Carolina, n. Georgia, n. Louisiana and ne. Texas; winters in Central America.") Robbins-Singer had a small map of the United States and Canada in the left margin, colored to show summer, winter, and year-round ranges and migration routes.[24] Rather than describing the calls, Robbins-Singer used a visual method, "sonograms," grids developed by Cornell's Laboratory of Ornithology that plotted pitch against time. These had, as the two-page explanation in the front admitted, to

The plate layout has Peterson's neutral background and common pose, but it included silhouettes for comparison as a standard feature.

This points toward the modern guide's use of poses of birds at rest and in flight, winter and summer, and the silhouettes serve not just to distinguish forms but, at the bottom, differences in the silhouettes of related species.

● **LOONS** (*Order* Gaviiformes, *Family* Gaviidae) are specialized for swimming and diving. Powerful legs attached at the rear of the body give extra leverage to the large webbed feet. Loons come ashore only to breed and to nest. They are silent in winter. In flight the head is lower than the body. The wingbeats are fast, uninterrupted by gliding. When diving, the swimming bird hops up and forward to begin the plunge, but it can also submerge stealthily from a sitting position. Loons eat fish, crustaceans, and some water plants. Eggs, 2-3.

COMMON LOON   *Gávia immer*
The most common loon, breeding along lakes and rivers. Its yodel-like laugh is given frequently, near the nest and in flight, especially at night. Varies considerably in size. Note its dark, evenly-tapered bill and, in summer, its cross-banded back. In winter the head and neck are darker than the Red-throated Loon's. Common Loons migrate in small flocks; most go to the coast.

YELLOW-BILLED LOON   *Gávia ádamsii*
The largest loon, and the most northern; breeds on lakes in the tundra. The bill is straw-colored; the upper half is straight, the lower half curved up, in contrast to the dagger-like bill of the Common. The head is darker and the white spots on back are larger and fewer than the Common Loon's. Both species have similar calls.

ARCTIC LOON   *Gávia árctica*
Nearly circumpolar, but rare in eastern North America. Breeds on tundra lakes. The Arctic is smaller than the two preceding loons; its light gray crown and white stripes on the side of the throat are diagnostic. In winter the back is gray with pale feather edgings. The bill is thin and straight, more slender than Common Loon's. The Arctic is so like the small race of the Common Loon that identification in winter is risky outside its normal range. Call is an ascending whistle.

RED-THROATED LOON   *Gávia stelláta*
Common in its breeding range on both fresh and salt water, wintering mainly along the coast. Often migrates in flocks. It is nearly as long as the Arctic Loon but is much slimmer. The light-colored, upturned bill is a good field mark. In summer plumage the white stripes extend up the back of the head. In winter the back is gray with tiny white spots. Call, a rapid quacking.

YELLOW-BILLED LOON
L 25" W 60"

cormorant scaup merganser loon grebe

mmer

winter

COMMON LOON
L 24" W 58"

winter

winter

summer

ARCTIC LOON
L 18" W 47"

winter

summer

winter

summer

RED-THROATED LOON
L 17" W 44"

Red-throated
raises wing
higher than
other loons.

Arctic Loon Red-throated Loon

The plate has no heading, for the text stands directly opposite.

Text, like illustrations, was a marvel of compression and arrangement, written, like Hoffman's New England guide of 1904, to answer the questions birders used to make identifications.

6.2 · *Robbins's Loons* · These plates added to paintings showing diagnostic patterns an array of shapes, and on the opposite page more information and maps that showed at a glance range and migration. It served a generation ready to move beyond Peterson's field marks. From *Birds of North America* by Chandler S. Robbins, Bertel Brun, and Herbert Zim, illustrated by Arthur Singer, © Western Publishing Company, 1966. Used by permission of Chandler S. Robbins and Alan and Paul Singer, The Estate of Arthur Singer.

be learned, but in theory they gave an immediate grasp of the song. Robbins-Singer addressed the problem of finding the right section of the book by listing families of birds on the inside cover and giving directions for marking the edges of the pages. A book on the presentation of graphic evidence and mapping described the book as having "a sense of craft, detail, and credibility that comes from gathering and displaying good evidence all together."[25]

Peterson emphasized plumage patterns, because they could be shown in pictures and novices easily grasped them, and downplayed form. He told readers to become acquainted with birds' shapes but used them only in the silhouettes, which were relegated to the endpapers or placed after the text.[26] Robbins-Singer put silhouettes throughout and arranged them for easy comparison. The first page of loons, for instance, had flying and sitting shapes of cormorant, scaup, merganser, loon, and grebe across the top of the page. On another the small tree-dwellers—chickadee, titmouse, nuthatch, creeper, and wren—marched across the top, three in characteristic poses on branches, and the nuthatch and creeper on the trunk, the first head down, the second head up. Robbins-Singer included extensive arrays of different plumages, again organized for comparison. Two pages showed heads of male warblers in the spring (shades of Merriam's *Birds of Village and Field*, but in color), one for those without wing bars, one with; two more had fall warblers, "Olive or Yellow immatures without wingbars" and "With wingbars and tail spots"; another two pages pictured sparrows with "Streaked Breasts" and "Unstreaked Breasts." Specialized plates showed other important groups: "Hawks in Flight," "Female Ducks in Flight," "Winter Plumage of Smaller Shorebirds," and "Immature Gulls."[27]

Birds of North America served a generation trained on Peterson's guides and using modern binoculars, and it pointed out how the community had changed. Merriam's generation had had books that treated a selection of common species and looked at them through opera glasses. Peterson's early readers found all the species treated in a uniform manner and, with the third edition's plates of "Confusing Fall Warblers," could move beyond simple plumages, and they had better optics. Peterson painted the plates for the first edition to show what could be seen through binoculars that magnified objects four times. After the war, bird-watchers had six- or eight-power glasses, and some lugged military surplus ten-power ones. By the 1960s, the market was large enough that binocular makers began catering to it, touting models light enough to carry all day, with better light-gathering ability, wider field of view, and quick-focus mechanisms that, the ads said, let you focus on the bird before it flew away. Good but not expert birders could identify birds in almost any plumage and pick out details of shape at greater distances. Robbins, recognizing that fact, included juvenal and female forms and common variations and emphasized shape. The advances in Robbins's guide owed more to other improvements in field identification besides optics, for in birding, unlike most field recreations, equipment did not give a decisive advantage. Expert birders ran up larger lists with up-to-date binoculars than they could with outdated glasses, but they relied primarily on knowing the significance of what they saw, and each generation of guides gave ordinary birders information gathered by the experts in the last. In a systematic way, Robbins-Singer helped readers use plumage variations, juvenal plumages, color morphs, body shape, postures and flight patterns, clues that had been the cutting edge of identification in Griscom's day.

Peterson knew his book needed revision, and he was concerned about Robbins's guide. Two years before it appeared, he warned Paul Brooks that it "may well cut us to ribbons," and eight months later said its publication would put Houghton Mifflin in a bad spot, for it would be three years before a new revision of the eastern guide would be ready. "I have not been worried about other competing guides since Dick Pough's books—and there have been several—but this one is something else again—a very powerful, astute publisher and the best possible choices of author and artist."[28] When the book appeared, he asked Brooks to look at it without prejudice, even if, as a competing publisher, he might find that difficult. "It certainly is a lot of *good* color for an incredibly low price. The color is far more accurate and cleaner than in our current eastern guide with its worn plates. Of course the book does not have our system but it is a lot for the money and supplements the field guide in many ways." It lacked the Peterson system, he went on, because of "my own pressure during the last two or three years on both Singer and Chan Robbins who are decent fellows. Zim," he said, "was all for taking over our system lock, stock, and barrel." In a second letter to Brooks, written that same day, he warned that the guide would "herald a complete series of Golden Field Guides eventually. How they managed to get 340 pages in color (good, clean color) plus bibliography and index for only $2.95 I shall never know."[29] Olin Pettingill agreed, writing to Robbins that the new guide, "covering all the species of North America under one small cover, in full color, and at modest cost, reached a milestone in publishing on birds for the amateur."[30]

Robbins-Singer lacked Peterson's relentless focus on comparison, but the treatment of these confusing species was a model of clarity.

This plate shows, more than most, attention to what was around the birds, perching each species on characteristic vegetation.

● **THE GENUS EMPIDONAX,** the most difficult genus of North American flycatchers, is commonly referred to by its Latin name. Species are frequently impossible to identify in the field. All are small short-tailed flycatchers with eye rings and wingbars. Wingbars of immature are more buffy than adult's. They flip their tails up and then down with rapid jerky motions. Size differences are slight and overlapping. With experience most can be identified on the breeding ground when singing and when habitat provides a clue. The eastern species and some western ones also have distinctive chips.

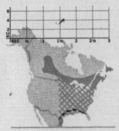

YELLOW-BELLIED FLYCATCHER *Empidonax flavivéntris*
Common on its breeding ground in spruce-fir forests, but rarely seen on migration. The only eastern *Empidonax* with a yellow throat. Acadian has yellow on flanks, especially in the immature, but its throat is white. No other eastern *Empidonax* has a whistled song—an ascending *per-wee* suggestive of Semipalmated Plover's call; also a single leisurely *che-bunk* similar to the oft-repeated *che-bek* of the Least Flycatcher.

ACADIAN FLYCATCHER *Empidonax viréscens*
Common in moist woodlands, especially deciduous floodplain forests, where it usually stays below the canopy. During migration, Acadian and Yellow-bellied Flycatchers can be seen in the same habitat; Acadian can be told by its white throat. Acadian is larger and heavier billed than Least, slightly greener above than Traill's, but not safely distinguishable except by its calls. Song is an explosive *peet-suh*, 2-4 times/min.

TRAILL'S FLYCATCHER *Empidonax trailli*
Common. Larger than Least, with greater contrast between white throat and olive sides. Browner backed than Acadian, Yellow-bellied, and the western species (p. 200). Songs and call note are distinctive—a whistle superimposed on a buzz. Northern birds in alder swamp sing a 3-syllable *fee-bee-o*; southern birds in dry brush a 2-syllable *fitz-bew*; 12-30/min. May be two species.

LEAST FLYCATCHER *Empidonax minimu*
Common in scrub growth, wood margins, and un sprayed orchards. This smallest eastern *Empidonax* ha less contrast between throat and side of breast than th Traill's, and little or no greenish on back. Told by it song, a dry *che-bek*, repeated 50-70/min.

EASTERN *EMPIDONAX* FLYCATCHERS

YELLOW-BELLIED
FLYCATCHER
L 4½"

im.

tail wag

ACADIAN
FLYCATCHER
L 4¾"

TRAILL'S
FLYCATCHER
L 4¾"

LEAST FLYCATCHER
L 4½"

The heading, unlike that on the loons, emphasizes the problems of identification, telling readers these are "frequently impossibly to identify in the field."

Songs are treated here in sonogram and text, and in detail, with differences for southern and northern specimens of Traill's Flycatcher.

6.3 · *Robbins's flycatchers* · Habitat, so important with these species, crept back into the illustrations, and songs appeared in the new, and sometimes baffling, form of "sonograms." From *Birds of North America* by Chandler S. Robbins, Bertel Brun, and Herbert Zim, illustrated by Arthur Singer, © Western Publishing Company, 1966. Used by permission of Chandler S. Robbins and Alan and Paul Singer, The Estate of Arthur Singer.

This groups related species both for patterns and form. In the silhouettes, non-ducks appear in blue rather than black.

The paintings show the wings at the bottom of the down stroke to make it easier to compare the important wing patches.

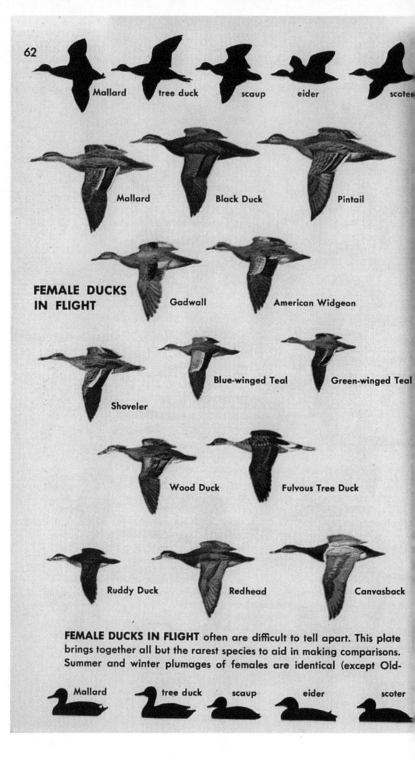

62

Mallard tree duck scaup eider scoter

Mallard Black Duck Pintail

FEMALE DUCKS IN FLIGHT Gadwall American Widgeon

Shoveler Blue-winged Teal Green-winged Teal

Wood Duck Fulvous Tree Duck

Ruddy Duck Redhead Canvasback

FEMALE DUCKS IN FLIGHT often are difficult to tell apart. This plate brings together all but the rarest species to aid in making comparisons. Summer and winter plumages of females are identical (except Old-

Mallard tree duck scaup eider scoter

merganser **Ruddy Duck** **loon** **coot** **alcid**

Ring-necked Duck **Lesser Scaup** **Greater Scaup**

Common Goldeneye **Bufflehead**

FEMALE DUCKS IN FLIGHT

Oldsquaw winter **Harlequin Duck** **Common Eider**

Common Scoter **White-winged Scoter** **Surf Scoter**

Common Merganser **Red-breasted Merganser** **Hooded Merganser**

Oldsquaw). Immatures usually are similar in plumage to females. Different species often flock together. Note the wing pattern, the most important field mark.

merganser **Ruddy Duck** **loon** **coot** **alcid**

The specialized plates in this new guide emphasized how many birders had moved from identifying species to trying to put a name on any bird they saw.

Text here did little more than remind readers what to look for, "the wing pattern, the most important field mark."

6.4 · *Robbins's ducks* · This plate, giving the duller females careful treatment, catered to a more advanced generation of birders than those who first read Peterson. From *Birds of North America* by Chandler S. Robbins, Bertel Brun, and Herbert Zim, illustrated by Arthur Singer, © Western Publishing Company, 1966. Used by permission of Chandler S. Robbins and Alan and Paul Singer, The Estate of Arthur Singer.

Peterson had reason to worry, for the market had changed since Houghton Mifflin had made the first printings of the 1947 edition almost a special production. Paperbacks and lower costs for color printing challenged a business model built around selling an unrevised volume for many years. A year after Robbins's book came out, Peterson wrote to Brooks that he was "a bit disturbed . . . when I learned that the Robbins-Singer bird guide was outselling us by a very considerable margin at the bookshop at the Massachusetts Audubon headquarters." Brooks said the competition was "stronger than I realized" but attributed it to the price difference: Peterson, only in hardback, cost $4.95, while the Golden Guide, in paperback, sold for $2.95. The firm's sales representatives, he said, wanted something at a competitive price—by which he meant a paperback version.[31] Peterson resisted, at least in part because of the difference in royalties, arguing that "the weakness in the Eastern book is not cheap competition but need of revision."[32] In 1969, he said the Golden Series "threatens to be very extensive" and the publisher was already preparing a new edition of the bird guide. "Incidentally, this item in its earlier edition sold well over three million copies."[33] That level of sales allowed frequent revisions, which made his own unrevised book even less attractive.

Wild America Meets On the Road

Peterson and Fisher's tour inspired Kenn Kaufman, but his memoir *Kingbird Highway* told of a new kind of search in wild America. Peterson and Fisher described a three-month expedition by a pair of accomplished, middle-aged naturalists, touring in a station wagon on a schedule arranged through an extensive network of friends and acquaintances, many of them eminent ornithologists and birders, with the North American year-list record (at least in the telling) an afterthought. In *Kingbird Highway* a teenager hitchhiked, took side trips for rarities discovered through community gossip passed on by telephone, had an enthusiastic audience following his progress, and the list was the thing. Looking back, twenty years later, he saw his teenage adventures not as a naturalist's journey but as part of

> an active game, even a competitive sport. [In the] early 1970s we were not birdwatching. We were *birding*, and that made all the difference. We were out to seek, to discover, to chase, to learn, to find as many different kinds of birds as possible—and, in friendly competition to try to find more of them than the next birder. We became a *community*

of birders. . . . [As] improvements in communication and in travel made it possible for people to seek birds from coast to coast . . . birding changed from a mild local pastime to a continent-wide craze. . . . Birding for the 1990s—indeed birding for the twenty-first century—was born in the brief period from 1970 to 1975.[34]

That turned the story inside out. It made the road central and put nature and conservation to one side. The postwar naturalists had wanted to see "everything that walked, hopped, swam, or flew, and the plants and rocks too," and they had looked at the land in the context of American history.[35] Their chapter titles recalled regions and events; searching for the Ivory-billed Woodpecker, Peterson and Fisher harked back to John James Audubon; and at the Dry Tortugas they looked at the old fort as well as the birds. Kaufman looked for birds alone and no further back in time than *Wild America*, which he took as a starting point and not a touchstone. Where Peterson lamented the loss of the wild, Kaufman mentioned conservation only in wondering how many birders would see the Cape Sable Sparrow before developers filled in the marsh it lived in. In a coda to that chapter, he described the fate of the Dusky Seaside Sparrow, forgotten as a subspecies, gone by the time taxonomists began to wonder if it might be a true species.[36] He put at the head of each chapter an outline map of the United States marked with the route traveled in the pages that followed. The *Wild America* tour told of the early years of the postwar boom, when long-distance travel was an adventure, war and the Depression recent memories, and the wild almost at hand. Kaufman hitchhiked on the interstates when conservation had moved out of being a cause that good citizens lobbied for, discreetly, to become the environmental movement.

Even as birders rallied to save the wild and the environment, devotees of recreational birding became a closer, more self-contained community. Griscom had spent a decade alone before finding "blessed companionship" and had competed within a small circle, but Kaufman knew about lists and competition from his childhood reading of *Wild America* and followed national birding events through newsletters from the American Birding Association—which set him dreaming. "I had thought that seeing 600 species in North America must be the result of a lifetime's effort by the most dedicated bird experts. . . . But by 1970 there were many birders with lists well over 600; one guy, Joe Taylor from New York State, was pushing seriously toward 700."[37] Guides allowed birders to master the details of identification in a few years rather than a lifetime, and the community told them where to find the birds across the country. It was possible for teenagers to dream. When Kaufman dropped out of school at sixteen to pursue his, he found a national network of birders ready to help, and the social barriers of Griscom's generation long gone.[38] At the American Birding Association Convention in 1973, Kaufman asked if he could "just sort of stick around and watch," since he could not afford registration or field trips, and while the local volunteer wondered what to do, not having "anticipated that bearded teenagers with backpacks would come to lurk around the edge of the otherwise orderly group," three of the association's officers spotted him, asked how the Big Year was coming, and swept him off to the members' meeting.[39]

The year had the frantic pace befitting a "natural obsession that got a little out of hand." Inspired by tales of six hundred birds in a year, he thought "more and more ... about what each new species would do for my list totals." He set out, but on learning that that Ted Parker had set a new record of 626 species, he quit. Six hundred seemed barely possible, but "626 loomed as an impossible figure to beat, especially by hitchhiking. So I quit." The next year he set off again. Marathon travel for birds, startling in Peterson and Fisher's day, was common enough to have a sardonic tag within the clan: "IDIOT, Incredible Distances in Ornithological Travel." In January, having picked up the common Arizona species, he hitchhiked from Tucson to Florida to find a Caribbean stray, the Loggerhead Kingbird, then north to Pennsylvania, on to New England, and south to the Outer Banks in North Carolina. From there he went south to spot Mexican Crows on the Brownsville, Texas, dump, back to Pennsylvania for a group outing after Boreal Owls, out to the Pacific Northwest, and back across the continent to the Dry Tortugas, off Key West. In April he caught the height of the spring migration on the Texas coast, joining a team for a day that began in Houston at 3 a.m., ended in Brownsville at midnight, and netted 229 species, of which he saw 214. Enthusiasm occasionally led him astray. Hearing of a European wanderer, the Spotted Redshank, at Brigantine National Wildlife Refuge, he hitchhiked from Tucson to New Jersey, only to find the identification had been mistaken. At the end of the year he had notched up 666 species. Floyd Murdoch had 669.[40]

The change in listing and records measured the growth of the birding community. Guy Emerson, reporting his tally in 1939, saw it as something new and played down the element of competition. Fifteen years later, Peterson and Fisher celebrated by sending Emerson a telegram, but only gave the new record publicity in *Wild America*. When Keith retraced the *Wild America* route in 1956, he earned an article in

Audubon, but in 1963, when he asked for life-list totals for an article on listing, he got fewer than two dozen (Ira Gabrielson, retired head of the Fish and Wildlife Service, stood first with 669, then Peterson with 638).[41] By the 1970s, the North American record had became the center of intense competition, followed by birders across the country. Kaufman knew who his competitors were and fielded questions all year about his progress. Like his predecessors, he relied on friends to arrange some of his outings, but he checked off pelagic birds on deepwater tours arranged for birders and picked up strays from Asia on Aleutian islands reached by flights arranged for birders. In ports on both coasts and at national wildlife refuges, birders could charter boats or planes, most run as occasional or seasonal businesses, but some full-time bird tour operations.[42]

Away from home, birders needed local information, and the growing market transformed finding guides. Pettingill's hardback books were useful but not current, and in the mid-1960s one enthusiast, Jim Lane, moved from birder to writer and publisher, turning his own and others' expertise into inexpensive, detailed, and frequently revised guides to small areas, books birders came to know simply as "Lane guides." The first, *A Birder's Guide to Southeastern Arizona*, appeared in 1965.[43] A typical example, the 1986 edition of *Birder's Guide to the Rio Grande Valley of Texas*, lacked even the pretense of production values. It had a cover of flimsy stock and cheaply printed pages held together by two staples that went through the spine, but the pages had a wealth of detailed information. In the Falcon State Recreation Area, for example, the "Hooded Oriole can usually be found in summer around the office. One year it nested in the light standard right next to the bulb." A good birding spot in Del Rio can be found by taking Spur 277 toward the international bridge and at a "sharp left turn marked by a 25-miles-an-hour sign turn right on a dirt road. Drive slowly and stop frequently to squeak or imitate a screech-owl."[44] Tables in the back showed the chances of finding any given species for each month, with bars ranging from a thick "Hard to Miss" to a line of dots signifying "How Lucky Can You Get." A separate page listed even less frequent visitors: "Seldom Seen but Possible."[45] The books changed, if not quite with the seasons, at least far more frequently than traditional publications. The 1986 Rio Grande guide was the fifth edition of a booklet that had first appeared in 1971.

Lists, the community that kept them, the guides, and the finding guides all changed, but some things remained the same. A young woman in a Mustang who picked Kaufman up near Brownsville found it hard to believe he was a birder. "Aren't birdwatchers all little old ladies with blue hair? Or old guys with skinny legs and funny-looking shorts and safari hats?" Did he have a girlfriend? No, and "not likely to either. Young women and birding just don't mix." Many women birded, but Kaufman lamented an "apparent lack of young female birders: unsolved mystery, the bane of all the young male birders."[46] That dated at least to the days of Linnaean Society of New York and the Bronx County Bird Club, and the Big Day had a certain macho air. Recall Teale's belief that Griscom's all-day expeditions would lead people "to elevate this robust, he-man activity to a place beside mountain climbing and the cross-country marathon."[47] When Teale made that comment the most prominent woman birder was Connie Hagar, who made her reputation by patiently combing the area around Rockport for species others over-looked, not with long lists compiled on marathon drives.

Birding had gone from strolls in the park or "a-birding on a bronco" to flights to isolated Aleutian islands, but Merriam, Wright, and Chapman would have recognized the standards for checking off spe-cies. What counted was still what the scientists counted as a species, found within the AOU's territory, and taxonomists' decisions changed the rules. When they divided a population once considered one species into two—"split," in the jargon—or decided that what seemed two were really one ("lumped"), the lists changed. "Once a bird was lumped," Kaufman said, "as far as the listers were concerned, it might as well not exist." The AOU's boundaries held. When Mexican Crows moved from the Matamoros dump to the trash heap maintained by Brownsville, Texas, they entered "the A.O.U. Check-list Area and [were] suddenly fair game for all the listers." Ross's Gull appeared in the North American books because it could regularly be seen in the fall in Pt. Barrow, Alaska. Birders could search Baja California, Bermuda, and Greenland because their bird life so closely resembled that of the United States that AOU scientists regarded the areas, biologically, as American territory.

The deeper appeals remained as well. The first guide authors spoke of the birds' world and the beauty and joy to be found in it, and while the rhetoric changed, the fascination remained. Like Peterson, Kaufman found in birds something that transcended his ordinary world. He wrote approvingly of a California birding guru who worked on his list but felt it was unimportant, who believed birds were "magical, and . . . searching after them was a Great Adventure . . . [with the list] just a friv-olous incentive for birding."[48] Florence Merriam or Neltje Blanchan, Ludlow Griscom or Joseph Hickey might have said the same, and so would millions of birders. Records, lists, and the fine points of field identification organized a great adventure whose appeal birders felt, though they could not define it.

Sales of *Birds of North America* demonstrated birding's rising popularity, and Kaufman's account the obsessive lure of the list, but the storm that followed *Silent Spring* changed birding by turning conservation from an aesthetic interest into an urgent moral concern involving humans as well as wildlife. In the short run, the environmental gospel disrupted established conservation groups, not least because it came entangled with the counterculture. The Sierra Club went through a very public battle, as David Brower changed it from a regional conservation organization interested in hiking into a national environmental group. The strains eventually brought the board to fire him. The National Wildlife Federation, originally a sportsmen's group, became a coalition that included both humane activists and trophy hunters. Audubon went through a less intense struggle—perhaps due to a lingering genteel tradition—but it, too, split over programs and priorities. To hardcore environmentalists, listing seemed a distraction from the necessary and all-absorbing crusade to save the planet. Recreational birders formed the American Birding Association and began the journal *Birding* at least in part because they felt *Audubon* neglected their interests to concentrate on environmental conservation.

The next chapter takes up birders' continuing engagement with conservation and recreation as environmentalism became a part of the mainstream culture and bird protection came to depend even more on science. Field guides incorporated ecological and environmental perspectives and developing electronic media. Recreation became more competitive, with world life-lists the new standard, and more cooperative, as ornithologists enlisted more birders into continuing programs surveying bird populations across the country and even the hemisphere. Recreation and conservation found, as they had in each generation since Florence Merriam went out with the Smith College bird club, a new relationship, one that aimed to preserve nature as part of American life and Americans' lives by encouraging the simple activity of identifying birds.

SEVEN

Environmental Birding

It's the wild and the urban
coming together in unexpected ways and places
that makes modern birding what it is.

—JONATHAN ROSEN,
THE LIFE OF THE SKIES (2008)

This layout emphasizes the many ways modern birders seek to identify a species, with the small pictures showing pattern, color, form, behavior, and range.

These small pictures, with bits of text attached, pack together various kinds of information rather than emphasizing the "uniform."

The running head on the page gave the family, the heading for the species the familiar English and Latin names, and the inclusion of length and weight (hardly useful for identification) harks back to natural history.

The text moves from the species' abundance to where to look for it to nesting and behavior, with the illustrations adding shape, pattern, and behavior that could be seen, such as hovering.

American Kestrel
Falco sparverius
L 9" ws 22" wt 4.1 oz (117 g)

Uncommon in many open habitats from desert grasslands to meadows to brushy fields; often seen on roadside wires or fenceposts, pumping its tail. Nests in tree cavities, birdhouses, or crevices in buildings. Solitary. Hunts within small range, mainly for insects and small mammals from perch or by hovering and dropping straight down. Our smallest falcon. Small size, habits, and rufous color distinctive. **Voice:** Shrill screaming *killy killy killy.* . . .

Prairie Falcon
Falco mexicanus
L 16" ws 40" wt 1.6 lb (720 g)

Uncommon in open deserts, grasslands, and agricultural land. Nests on cliff ledges. Solitary. Hunts from perch, from low contouring flight, or from high in the air. Feeds mainly on small mammals such as ground squirrels, but also takes many birds and some insects. Slightly longer-tailed and rounder-winged than Peregrine Falcon. Best distinguished by sandy-brown color with contrasting dark flanks and underwing coverts. **Voice:** Similar to Peregrine, but higher.

T his latest phase in birding's story comes in three related parts: the boom in recreational birding, field guides' assimilation of ecology and environmentalism, and conservation in the environmental age.[1] The books, and the media supplementing or replacing them, show the first two. In the last thirty years, the number of new guides and their variety have come to rival the early, experimental years, as publishers compete for the niches of a large, segmented market. The new standard, David Sibley's *Sibley Guide to Birds*, published in a large-format edition in 2000, and three years later in two field-guide-sized volumes (east and west), dominates the general field guides, a fiercely competitive market segment. The American Bird Conservancy's *All the Bird of North America*, plastic-covered and hip-pocket-sized, with "a revolutionary system based on feeding behaviors and field-recognizable features, color-coded with icons for instant identification," exemplifies *Sibley's* competitors, each with its own special features. Birders have also had a variety of specialized guides, books like *Hawks in Flight,* by Pete Dunne, David Sibley, and Clay Sutton, and *A Guide to the Identification and Natural History of the Sparrows of the United States and Canada,* by James D. Rising—less field guides than shelf books intended for close study of the fine points of identification of a particular family.[2] *Local Birds of Central Texas*, billing itself as a "'Quick-Guide' to commonly seen local birds," represents the market in novice guides, a five-and-a-half- by six-and-a-half-inch plastic-covered sheet unfolding to six

7.1 · *Sibley's hawks* · The focus here lies not in separating similar species but the more advanced skill of identifying every form of each one—by plumage, flight, form, and behavior. From *The Sibley Guide to Birds of Eastern North America* by David Allen Sibley, copyright 2003 by Chanticleer Press, Inc. Used by permission of Alfred A. Knopf, a division of Random House, Inc.

panels, printed on both sides, with thumbnail pictures and field marks. Finding guides directed birders to hot spots in states, cities, and particular national parks, though wider horizons could be found in Peter Alden's *Finding Birds around the World*.[3] The American Birding Association's catalogs and websites, along with various leaflets and flyers, present an astounding range of goods and services, from products for the backyard feeding station to trips for the adventurous, such as a two-week birding tour in Turkey (cost exclusive of airfare $3,895) that promises to reveal "the avian riches of Asia Minor." The magazine *Birds and Blooms* (shades of Mabel Osgood Wright and Neltje Blanchan) and books like *The Big Year*, by Mark Obmascik, or Dan Koeppel's *To See Every Bird on Earth* appeal to other parts of the market.[4] The books about record runs and obsessive listing suggest a general public interest in the hobby, only partly explained by the ordinary human fascination with other people's obsessions.[5]

In the last twenty years, field guides and other birding essentials began migrating to the Internet and handheld electronics, and field and finding guides now come in downloadable form. Books like Donald Kroodsma's *Singing Life of Birds* include CDs of birdsongs illustrating the differences within a single species.[6] Websites took over rare bird and migration alerts, once carried on informal telephone trees, and now carry material once confined to print. At the Cornell Laboratory of Ornithology's page, viewers may gather information about birds and sign up for the lab's citizen science projects; at the Fish and Wildlife Service's page, one may pore over reports from the continental breeding bird survey showing changes in populations and ranges.[7] Even in print, the field guide has taken new forms. Ordinarily concerned with organisms, it has been adapted to help people catalog ecosystems (not quite the same as checking off warblers but not impossibly different) or learn about humans' environmental impact (an approach harking back to the wide-ranging curiosity that grounded that bible of Progressive nature study, Anna Comstock's *Handbook of Nature-Study*). Finally, conservation changed. Scientists who needed more and more detailed information than even an army of graduate students could gather mobilized birders, from experts to those who just looked out the kitchen window, to do the job.

Books, CDs, websites, and catalogs reveal much about the consumer side of birding in the environmental age, but less of the dominant theme of the last generation: recreation's engagement with environmental conservation. When it became apparent, somewhere in the 1970s, that industrial civilization was not going to collapse or the revolution sweep away everything, conservationists took up the old task of saving birds under the conditions of the environmental age: programs had to cover the nation or the hemisphere. Ornithologists recruited the enthusiastic army of amateurs to help them, and as computers and the Internet cut costs, used modern statistical methods to show bird populations and changes in them over time, in the process forging a new balance and relationship between conservation and recreation.

Guides for Every Birder

By the late 1970s, Peterson was a national figure—honored by President Jimmy Carter with the Medal of Freedom, his books part of the culture, and a new edition of his field guide a public event. Now, though, he faced stiff competition. In the spring of 1979, an article in the *New York Times Sunday Magazine* described a "Battle of the Bird Books" among Peterson, the Golden guide, and the Audubon Society guide.[8] Peterson was in no need of this article to alert him to the threat. In 1972 he told Guy Montfort, his collaborator on the European guide, that revision was "long overdue." An edition would not last more than ten years, and this one had been unchanged for twenty-five. He planned radical revisions, including more color and range maps "to compensate for some of the advantages of [Robbins's guide]."[9] His pride as well as his position was involved; he later said that he did "not want to go to my grave with the old one as my creative legacy."[10] The new version had 136 plates, all new or redrawn, and 390 range maps. Houghton Mifflin, as it had with the 1947 edition, invested substantial time and money in the production. It tried twelve engraving companies before settling on one, and Peterson oversaw all the details. Three times he and his wife worked with pressmen until 3 a.m., checking each proof of range maps and plates with a magnifier. He overhauled even minor elements. The section "How to Use This Book" got a new title, "How to Identify Birds," broke birds down into nine groups based on form, and then discussed size, shape, wing shape, and other clues. The almost apologetic comments in earlier editions about watching birds as just a game vanished, and what had been "My Life List" became a "Systematic Checklist." Three new paragraphs described coverage and scientific naming and pointed readers to the American Birding Association for a complete continental bird list.

Time and *People*, rarely concerned with nature or conservation, noted its appearance, and both hardcover and paperback made the *New York Times* best-seller list. Peterson was pleased. A year later, he wrote to

Montfort that it had "already sold upwards of one-half million copies. Whereas its main competitor, the Golden Field guide, was outselling my old one three to one, the reverse is now true."[11] The public snapped it up, but hard-core birders were less enthusiastic. The American Birding Association's journal, *Birding*, printed five reviews and Peterson's response under the heading "Bird Book Wars: The Emperor Strikes Back."[12] The critics felt it was all right for beginners, but found the art deficient in "such crucial features as bill-shapes and plumages of shorebirds and gulls," as well as color reproduction ("satisfactory if a bit faded in some cases"). They particularly disliked the handling of complex problems in identification, a reaction Kenn Kaufman later described as kicking the book "around because it did not include all the groovy new field marks we thought we had discovered."[13] Peterson responded not as birder but as author. "Most people are naïve about the realities of publishing." The range maps went in the back so they could be larger and because it made revision easier. He had so many plates, a good thing, because "the field guide has built up its own market to the point" that the publisher could afford them. Still, the firm was in business to make money, and "space is the final dictator." *Birding*, he pointed out, had devoted thirteen pages in its December issue to Thayer's Gull. No general guide could afford that level of detail.

New field guides continued to appear, not simply general guides but specialized ones and guides to other parts of nature. The modern bookstore browser found a wide array on birds and everything else, testimony to public enthusiasm for this form of informal education. Stores usually carried Peterson's fifth edition, completed after his death in 1996, and the new *Peterson Field Guide to Birds of North America*, published in 2008, along with the latest revision of the National Geographic guide to birds, David Sibley's book in both one- and two-volume editions, and some of the others, a list now running to close to a dozen.[14] Beside the general guides stood specialized publications devoted to hawks, gulls, warblers, or sparrows or telling how to identify birds at great distances. At the other end of the spectrum of expertise, several basic guides to common birds competed for the customer's dollars. Further along the shelf stood the troops of the expanding field guide empire: the four dozen volumes of Roger Tory Peterson's series, the Audubon series, slightly taller and narrower volumes with limp plastic covers, Golden Press's paperbacks, the Stokes Guides ("More than 3 million readers rely on Stokes Guides"), Kenn Kaufman's Focus Guides ("The best guides for getting started"), and perhaps a combination volume like the *Reader's Digest's North American Wildlife*, which promised "birds and butterflies, ferns and frogs, mushroom and manta rays, sea-shells and salamanders," helping readers identify more than two thousand species in all.[15]

The general field guide to the birds remained at the center. Peterson still held his target audience, beginners, but many other birders wanted a more advanced treatment. In 1983, Golden Press put out a second edition of the Robbins-Singer guide, and the National Geographic Society published its *Field Guide to the Birds of North America*, with an initial printing of 250,000 copies. Knopf upped the ante with the three-volume *Audubon Society Master Guide to Birding*, at $41.85. Though the preface cheerfully spoke of "three volumes, each of which may be conveniently carried into the field," carrying one meant looking at only, say, "Old World Warblers to Sparrows," and taking three meant a load.[16] Besides field marks, the *Master Guide* dealt with flight, flight silhouette, behavior, and shape. The "Sharp-shinned Hawks," it said, are "the most buoyant fliers [with] Cooper's Hawk intermediate in this respect; Goshawks . . . flap most slowly and appear heaviest in flight," characteristics useful only for experienced birders.[17] *Birding*'s reviewer recommended the National Geographic guide for the field, except for beginners, who should use Peterson, "but no birding enthusiast is going to want to be without the *MGB* on his/her shelf, and I predict that s/he will spend a lot of time transferring information from it to the guides which are carried into the field."[18]

All included far more detail than Peterson. The National Geographic guide gave comprehensive coverage to immature birds and illustrations for more than eight hundred species, including some escaped cage birds that might not have established breeding populations. Four Asian buntings that occasionally appeared in western Alaska in the summer had their own plate, even though, as the reviewer for *Birding* noted, he knew no one who had seen all of them in North America.[19] There were seven parrot species, not only escaped cage birds but the Thick-billed Parrot, possibly a "fall or winter vagrant to southeastern Arizona [even though there had been] no reliable sightings since the 1930s." It treated "four races of the Seaside Sparrow . . . five races of the Song Sparrow . . . and six races of the Fox Sparrow . . . thus doing," the reviewer said, "a good job of illustrating the variations one can find in some species."[20] It had plumages of all the immature gulls, some of which took four years to reach adulthood, and the information that "Western Gulls hybridize extensively with Glaucous-winged Gulls in the northwest; hybrids are seen all along the west coast in winter."[21] Western birders found it particularly useful for sorting out the confusing set of local races that could be distinguished in the field.

Environmental Birding

Ring-billed Gull

breeding adult

2nd winter

winter adult

breeding adult

1st winter tail

juvenile

1st winter

1st winter tail

winter adult

2nd winter

breeding adults

juvenile

Mew Gull
brachyrhynchus

1st winter

kamtschatschensis

winter adult

1st winter

winter adult

canus

adult
kamtschatschensis

1st winter

adult
canus

· The layout had the classic Peterson arrangement: on the right, pictures showing gulls, though now with such things as the pilings under their feet; text and range maps were on the facing page.

· The illustrations included diagnostic parts, for gulls, as wings and tails, a return to the partial views common in works like Coues and Ridgway's *Manuals*, but these were color paintings, not line drawings.

· Again on the Peterson model, the page had no heading and even the facing one the running head of taxonomic families, here "Gulls, Tern, Skimmers."

· Annotations on the illustrations cover seasonal plumages but also races that could be picked out in the field, identified by their Latin adjectives.

Both guides and the business of making them changed. Peterson's 1947 edition set a standard for production, but publishers had at any rate generally looked for quality in a book that would be used constantly and sold for many years. In the new guides, a reviewer complained, "some care and excellence . . . was forsaken for speed in a race for competitive publication dates."[22] Guides had usually been the work of a single author or an author and illustrator, but the National Geographic listed eight "writers" and thirteen artists, while the *Audubon Master Guide* had sixty-one authors, "nine well-known artists," and an unspecified number of photographers contributing the "tens of thousands of transparencies" that the editorial committee reviewed.[23] Peterson pointed out to Chandler Robbins that the National Geographic Society artists had worked for a total of thirty-nine person-years, gloomily adding that it was "becoming harder and harder for the individual to buck the corporate world."[24]

General guides continued to appear at frequent intervals. In 1994 the Audubon Society brought out a revised edition of its regular guide, in 1996 Donald and Lillian Stokes their two-volume guide (east and west), and in 1997 the American Bird Conservancy its one-volume national guide, sized for the back pocket of a pair of jeans. In 2000, Kenn Kaufman's first Focus Guide and David Sibley's large-format guide appeared. The next year saw a revised Golden Guide; two years later Sibley's smaller format two-volume set appeared; and the National Geographic kept pace with new editions in 1987, 1999, 2002, and 2006. Guides bearing the names of the National Wildlife Federation and the Smithsonian Institution entered the competition in 2008.[25] All followed Robbins in putting all the information for a species on a two-page spread, used maps to show ranges, emphasized shapes, and—recognizing that birders would not memorize the order of families—often had tabbed or marked pages to make it easier to find the right section. They took a higher level of expertise for granted. Guides had previously used males in spring to illustrate (they were easiest to identify) and ignored or downplayed juvenals, races, and color variations. All these now received full coverage and females equal treatment—Sibley, for instance, put them first in the warblers' section

7.2 · *National Geographic gulls* · Gulls, whose plumage commonly changed for more than one year before reaching the adult pattern, came in for detailed treatment, as more and more birders looked for challenges. From the National Geographic's *Field Guide to the Birds of North America*. Reprinted by arrangement with the National Geographic Society from *Field Guide to Birds of North America*, 5th edition. Copyright © 2006 National Geographic Society.

Environmental Birding

and showed nonbreeding plumages before breeding dress among shorebirds. Anyone, the new guides seemed to say, could tell the easy forms; they would help with the harder ones.

Guides touted special features. The Stokes guide had "Learning Pages" for novices, showing such groups as "Most Common Shorebirds on Mudflats and Beaches" or "Common Eastern Gulls" (an aid that harked back to Hausman's 1946 *Field Book of Eastern Birds*), while the Audubon guide arranged perching birds by color, put a colored silhouette at the edge of the pages, and had plasticized, waterproof covers and a format that fit a hip pocket. The American Bird Conservancy guide has the same shape, waterproof covers, and its promise of a "revolutionary system based on feeding behaviors and field-recognizable features." Kaufman used technology to overcome the greatest disadvantage of photographs: any one photograph showed only one state of a bird's plumage in one light, while birders saw all stages, lit by anything from bright sunlight to fading twilight. Paintings usually presented an average specimen under average conditions, and digital manipulation now allowed photographs to duplicate that effect. It quickly became common practice.

The new guides also put the birds back into the world. Habitat had never been completely absent, though Peterson kept it out of the illustrations and used it only in the text to locate or identify the species. The newer guides made it part of the text and illustrations. The Golden Guide showed birds on perches in typical habitat. The Red-headed Woodpecker, Lewis's Woodpecker, and the Yellow-bellied Sapsucker perched on a paper birch with a broken-off stub and several series of holes drilled by sapsuckers. *All the Birds of North America* went the furthest. It used ecology to organize the birds, dividing perching birds by bill type—flycatching bills, curved, straight, and conical—to emphasize distinctive features related to food, feeding behavior, and ecological niche, and treating others by similar criteria. It emphasized environmental change by giving a special place to recent extinctions and endangered species. The Whooping Crane stood on a dried out lake bed, with the caption "Drained wetlands—lost habitat," and other pages covered the Great Auk, Passenger Pigeon, Ivory-billed Woodpecker, Labrador Duck, Carolina Parakeet, Heath Hen, and Bachman's Warbler (though hope still existed for the warbler). Each of these had a picture and a range map, and they were distinguished only by appearing as a group in the front rather than in their taxonomic places. Descriptions included changes in abundance and reasons for them, and those at risk had "their names highlighted at the head of their species accounts. [Those] in red are in the greatest danger . . . in yellow are either at risk of requiring human intervention . . . or they are already disappearing from a significant potion of their range."[26] The backgrounds to the illustrations took in not only nature but culture; in the background of the scene showing Common and Red-breasted Mergansers on a lake, there was a bridge and on the shore a group of birders with binoculars and spotting scopes.

While general guides more clearly placed birds in the world, more specialized books pulled birders into the world of field identification. A review of Clark and Wheeler's *Field Guide to the Hawks of North America* pointed out that the "Peterson and Robbins field guides were okay as far as they went (which wasn't very far). In 1983 the 'advanced' Master and Geographic guides took field identification a step further, but even these were too often incomplete and oversimplified." Now birders had a new generation of "specialized field guides": "e.g., Grant's guide to gulls, the shorebird guide by Prater, et[.] al., and now Bill Clark's guide to the 39 species of diurnal raptors that have been recorded north of Mexico," covering "every race and color morph, [with] field marks that even experts will find revealing."[27] The next year *Hawks in Flight*, by Pete Dunne, David Sibley, and Clay Sutton, a "field guide without field marks," downplayed individual features of birds' plumage "in favor of more subjective considerations—call it *jizz* or gestalt or the holistic method . . . a step beyond the Peterson system of arrows pointing out unequivocal field marks," relying on "features such as behavior, shape, manner of flight, and size [that were] as diagnostic as the Red-tail's red tail."[28] Identification moved toward Chapman's dictum that you learned "to recognize bird friends as you do human ones—by experience," and the reviewer discussed this new book in just those terms, noting that people could put a name to their "spouse or best friend a block away," a distance too great to allow recognition of diagnostic features.[29] As "jizz," "gestalt," or what one enthusiast described as "'birding by impression,' because it relies on being able to recognize quickly the unchanging physical features of a bird along with important behavioral and geographic variables," the method moved from experts to ordinary birders.[30] A 2006 article in the Cornell Laboratory of Ornithology's bulletin for backyard birders sorted out the House Finch, the Purple Finch, and Cassin's Finch by body and bill type, treating first the females, then the males, describing tails as "relatively long" or short and Cassin's Finch as having "a slightly larger body with a large head that often appears peaked." Then it described variations in shading and regional differences.[31]

Better guides and finding guides, quicker communications and travel, and the growing popularity of birding made for more frantic and

Rather than the reader's eyes moving from left and right, here they would move up and down; otherwise this is the standard format.

With the habitat part of the illustration the illustrator had to create a multi-layered scene: the lake with its floating mergansers, the line of flying mergansers above which might be part of the scene but also could be a separate picture, and at the top more species, clearly separate. The painter relied on the familiar convention that blank space around an image meant it had no relation to its neighbors.

This uses a taxonomic "heading," placed at the lower right, written up and down, which allowed readers to flip through the book for the section they needed by name or outline.

This had two kinds of text, a general section on the family and identification (with an explanation for the Pied-billed Grebe's presence), and the individual species' descriptions and range maps.

Mergansers are rakish-looking ducks. Most sport swept-back crests, and all have long, slender bills. Only the hooded merganser has a dark bill (note the yellow-orange at the base of the female's lower mandible), and the male hooded certainly has the most arresting crest. The crest is scant in the male common merganser. The best mark for separating female common and red-breasted mergansers is the clean line beween the neck and breast in the common. Also, note the white collar on the male red-breasted. On the pied-billed grebe the bill changes color seasonally, but the chicken-like bill shape is constant. The pied-billed is more easily confused with the birds on Key 41 than with the grebes on Key 40.

◀Hooded Merganser *Lophodytes cucullatus* 18"
Fairly numerous on fresh water, esp. woodland streams, ponds; rarely on salt water. Often in small flocks in winter. Can jump into flight like dabbler. ● Bushy crest, steep forehead, thin bill with serrated edges. Male has white patch on crest. Female dull brown with rufous tinge to crest, yellow on bill. In flight, male shows some white in wing; female, less. In all mergansers, eclipse and imm. males resemble female. Imm. male molts to adult during 1st winter and spring.

Least Grebe

summer

downy young

summer

Pied-billed Grebe

winter

red-breasted

♀

♂

Red-breasted Merganser

♂

♀

♂ molting
imm.

◀**Common Merganser** *Mergus merganser* 25"
Numerous, widespread on fresh water, occasionally brack-ish inlets in winter; often in large flocks. ● Long red bill, thicker than in other mergansers; sloping, elongated head. Male mostly white with dark, greenish head. Female has chestnut-brown head, ragged crest, well-defined border to white throat patch and breast. In flight, male shows single black bar crossing white on upperwing; female has white speculum crossed by bar.

◀**Red-breasted Merganser** *Mergus serrator* 22"
Numerous along coasts in winter. Can be tame, attend fishing piers with cormorants. In summer, most migrate to fresh water. ● Forehead steeper than in common merganser; bill thinner at base, nostrils closer to base; eyes red in adults. Male has dark breast, shows two dark bars on upperwing in flight. Brown on female's head blends into white breast.

Pied-billed Grebe *Podilymbus podiceps* 14"
◀Numerous on fresh and brackish water; scarce on salt water in winter. Usually alone. Often submerges with only head remaining above water; other grebes seldom do this. ● Stubby, chicken-like bill; round head; dark eye with white eye-ring. Brown with black throat, black band on bill in sum-mer. In winter, pale throat, plain bill. Juv. has striped head.

Least Grebe *Tachybaptus dominicus* 10" Scarce, local resident in s. TX. Records to se. AZ and along TX coast. ● Thinner bill than in pied-billed, yellow eyes.

7.3 · *American Bird Conservancy, mergansers* · A guide built on ecological relations showed species in their habitat, included human works and even a gaggle of birders on the shore. From American Bird Conservancy, *All the Birds of North America* (New York: HarperCollins, 1997).

public Big Years. Looking back, Kaufman said that when he made his run a birder with little money could still compete, but soon emphasis shifted "away from knowledge and planning and experience, toward contacts and hotlines and money. . . . In 1979 a Mississippi businessman [who] admitted that he was a novice . . . hired experts to plan his trips and show him the birds, and he ended the year with a list of 699 species."[32] Publicity grew, too. Kaufman's run had been a matter of community gossip; in 1983 *Birding* covered from start to finish Benton Basham's attempt to eclipse the Mississippi businessman's record, which he did with a tally of 711 species. Since this was thirty-six more species than were known to breed in the area covered by the AOU, new records depended on finding even more strays.[33] Twenty years later, the subject leaped from the specialized birding press to trade books, as Free Press printed *The Big Year*, Mark Obmascik's chronicle of three men's pursuit of a new North American record in 1998. Though one, Greg Miller, had been inspired by Kaufman's *Kingbird Highway*, this was far from a teenage birder's shoestring venture. Sandy Komito was an industrial contractor from New Jersey, Al Levantine a retired industrial chemist living in Aspen, Colorado, and Greg Miller a divorced software engineer from Maryland. Miller spent $31,000, flew 87,000 miles, and drove another 36,000; Levantin ran through $60,000 and 135,000 miles on United Airlines, besides what he accumulated on other airlines; and Komito racked up 270,000 miles. They saw pelagic birds and Asiatic strays on scheduled tours booked months in advance with birding companies and relied on websites to alert them to rarities that let them wring every last checkmark out of the year. All of that, plus an exceptional El Niño and a Siberian storm that pushed flocks of rarities onto Attu Island during the birding season, brought the winner, Komito, a total of 745 species.[34]

By the time the public began buying books about Big Years in North America, the birding elite was looking beyond the United States to the world. Peter Alden's global analog of Pettingill's postwar books, *Finding Birds around the World*, foreshadowed a flood of specialized finding guides and high-end bird tours. The well-heeled, at least, could try, as the title of a recent book had it, *To See Every Bird on Earth*.[35] At that end of the spectrum, money and fanaticism ruled, and books about these pursuits had the attraction of accounts of any obsessive quest, but birders also bought them because they, too, dreamed of far-off countries. Just as the postwar generation had come to see the nation as a range they might explore, if not fully cover, the new generation looked to the globe. Field guides appeared for areas beyond North

America, Europe, and Central America—for Africa, Asia, even Antarctica—and finding guides followed. Princeton University Press, with a strong list in the biological sciences, served the growing interest in bird tourism, but as the ABA catalogs showed, it had competition. Bird tourism expanded from cottages near flyways and a sideline for fishing boats into full-fledged businesses, and from North American parks and wildlife refuges to forest lodges in Costa Rica and treks in the Himalayas, adventures at every level from roughing it to four-star hotels in the jungle.

While birders ranged or dreamed of ranging around the world, they also plunged more deeply into bird study. In 1964, Peterson saw growing sales of local ornithologies as "an interesting trend"; thirty years later, birders had local finding guides, state checklists, and books giving information about all the species in their state, including abundance, migration, habitat, and recent changes in population. Usually done by or with the cooperation of the state ornithological society, these were not hardbacks from university presses, aimed at ornithologists and amateur naturalists, but paperbacks destined for the local bookstore's sections on "Nature" or "Regional Publications."[36] A new genre developed of books on biology and life-history for the amateur. Paul R. Ehrlich's *Birder's Handbook* led the way in 1988. Touted on the cover as an "essential companion to your identification guide," it had almost eight hundred pages of thumbnail life-histories, interspersed with essays on territoriality, nest materials, egg colors, hybridization, bird invaders, and prominent ornithologists.[37] Kenn Kaufman followed in 1996 with his 650-page *Lives of American Birds*. He left out the biographies of the scientists. Five years later, Knopf published a companion to David Sibley's large-format field guide, *The Sibley Guide to Bird Life and Behavior*, written by Sibley and a team of some forty experts.[38] Three years after that, the Cornell Laboratory of Ornithology added the *Handbook of Bird Biology*, published in association with Princeton University Press. The second edition of the text for its home-study ornithology course (serving some ten thousand students since Olin Pettingill set it up in 1972), it ran to eight hundred large-format pages (eight and a half by eleven inches) and covered birds inside and out, from physiology to ecology. It even had a section on birdwatching.[39] In 2006, *Pete Dunne's Essential Field Guide Companion* added another 650 large pages to birders' shelves, and the *National Geographic Complete Birds of North America*, billed as a companion to the field guide, as many more. At just over four pounds, the *National Geographic* weighed just a bit more than the book Florence Merriam relied on, Robert Ridgway's *Manual of North American Birds*.[40]

Environmental Birding

At the other end of the spectrum, casual birders and novices chose among a variety of new basic guides, often cut-down versions of general guides. The Peterson series, for example, had a "First Guide," covering almost two hundred species, with roadside silhouettes and eight pages on how to identify birds, and the American Bird Conservancy offered *All the Backyard Birds*, with eastern and western sections printed back to back, eighty-four eastern species on one side, ninety western ones on the other.[41] Like the introductory guides of the 1890s, it had "Common Birds of Parks and Roadsides" and listed species in an intuitive rather than taxonomic order (the House Sparrow, *Passser domesticus*, appeared with the sparrows, though it belongs to a different family), but—following modern ideas—did include the bird-eating hawks. An even more basic form appeared: laminated sheets unfolding from five by six inches to fifteen by twelve inches. One example, *Local Birds of Central Texas*, had 136 species, "Local Backyard and Trail Birds" on one side, "Local Shore and Water Birds" on the other, arranged by size, with thumbnail pictures and descriptions. Nesting boxes and bird feeders, once products of handicrafts, school projects, or local industry, came to nature stores at the mall, and supermarkets stocked fifty-pound bags of birdseed in the pet aisle, with mixtures formulated for different species' needs. Lower costs and a larger market allowed publishers and local groups to sell inexpensive books for small areas, an impulse buy for birders or casual nature watchers on vacation. Shops and restaurants around the Great Smokies National Park stocked *Birds of the Smokies*, six by five inches, with photographs, descriptions of a hundred species, information about seasons and abundance, and the obligatory checklist. In 1997 Waterford Press had ten local guides for American parks, from Yosemite to Central Park, each covering up to 150 plants, animals, and natural phenomena; thirty-three regional guides, including three on golf course wildlife (Arizona, South Florida, and the southern coast from North Carolina to northern Florida); seventeen city guides; eight Canadian ones; and fourteen international guides.[42]

Magazines and websites grew to serve a community that needed more, and more immediate, information than the monthly issue of *Audubon* contained. The magazine still alerted readers to conservation crises, scientific developments, childhood education, national programs, and new books, but other publications served parts of the community. The Cornell Laboratory of Ornithology began *Living Bird* in 1962 as part of its expanding program of public education, and at the end of that decade the new American Birding Association had its own journal, *Birding*, and had taken on the issuing of Audubon's more technical publications. Casual birders had *Birdwatcher's Digest* and *Birders' World*; the Backyard Beautiful movement had *Birds and Blooms*, with come-ons on the cover: "Simple Suet: Woodpeckers can't resist these recipes" and on its website, among other offerings, a book of *1,029 Backyard Birding Secrets* (so much to learn).[43] Websites reported migrants and wanderers.

Birding's popularity brought more consumer goods, but the hobby did not fundamentally change. More naturalists and field guide authors made their livings by guiding birders or running tours, but birding did not develop a professional class—or has not yet done so—possibly because it does not readily fit well into the consumer economy. Birding did not lend itself to television and, unlike sports such as bass fishing, offered few niches for equipment manufacturers. Binocular companies got well-known birders to endorse their products and sponsored teams in competitive events, but birding remained very largely a noncommercial enterprise. New books and software made it easier to learn the birds, finding guides reduced the number of empty hours on the road, and companions to the field guide let people learn about bird biology and ecology at their own pace and without a formal course of study, but they did not give a decisive edge in competition. Their greatest effect was to move many birders more quickly to the sort of expertise Diamond found among the Ketengban in New Guinea, knowing the birds by a variety of clues, but the birders also knew them as part of a larger set and within an understanding of their populations and changes in abundance. Birding's appeal remained what it had been in Merriam's day: the rewards of knowledge and skill, and the occasional surprise or insight.

Books, money, gadgets, and tours changed the hobby at the competitive margins but not the core because most people pursued birds for fun and, in the end, valued knowledge more than lists. The novice Mississippi businessman had a lengthy list, but it was the birders' equivalent of the trophy den filled with heads of game shot on guided safaris—testimony to money and a basic level of skill, but not the skill and understanding of nature that the trophies were supposed to stand for. In any event, lists only gestured at the deeper interest that led people back to nature: the chance to encounter the world beyond society and glimpse the processes and rhythms of life in which Rachel Carson found symbolic as well as actual beauty. This was the lure that made birds, for many, magical.

Even as recreational birding became more intense and focused, conservation became more pressing, and it reshaped not only policies and politics but birding guides and the field guide genre. Environmentalism taught people to think of nature in terms of relationships and systems, but when they went outside what they saw were plants and animals, and they had a familiar tool for understanding them, the field guide. By the early 1970s, publishers had guides to ecosystems, including urban ones, and to environmental concerns ranging from grizzlies in the wilderness to rats in city buildings and nematodes in the lawn. The new books showed the power and flexibility of a form built around natural history, for the field encompassed all life, allowed lifetime self-education, and used observations but also led to deep insights. Making a field guide that illuminated processes and relationships required changes in format and coverage, for ecosystems did not fall into a taxonomic scheme and rarely had unambiguous marks and defined boundaries. Identification usually required finding several indicators, such as characteristic species, but they could be checked off, even if the practice lacked the comforting precision of listing warblers.

When the Peterson Series took up the environmental challenge with volume number thirty-seven, John Kricher's *Eastern Forests*, editor and author acknowledged the change.[44] Peterson described the book as "one of a new generation of field guides" that tried to "pull things together (or apart)," extending his system from organisms to forest types, identifying each by its "unique combination of plant and animal species." Kricher said that while "the concept admittedly requires some stretching, the Peterson system can be adapted to a functional, interpretive approach as well as a taxonomic approach."[45] The text showed the same stretching. One chapter dealt with "Forest Field Marks" and another the various communities, but the next described disturbance and pioneer plants, another covered adaptation, and three discussed the seasons. All went beyond identification to include a miscellany of information. "Adaptation" had sections on hibernation, migration, insectivorous plants, differences in tree bark, the thick zigzag strands in some spider webs, and natural selection. The plates, in the center rather than spaced through the text, kept illustrations on the right, notes about the species shown on the left, and taught identification, but they arranged their subjects not by taxonomy but by function, usefulness as indicators, life-history, or niche. Some showed "nonindicator species," which might be found in many communities, and even those dealing with a particular community took a broad view. A plate on the "Southern Hardwood Forest," for instance, showed Trumpet Creeper, Virginia Live Oak, Tufted Titmouse, Spanish Moss, Northern Mockingbird, Southern Magnolia, Laurel Oak, Sweetbay, Laurel Oak, Red-bellied Woodpecker, Common Persimmon, Virginia Opossum, and Pecan— with the birds and small parts of the plants in color and black-and-white sketches in the background showing tree shapes. Other plates covered birds that formed "Mixed Foraging Flocks," the "Herbs of Old Fields— Alien Annuals," the insects involved in "Milkweed Natural History," and the "Adaptations of Reptiles."

Kricher organized the book by natural history, which he saw not just as a field of science but a way of knowing, "an extraordinary subject, [that] fascinated Aristotle no less than it did Charles Darwin centuries later [and] still fascinates us today. Few subjects so clearly and simultaneously appeal to both the emotions and the intellect."[46] Leading field trips and nature seminars gave him the idea for the book, but its "inspiration comes directly from John Burroughs's philosophy," the belief that the gold of nature does not seem to be gold, that nature's facts seem insignificant "'until they are put through some mental or emotional process and their true value appears.'"[47] Burroughs, Emerson's last disciple and the premier bird-watcher of his generation, looked to nature for secular, but spiritual, insight; Kricher looked to it for a less spiritual but still hidden understanding. As much as Carson, Kricher appealed to a sense of wonder, the encounter with nature as the opening to awe and insight, and like Comstock, he cultivated an omnivorous curiosity. Olaus Murie had taken that approach in an earlier volume in the Peterson series, his *Animal Tracks*, but Kricher, using the framework of ecosystems, organized that interest and encouraged readers to look at anything and try to see its relation to the rest of the environment.[48]

Other guides responded to the growing concern about humans' impact on the environment by using the field guide form to examine the ways nature entered humans' lives. The Peterson First Guide to *Urban Wildlife*, a slim volume of 128 pages, touted on the cover as a "concise field guide to more than 250 animals and plants of our cities and towns," covered organisms from bacteria to vertebrates. It had sections on intestinal bacteria, scale insects on fruit trees, and cockroaches and rats in houses.[49] While acknowledging taxonomic categories and following the familiar Peterson format, it gave only casual field descriptions, omitted scientific names, and included odd bits of cultural knowledge— that prize koi in Japan, for instance, might sell for as much as $4,000.[50] John Brainerd's *Nature Observer's Handbook*, subtitled "Learning to

This has the Peterson guide layout—plate on right, text on left—adapted to the subject. No comparison of similar species here.

To deal with ecosystems, the illustrations combine paintings of animals and birds with tree leaves and flowers and, a bit ghostly in the background, line drawings of tree shapes. The different presentations rather than blank space indicated changes of subject or scale.

This guide put the plates in the center rather than scattering them through a text, possibly because of the subject, and used, on the facing legend page, a simple ecological title, here "Southern Hardwood Forest."

Text shows the common format of the Peterson series, from its species names on the plate to the arrangement of names and characteristics on the legend page.

PLATE 16

Southern Hardwood Forest
(p. 76)

A forest of mixed deciduous and evergreen species, characteristic of upland and coastal areas.

TRUMPET-CREEPER
See Pl. 57 for description.

VIRGINIA LIVE OAK
A beautiful spreading crown. Grows to 50 ft. Leaves evergreen, oval, shiny green, untoothed, hairy underneath.

SPANISH MOSS
A wispy air plant, suspended in long, gray-green strands from trees and telephone wires. Tiny, pale green flowers. Single strands may be up to 25 ft. long.

TUFTED TITMOUSE
A 6-in. gray bird with a crest. Wash of rufous on flank.

SOUTHERN MAGNOLIA
Up to 80 ft. tall. Evergreen, alternate leaves, very shiny green, oval, untoothed but with edges curled under. Large, white, fragrant blossoms.

NORTHERN MOCKINGBIRD
Slender gray bird (9–11 in.) with large white wing patches. Sings from wires and often sings at night. Mimics many other bird species.

LAUREL OAK
Up to 80 ft. tall. Shiny green, alternate, slender, oval leaves. Basically evergreen, though it sheds many leaves in early spring.

RED-BELLIED WOODPECKER
A ladder-backed woodpecker. Male has red on neck and top of head; female has red neck only. Shows small white wing patches in flight.

SWEETBAY
Up to 60 ft. tall. Deciduous in northern areas, evergreen in Deep South. Leaves alternate; light, shiny green above, very pale below; oval, untoothed. Flower like that of Southern Magnolia.

COMMON PERSIMMON
Up to 70 ft. tall. Deciduous. Leaves alternate, oval, untoothed, with a slight point at tip. Fruits orange-red in color.

PECAN
Up to 100 ft. tall. Alternate, compound leaves with 11–17 sharply pointed, oval, yellowish green leaflets. Nut has dark brown husk.

VIRGINIA OPOSSUM
Gray fur, pointed snout, naked tail. Cat-sized. Nocturnal. Good tree-climber, using prehensile tail. Plays dead when threatened.

TRUMPET-CREEPER

TUFTED TITMOUSE

VIRGINIA LIVE OAK

NORTHERN MOCKINGBIRD

SPANISH MOSS

SOUTHERN MAGNOLIA

LAUREL OAK

SWEETBAY

RED-BELLIED WOODPECKER
male

COMMON PERSIMMON

VIRGINIA OPOSSUM

PECAN

7.4 · *Eastern Forests* · The Peterson series pushed the application of his principles of identification beyond organisms to ecosystems, with indicator species standing in for field marks. From *A Field Guide to Eastern Forests, North America* by John Kricher and Gordon Morrison. Illustrations copyright © 1988 by Gordon Morrison. Reprinted by permission of Houghton Mifflin Harcourt Publishing Company. All rights reserved.

appreciate our Natural World," sacrificed the field guide's organization by forms of life for examples of humans' connections to the world to help readers "observe, record, and experience the intricate beauty of nature everywhere—from an untamed wilderness to an urban landscape," a Comstockian program for an urban population.[51] He discussed "Nature's Patterns," from the sky to the soil, and "People's Patterns," which took in farms, bicycle paths, bridges and causeways, towns and cities, assumed little knowledge, and rather than giving information, concentrated on getting people to think about the ways their lives were part of the world and how their goods came from nature.[52]

The new format and focus supported the familiar aim of getting people interested in nature as a prelude to working to preserve it. Ecological research, showing our dependence on nature and the ways the chemicals we put into the world came back into our bodies, made conservation a matter of human survival as well as aesthetics. With numbers and technology, humans have shaped the world and the course of life on earth. Natural history served this new understanding, for it saw humans within nature, even as they stood outside it putting plants and animals in filing cabinets. People turned to this new generation of field guides to understand their situation, and a form developed to identify birds showed them how they were part of the natural world and how that world came into their lives, homes, and bodies.

Conservation Recruits Recreation

As humans reshaped ecosystems on larger and larger scales, the nation, the hemisphere, and in some cases the world became the essential contexts of conservation. Programs on this level required information on a new scale, and scientists' need for a continuing stream of detailed, nationwide data led to a new stage in their relationships with birders. What had begun with the use of a few sight records for a local ornithology of the New York City region became a continuously updated national picture of bird populations. Even the largest and most enthusiastic army of graduate students could not gather what was needed, and ornithologists, almost all of them birders, enlisted their amateur fellows, everyone from experts to backyard birders. Over a generation, they built a network of connections between scientists and ordinary citizens unprecedented in scope and producing an equally new understanding of bird populations and how human civilization affected them.

Some birders became deeply involved in this work, most conspicuously Ted Parker, to whose memory Kaufman dedicated *Kingbird*

Highway. He began as a teenage lister, made his name with his Big Year in 1971, and went from American birds to the more complex avifauna of South America. By the time he died he was a legend among field ornithologists. Besides finding birds in the field, he could identify them from tapes, including background birds the ornithologist was not concerned with; at times he used his knowledge of ranges to say where tapes had been made. He helped make the Library of Natural Sounds at the Cornell Laboratory of Ornithology a major archive for recordings of calls, work that an obituary called an aspect of his "unwavering commitment to conservation of neotropical biodiversity."[53] His enthusiasm might have led him, as it had Hickey and Chandler Robbins, into a career in ornithology, but while he had a deep interest in science and contributed to it, he did not want to become an academic or, like Robbins, a government researcher. He worked, though, with scientists, and he died in a plane crash while helping an international conservation organization assess the biotic riches of areas under immediate threats from development.

Parker's feats with sound recordings pointed to advances in field identification as revolutionary as Peterson's first guide: technologies that allowed birders to compare sounds as easily as Peterson's plates allowed them to compare plumage patterns. Good birders had always used sounds, and in the forest depended on them, but printed guides had done a wretched job of conveying sounds. After World War II, birders bought records, but these, as well as being confined to the home, reproduced songs in a set order. As the size and cost fell and quality improved, recording became more common, and now electronics give birders searchable databases in very small packages. They can study sounds as they did feathers, moving quickly from one to another and noting characteristic differences.[54]

Equally important, advances in data collection and processing allowed scientists to organize information on a new scale. Chandler Robbins, enthusiastic birder and lister, then federal ornithologist and field guide author, organized the most ambitious effort, the Fish and Wildlife Service's Breeding Bird Survey. It used expert amateurs collecting data in a standard way. At regular intervals during the nesting season, volunteers followed mapped routes twenty-four and a half miles long, randomly located in common habitats, stopping every half mile for three minutes to record all birds heard and seen within a quarter mile. Repeated visits and many birders gave, if not a count of the birds, a measure of relative abundance tracking population changes. The Fish and Wildlife Service launched the program in 1966 in the eastern United

States and Canada, expanded it to the West the next year, in the 1980s added northern Canada and Alaska. After twenty years, it had 3,700 active routes, some 2,900 of them surveyed annually, providing data on some four hundred species. The agency's website, besides breakdowns of data for researchers, offered a continental version of Griscom's portrait of the New York City region, a map and not a book, covering forty-five years rather than a century, but in essence the national equivalent of a local ornithology.[55] It also, quite incidentally, showed the distribution of birders. Routes were densest in birding's historic heartland, New England and the middle Atlantic region.[56]

Private groups did not have the government's resources, but they also organized research. The Cornell Laboratory of Ornithology took a large role. Originally a graduate program in ornithology, after World War II it became a self-supporting research institution, associated with Cornell, devoted to research and conservation.[57] It began its own magazine, *Living Bird*, in 1962, and a decade later an ornithology home-study course. In the 1980s it used that base to enlist birders of all skill levels. Project Feeder Watch began in 1986, and by its twentieth anniversary counted a million checklists sent in by tens of thousands of watchers. Following an outbreak of conjunctivitis in birds in the winter of 1993–94 (reported by backyard watchers on the East Coast), it set up the House Finch Disease Survey, "the first [research project] to document how disease spreads in a natural population of wild birds."[58] The Internet let the Laboratory collect data and make the results available more quickly and widely than scientific papers, and by 2007, it had a suite of Citizen Science projects: Birdhouse Network, Urban Bird Studies, PigeonWatch, and the "Great Backyard Bird Count," a "four-day window survey of birds," with the results available "in real time over the Internet." "Birds in Forested Landscapes" and the "Golden-Winged Warbler Atlas Project" relied more on professional observations but asked citizens to help. Another project, "eBird," started in 2002 by the Laboratory and Audubon as a "continent-wide, year-round survey," used "State-of-the-art Web technology" to gather data that went to the Avian Knowledge Network, covering the Western Hemisphere, and then to the Global Biodiversity Information Facility. Just as reports from the Audubon Christmas Bird Count moved from backyards to the countryside as cars became common, information from backyard feeders followed technology. In the early years reports arrived in the mail, but by 2006, 77 percent came in online, and people signed up on the website instead of mailing a form to the lab.[59] Analysis followed a similar path. While doing his doctorate at the University of

Michigan in the early 1940s, Joseph Hickey had applied modern statistical methods to paper-and-pencil reports and put his conclusions into scientific journals that went out to ornithologists and academic libraries every few months. By 2008, birders' data existed in what one article on changing technology called "a flexible, adaptable, globally accessible data archive complete with documentation and verification as part of a permanent record."[60]

Collaboration on this scale, with analytical tools unimaginable twenty years before, produced a picture of continental bird life that was astonishing in scope and detail—but that Elliott Coues, Florence Merriam, and Frank Chapman would have found familiar. Underneath all the computer maps of shifting populations of Dickcissels on the Great Plains and Scarlet Tanagers in the eastern United States lay the view that began in natural history and passed into ornithology, the concern with the distribution of life on the land. Both sides in this collaboration changed after the 1920s, along with their relationship. Ornithology moved from observations to rigorous testing of hypotheses framed by ecological theories, birdwatching sharpened its field techniques, and bird conservation turned from defending a few species on humane or aesthetic grounds to defending all, first as part of wild America and then as elements of ecosystems. Like other scientists, ornithologists built professional research programs, but the nature of birds and field research, and birds' popularity, meant that the professionals could never fully exclude the amateurs, and did not want to. Some scientists maintained dual citizenship, and a few even took as their task encouraging cross-border traffic. From Frank Chapman to Chandler Robbins, scientists birded, wrote guides, aided birders, and gave them a place in research. On the other side, some birders, like Ted Parker, became deeply involved in field ornithology.

Birding looks like a Frank Gehry building on a foundation by H. H. Richardson—a fully modern recreation with a late Victorian base, its modern structure the result of several generations of enthusiasts and scientists working out the problems of field identification, its old foundations grounded in human needs and American culture. Birding grew from a common human fascination that was directed by the culture's accepted authority about the world—science—and was driven by a desire to keep and keep touch with a nature while living in a society that threatened it. The latest software of songbird calls had the same goal as *Birds through an Opera-Glass*, helping people put the right name on what they saw as a first step toward seeing and defending nature's wonders. Field guides anchored the hobby because they fit the ways people learned. The form survived as natural history gave way to ecology, illustrations changed from wood engravings and color reproductions of fine art to pictures on a computer screen, and the "wild," once at hand, first moved out past the suburbs, then became the topic of essays that mourned the death of nature. Guides served as catalog, teacher, and scorecard. To say that guides made the hobby, though, would be inaccurate. Books and birding developed together, each forming the other. The first generation introduced the activity, and as people gained experience and the community learned more about identification, they demanded new guides. Peterson met that need, and by making it easier to start, helped the community grow. That larger community, in turn, learned more, which improved the next generation's guides, which further encouraged the hobby and extensions of the field guide form to other forms of life and other topics in nature.

At the start of the twenty-first century, birding is extremely popular, and the genre it fostered, the field guide, fills every niche in amateur nature study. Even if guides become electronic ghosts of their paper selves, the form will remain. A fascination with nature almost necessarily leads to naming, and the urge to make a list, and then a longer one, has deep roots. There will remain as well the great territory beyond the guide, the unpredictable interests, enthusiasms, and insights that come from learning about the world that we are both a part of and apart from.

Conclusion: The Gyre

Gyre: by usual dictionary definition a circular or spiral turn, applied in falconry and birding to the rising and widening circles of a hunting raptor or vulture that reveal with each revolution more of the land.

We see the same birds the Victorians did, with some losses, but we understand them in very different ways, and we use very different guides. Florence Merriam's *Birds through an Opera-Glass* (1889) bears little resemblance to David Sibley's *Sibley Guide to Birds* (2000). The first has all the marks of a conventional trade book, down to the dark blue covers and gilt lettering, and its wood engravings only occasionally interrupt a text describing some common birds in general (and genteel) terms. The second has plasticized covers and water-resistant pages, covers all the birds, and minimal text that is tucked around maps and pictures showing species in all their plumages. Although they look very different, they have the same goal, helping people enjoy identifying birds, and Merriam's college friends, shooting birds in the park with opera glasses, were just as enthusiastic as their descendants in the wildlife refuge with eight-power binoculars and sixty-power spotting scopes—and just as committed to saving them.[1] Over the generations, these books shaped Americans' approach to nature in important, if not always measurable, ways. They standardized names and taught people to think in terms of species, made them conscious of birds and nature and so encouraged them to become advocates for protection. More subtly, they taught readers to see and encounter nature in particular ways, and in the last generation to be aware of their collective impact on it. Birds proved good to think with, and field guides started millions thinking.

The books taught people to look at characteristics of the organism, and in particular those that made for identification.[2] In "The Deer Swath," Aldo Leopold divided outdoor people into four categories: the deer hunter, always watching the next bend; the duck hunter, checking the skyline; the bird hunter, who watched the dog; and "the non-hunter," who "does not watch."[3] Birders watched. What marked them out from those who shot was that they watched not just in the field but in the park, around home, even at the dump. Birding developed a sensitivity to the flicker of a wing or a call note that became an almost unconscious but ever-present awareness of the surrounding world.

Guides directed people to birds both as a class and as part of the life of the land. Naturalists learned birds as physical organisms as they made carcasses into specimens, sprinkling arsenic powder on every surface and arranging wings, feathers, and feet, but they also learned birds as an ordered array by measuring wing length, counting tail feathers, and thumbing through ornithology texts to find out what they had. Birders did not need the full panoply of taxonomy, as is evident from the popularity of indexes in field guides, but they learned basic arrangements and made full use of the naturalists' detailed knowledge of plumage and plumage variations. Ludlow Griscom, for one, owed some part of his prowess to hundreds of hours spent in the museum comparing specimens. Birders' knowledge of birds on the land came from the approach that organized Comstock's *Handbook of Nature-Study*. Comstock's readers knew the Eastern Phoebe less as one species in the family of Tyrant Flycatchers (the collector's perspective) or a checkmark on a list (the birder's) than as the species that nested each year under the eaves of the shed or by the brook.

Birding borrowed natural history's categories to measure competition and accomplishment, but unlike naturalists, who worked within the framework of the culture's authoritative knowledge of the world and, at least implicitly, worked to add to it, birders sharpened their field skills for their own enjoyment. Only a few contributed to the community's craft knowledge. The hobby adapted nature study's program of personal life-time learning, putting it in the context of play, not work, a view that owed much to consumer society. Birding made nature a place to visit for a certain kind of activity (identifying species), experiences that could be collected, compared, and used for status within a community of enthusiasts—one reason birding began and remained an intensely social activity. Many birded alone or with a few friends, but from the days of Merriam's Smith College bird club to today's offshore birding trips, birders went in groups.

Birding lacked, necessarily, something of the perspectives of nature study and natural history, but it had the great advantage of opening a way to nature from within modern life, a way people could follow as far as they wished and in whatever direction they chose. They might watch the backyard feeder or try to see every bird on earth, make lists or become ornithologists without degrees. Whatever their path, their accumulated experiences over the years, seeing populations wax and wane, new birds arrive, some leave, and the ways weather and development affected migration, they gained a vivid if unsystematic understanding of the connections between species and the environment. From the campaign for a model songbird protection law to tracing the spread of disease through a population, individual study and local efforts served a larger cause. Birding's greatest contribution to American life was to give people an activity that involved them in nature and to give them a voice in preserving it.

Field guides played crucial roles. They initiated people into the community and instructed them in its ways and lore. In text and pictures they said what was important, told how to practice the craft, even what to call the birds. In the field they served, as much as binoculars, as a member's badge and an introduction ("I think for the immatures you will be finding around here my guide would help you more"). As guides replaced family and neighbors as the common means of learning about birds, local names gave way to "standard" ones. "High-hole" or "Yellow-hammer" became "Northern Flicker" or simply "Flicker," and an array of "hawk" names fell into disuse. The effect can be seen by looking at field guides from countries where natural history rather than identification remained the center of bird study. Graham Pizzey's 1980 guide to Australian birds, for instance, listed twenty-one "other names" for the Laughing Kookaburra, including "Alarmbird, Bushman's Clock, Jack, Jacky, and Ha Ha Pigeon."[4] Guides presented a standard, and not always intuitive, set of birds, the ones the scientists decided on. After the AOU "lumped" them, millions learned to see the "Oregon" and "Slate-colored" Juncos as the same species, the "Dark-eyed Junco," or apparently indistinguishable birds as two different species, based on call or geography, or others as members of a group in which individuals could be named when at home but not on migration. Only in rare cases—as when the Committee on Nomenclature, reviewing evidence of hybridization, reduced the "Baltimore Oriole" to a subspecies of the "Northern Oriole"—did anyone protest. Implicitly, and occasionally explicitly, the guides taught humane values. Birders watched and did not collect, and did not unnecessarily disturb birds, especially around their nests.

Birding began with the search for beauty, diversion, and self-education, a combination treasured in genteel nineteenth-century culture, and retained these values even as it probed our relation to nature and our species' place in the world. These motives lay in the background of Griscom's book on New York City's birds, appeared more clearly in

Peterson and Fisher's *Wild America* and Kenn Kaufman's *Kingbird Highway*, and in the last generation infused the culture. In the early 1980s, Terry Tempest Williams used birds and birding as a respite from caring for her cancer-stricken mother. In *Refuge: An Unnatural History of Time and Place*, she meditated on family history, feminism, environmental commitment, and their links in her life. In 2008 Jonathan Rosen examined his own quest in nature, his interest in literature, and the environmental crisis in *The Life of the Skies: Birding at the End of Nature*.[5] Birding, which began as a specialized hobby, became a way to frame personal tragedy, climate change, or existential questions.

Williams faced a usual tragedy—her mother's illness and death—under unusual circumstances. Her family had been exposed to the fallout drifting downwind from postwar atomic tests in Nevada, and she belonged to "a Clan of One-Breasted Women. My mother, my grandmothers, and six aunts have all had mastectomies. Seven are dead. The two who survive have just completed rounds of chemotherapy and radiation."[6] Birds and birding helped her escape but also deal with this horror, and birds organized her account of it. She used bird names as chapter titles and anchored family memories in birding. She wrote of her own visits to Bear River Migratory Bird Refuge, childhood trips with her grandmother, and conversations while birding with her mother. Checking off familiar birds, she renewed her ties to the land, while unfamiliar ones hinted of the larger world. Finding a dead swan on the shore of the Great Salt Lake, she straightened its body, washed its feet, and put stones on its eyes, rehearsing in nature a death rite from the culture. Linking the rising waters of the Great Salt Lake that were killing the refuge with her mother's growing tumor, she tied nature and culture together in a way that inverted John Burroughs's sunny view of a century before—that the "birds link themselves to your memory of seasons and places [and] set going a sequence of delightful reminiscences in your mind"—but kept the center of Burroughs's view: birds help us bind our lives to the life of the land.[7]

While Williams turned inward, Rosen used his newfound hobby to look at nature in the environmental age. He wrote of birds he saw or wanted to see (the Ivory-billed Woodpecker, naturally), places he birded, from Central Park to Israel, and writings about birds by, among others, Audubon, Darwin, Wallace, Thoreau, Walt Whitman, Robert Frost, Bill McKibben, Teddy Roosevelt, and Emily Dickinson. He spoke of loving to see "birds against the silver silhouette of the World Trade Center, incorrectly perceiving this as a poetic juxtaposition of the permanent towers and the evanescent birds."[8] All these excursions

Conclusion

served a larger purpose. Something in birding, he believed, "connects us to that word, 'soul,' which—however much it seems an embarrassment in contemporary culture—nevertheless is as hard to kill off as our animal heritage. I can't think of any activity that more fully captures what it means to be human in the modern world than watching birds." It was something "intimately connected to the journey we all make to find a place for ourselves in a post-Darwinian world."[9]

Those explorations pointed to birding's deepest appeal, its capacity to help us discover ourselves and our relation to the world on every level from the material to the transcendent. Birding showed nature's wonders, small to great, surprising to reassuring, at home or in the wilderness—a new warbler in the park, a bird's nest in a woodlot, a covey of quail exploding from underfoot in a meadow, a Bald Eagle glimpsed from a city street as it soared above a river or seen from a wilderness lake as it labored back to its nest with a fish. Over the years, seeing migrating flocks, watching swallows or wrens or phoebes nest in familiar spots in the backyard, and seeing their children or grandchildren repeating their discoveries, birders gained insight into those "repeated refrains of nature" that Carson found "infinitely healing." And, as Williams and Rosen found, birds helped us face questions about our lives and purpose in the world.

But what use was it to check off species while ecosystems collapsed, even if it helped us understand our lives? That complaint, dating to the early days of environmental enthusiasm, ignored another aspect of our thinking with birds, one that went back to Merriam's generation. In *A Sand County Almanac* Aldo Leopold, calling for an ethical relation to the land, declared that it was "inconceivable that [this] can exist without love, respect and admiration for land, and a high regard for its value, and these depended, as a first step, on knowing the land."[10] Birding, more than any other activity, offered everyone that chance. It catered to a common fascination with birds without requiring study or even much initial knowledge, and opened doors to science, art, conservation, and insight. It began with an appeal to learn about our bird neighbors and now supports learning about the systems of life on which we depend, a simple activity from which, to borrow from Darwin, "endless forms most beautiful and most wonderful have been, and are being evolved."

Notes

INTRODUCTION

1. Florence Merriam, *Birds through an Opera-Glass* (Boston: Houghton Mifflin, 1889). David Allen Sibley, *The Sibley Guide to Birds* (New York: Knopf, 2000). For a listing of the recent guides, mainly since 1980, see Diane Schmidt, *A Guide to Field Guides: Identifying the Natural History of North America* (Englewood, Colo.: Libraries Unlimited, 1999) with its thirty pages, 174–204, of bird guides to North America. On the history of birdwatching see Mark Barrow, *A Passion for Birds: American Ornithology after Audubon* (Princeton, N.J.: Princeton University Press, 1998), especially chapter 7; Stephen Moss, *A Bird in the Bush: A Social History of Birdwatching* (London: Aurum Press, 2004); Felton Gibbons and Deborah Strom, *Neighbors to the Birds: A History of Birdwatching in America* (New York: Norton, 1988); Joseph Kastner, *A World of Watchers: An Informal History of the American Passion for Birds—from Its Scientific Beginnings to the Great Birding Boom of Today* (New York: Knopf, 1986); Scott Weidensaul, *Of a Feather: A Brief History of American Birding* (Orlando, Fla.: Harcourt, 2007). Related matter for the period since World War II is in Mark Cocker, *Birders: Tales of a Tribe* (2001; reprint, New York: Grove, 2001).
2. Suzanne Zeller, *Inventing Canada* (Toronto: University of Toronto Press, 1987) provides a good introduction to natural history's activities.
3. Terry Tempest Williams, *Refuge: An Unnatural History of Family and Place* (New York: Pantheon, 1991; reprint, New York: Vintage, 1992), has one of the fullest accounts of memory, land, and birding.
4. U.S. Fish and Wildlife Service, *Birding in the United States: A Demographic and Economic Analysis, Addendum to the 2001 National Survey of Fishing, Hunting and Wildlife-Associated Recreation* (Washington, D.C.: Government Printing Office, 2001), 4, 15; available at www.fs.fed.us/outdoors/naturewatch/start/economics/Economic-Analysis-for-Birding.pdf.

CHAPTER 1

1. Florence Merriam Bailey, *Handbook of Birds of the Western United States* (Boston: Houghton Mifflin, 1902). Frank Chapman, *Handbook of Birds of Eastern North America* (New York: Appleton, 1895). Florence Merriam, *Birds through an Opera-Glass* (Boston: Houghton Mifflin, 1889), and *Birds of Village and Field* (Boston:

Houghton Mifflin, 1898). Neltje Blanchan, *Bird Neighbors* (New York: Doubleday, 1898). Mabel Osgood Wright, *Birdcraft* (New York: Macmillan, 1895). John B. Grant, *Our Common Birds and How to Know Them* (New York: Scribner's, 1891). Edward Knobel, *Field Key to the Land Birds* (Boston: Bradlee Whidden, 1899).

2. Florence Merriam, *A-birding on a Bronco* (Boston: Houghton Mifflin, 1896). Ridgway's Manual is Robert Ridgway, *Manual of North American Birds* (Philadelphia: Lippincott, 1887).

3. For summaries of Bailey's career, see Keir B. Sterling, Richard P. Harmond, George A. Cevasco, and Lorne F. Hammond, eds., *Biographical Dictionary of American and Canadian Naturalists and Environmentalists* (Westport, Conn.: Greenwood, 1997), and Marcia Myers Bonta, *Women in the Field* (College Station: Texas A & M University Press, 1991), 186–96.

4. Merriam, *A-birding*, 2, 140, punctuation in the original.

5. Ridgway, *Manual*, 468, 476–77.

6. Elliott Coues, *Key to North American Birds* (Boston: Estes and Lauriat, 1887).

7. Coues, *Key*, 1–2, 12–13, 13, 28–40, 56.

8. William Zinsser, "Watching the Birds," in Roger Tory Peterson and Rudy Hoglund, eds., *Roger Tory Peterson: The Art and Photography of the World's Foremost Birder* (New York: Rizzoli, 1994), 23.

9. Preface to Chapman, *Handbook*, unpaged. Advertisement in Bailey, *Handbook*, unpaged matter in back.

10. Chapman, *Handbook*, 23.

11. Chapman, *Handbook*, 401.

12. Bailey, *Handbook*, 115.

13. Merriam, *Birds through an Opera-Glass*, 1. John Burroughs, introduction to Blanchan, *Bird Neighbors*, vii–viii.

14. Merriam, *Birds through an Opera-Glass*, 61. Blanchan, *Bird Neighbors*, subtitle. Basic guides, such as these, generally included 70–150 species. See for example the advertisement for the Audubon chart in *Bird-Lore* 5 (January–February 1903), unpaged matter inside cover, and in the review of *Land Birds of Northern New York*, by Edmund J. Sawyer, *Bird-Lore* 18 (September–October 1916), 323.

15. For instance, Sheri Williamson, "Choose Your Wardrobe Wisely: Good Birders Don't Wear White," in Lisa White, ed., *Good Birders Don't Wear White* (Boston: Houghton Mifflin, 2007), 33–37.

16. Merriam, *Birds through an Opera-Glass*, 1–3.

17. Merriam, *Birds through an Opera-Glass*, 60.

18. Merriam, *Birds through an Opera-Glass*, 4–5. Blanchan, *Bird Neighbors*, ix.

19. Blanchan, *Bird Neighbors*, 109.

20. Coues, *Key*, 402. Merriam, *Birds of Village and Field*, 98–99. On the other hand, she quoted Coues on the Cowbird in *Birds through an Opera-Glass*, 106. Wright, *Birdcraft*, 168.

21. Wright, *Birdcraft*, 126–27.

22. H. E. Parkhurst, *The Birds' Calendar* (New York: Scribner's, 1894), 42, quoted in Blanchan, *Bird Neighbors*, 151.

23. Merriam, *Birds of Village and Field*, 271. Wright, *Birdcraft*, 216.

24. Grant, *Our Common Birds*, 122.

25. Grant, *Our Common Birds*, 14–18, quote from 16.

26. William E. Davis, Jr., *Dean of the Birdwatchers: A Biography of Ludlow Griscom* (Washington, D.C.: Smithsonian Institution Press, 1994), 5.

27. Merriam, *Birds of Village and Field*, iv, 346–47, 252–53.

28. Merriam, *Birds of Village and Field*, 170.

29. Roger Tory Peterson, *A Field Guide to the Birds* (Boston: Houghton Mifflin, 1934), xix.

30. F. Schuyler Mathews, *Field Book of Wild Birds and Their Music,* rev. ed. (New York: Putnam, 1921; originally published 1904).

31. Laura Dassow Walls, *The Passage to Cosmos* (Chicago: University of Chicago Press, 2009), especially the section "Manifest Destinies, 99–147.

32. Edward O. Wilson, *Biophilia* (Cambridge, Mass.: Harvard University Press, 1984).

33. Here see Scott Atran, *Cognitive Foundations of Natural History* (New York: Cambridge University Press, 1990).

34. Coues, *Key*, 9. George Miksch Sutton, "Fifty Years of Progress in American Bird-Art," in American Ornithological Union, ed., *Fifty Years' Progress of American Ornithology, 1993–1933* (Lancaster, Pa.: American Ornithologists' Union, 1933), 181–97.

35. Kenn Kaufman, *Kingbird Highway* (Boston: Houghton Mifflin, 1997), 154, 49, 81, 97, 294–95, 43.

36. David Allen, *The Naturalist in Britain* (London: A. Lane, 1976), and "Tastes and Crazes," in N. Jardine, J. A. Secord, and E. C. Spary, eds., *Cultures of Natural History* (New York: Cambridge University Press, 1996), 394–407.

37. Mark Barrow, *A Passion for Birds* (Princeton: Princeton University Press, 1998), 97.

38. Thomas Nuttall, *A Manual of the Ornithology of the United States and Canada*, 2 vols. (Cambridge, Mass.: Hilliard, Gray, 1832–34), 1:273.

39. On the modern market see Bill Steiner, *Audubon Art Prints* (Columbia: University of South Carolina Press, 2003), 16–25.

40. On cost, Richard Rhodes, *John James Audubon: The Making of an American* (New York: Knopf, 2004), 403; on production, William Souder, *Under a Wild Sky: John James Audubon and the Making of The Birds of America* (New York: Farrar, Strauss, and Giroux, 2004), 283.

41. Ann Shelby Blum, *Picturing Nature: American Nineteenth Century Zoological Illustration* (Princeton: Princeton University Press, 1993).

42. I treated this extensively in *Nature and the English Diaspora* (New York: Cambridge University Press, 1999), and while I stress American motives here, this movement formed part of a common "Anglo" tradition.

43. Frank Graham, Jr., *The Audubon Ark* (New York: Knopf, 1990), 12–13.

44. Graham, *Audubon Ark*, 15. Editorial, *Osprey* 1 (April 1897), 114.

45. Graham, *Audubon Ark*, 6–7.

46. Jenny Price, "When Women Were Women, Men Were Men, and Birds Were Hats," 57–109, in Price, *Flight Maps: Adventures with Nature in Modern America* (New York: Basic Books, 1999). Robin Doughty, *Feather Fashions and Bird Preservation: A Study in Nature Protection* (Berkeley: University of California Press, 1975).

47. Doughty, *Feather Fashions*. Charles G. D. Roberts, "The Aigrette," in Charles G. D. Roberts, *The Secret Trails* (New York: Macmillan, 1916), 77–89.

48. *Bird-Lore* 3 (February 1901), 40–41.

49. Unsigned (presumably Daniel J. Philippon, ed.), introduction to Mabel Osgood Wright, *The Friendship of Nature* (1894; reprint, Baltimore: Johns Hopkins Press, 1999), 3–6. Sterling et al., *Biographical Dictionary*.

50. Sterling et al., *Biographical Dictionary*.

51. *Bird-Lore* 1 (August 1899), 136. The others were Tennessee, Texas, and California and a West Virginia affiliate of Pennsylvania Audubon.

52. Ralph Hoffman, *Birds of the Pacific States* (Boston: Houghton Mifflin, 1927).

53. The clubs proved so successful that the Australians copied them, and the Gould League of Bird Lovers (named after John Gould, the great British Empire producer of bird books and pictures) became a force in Australian bird protection. Thomas R. Dunlap, *Nature and the English Diaspora* (New York: Cambridge University Press, 1999), 116–17.

54. Anna Botsford Comstock, *Handbook of Nature Study*, 2 vols., rev. ed. (Ithaca, N.Y.: Cornell University Press, 1986) (originally published Ithaca, N.Y.: Comstock, 1911). On nature study and agriculture see James G. Needham, *The Natural History of the Farm* (Ithaca, N.Y.: Comstock, 1916). On its influence abroad, see Dunlap, *Nature and the English Diaspora*, 116.

55. Comstock, *Handbook*, 1:1.

56. They still serve that purpose. A set of field guides for Brazilian birds, in preparation in 2006 at the Bronx Zoo (formally the Wildlife Conservation Society), planned to encourage the idea of birds as a national heritage by marking endemics (birds found only in that region) with a tiny national flag beside the description. Author's interview with John Gwynne, August 3, 2006. This was done; see John A. Gwynne, Robert S. Ridgely, Guy Tudor, and Martha Argel, *Birds of Brazil: The Pantanal and Cerrado of Central Brazil* (Ithaca, N.Y.: Cornell University Press, 2010).

CHAPTER 2

1. Chester A. Reed, *Bird Guide: Water Birds, Game Birds and Birds of Prey East of the Rockies* (Worcester, Mass.: Chas. K. Reed, 1906; reprint, 1913), *Bird Guide*, pt. 2, *Land Birds East of the Rockies from Parrots to Bluebirds* (Worcester, Mass.: Chas. K. Reed, 1906; reprint, New York: Doubleday, Page, 1912), and *Western Bird Guide: Birds of the Rockies and West to the Pacific* (Worcester, Mass.: Chas. K. Reed, 1913; reprint, New York: Doubleday, Page, 1923). Ralph Hoffman, *A Guide to the Birds of New England and Eastern New York* (Boston: Houghton Mifflin, 1904). Frank M. Chapman, *Color Key to North American Birds* (New York: Doubleday, Page, 1903).

2. Reed, *Water Birds*, 5.

3. Reed, *Water Birds*, 30, 98.

4. Reed, *Water Birds*, 90, 122, 123.

5. Advertisement, *Bird-Lore* 7 (November–December 1906), front, n.p. Reed, *Land Birds*, unpaged back matter.

6. Joseph Grinnell to Florence Merriam Bailey, August 31, 1908, July 29, 1910, December 22, 1913; Bailey to Grinnell, December 5, 1913, correspondence files, Museum of Vertebrate Zoology (MVZ) University of California, Berkeley.

7. Chapman, *Color Key*, iii.

8. Roger Tory Peterson and Rudy Hoglund, eds., *Roger Tory Peterson: The Art and Photography of the World's Foremost Birder* (New York: Rizzoli, 1994), 23. George M. Sutton, *Bird Student* (Austin: University of Texas Press, 1980), 8.

9. Chapman, *Color Key*, iii.

10. Chapman, *Color Key*, 207.

11. Chapman, *Color Key*, iv.

12. Ernest Seton-Thompson [author varied name in this period], "Recognition Marks of Birds," *Bird-Lore* 3 (November–December 1901), 187–89; quote from 188. The previous article, written under the name Ernest Seton Thompson, was "Directive Color of Birds," *Auk* 14 (October 1897), 395–96.

13. Roger Tory Peterson, *A Field Guide to the Birds* (Boston: Houghton Mifflin, 1934), v.

14. The categories, obviously, overlapped. Audubon's fine art combined natural history's detail with glimpses into the wilderness; the lithographs in the federal reports of the post–Civil War natural history surveys of the West are now treated (and sold) as fine art; and wood engravings could show birds and even rise to fine art.

15. Frank M. Chapman, *Bird Life* (New York: Appleton, 1897), v.

16. Mabel Osgood Wright, *Birdcraft* (New York: Macmillan, 1895). Mabel Osgood Wright to Arthur Allen, March 23, 1895, and June 23, 1895, Historical Correspondence, Chapman Papers, Department of Ornithology, American Museum of Natural History (AMNH), New York.

17. Review signed W.A.J., *Osprey* 2 (February–March 1898), 91.

18. Compare, for example, Hoffman, *Guide to the Birds*, 94, and Florence Merriam, *Birds of Village and Field* (Boston: Houghton Mifflin, 1898), 207.

19. Hoffman, *Guide to the Birds*, 87, 145, 218, 130, 95, 191, 274.

20. Reed, *Water Birds*, 5.

21. Merriam, *Birds through an Opera-Glass*, 211–19.

22. Chapman, *Handbook*, 34, *Bird Life*, 76–77, *Color Key*, 170.

23. Wright, *Birdcraft*, 283.

24. Merriam, *Birds of Village and Field*, xxix–xlix, xiii.

25. Chapman, *Handbook*, 404. Bailey, *Handbook*, 479.

26. Joseph Grinnell to Florence Merriam Bailey, August 31, 1908, MVZ.

27. Chapman, *Handbook*, 404–10.

28. Florence Van Vechten Dickey, *Familiar Birds of the Pacific Southwest with Size and Color Key* (Stanford: Stanford University Press, 1935). Lou Blachley and Randolph Jenks, *Naming the Birds at a Glance* (New York: Knopf, 1963). Mike Lambert, *Birds by Colour: The Simplest Identification Guide* (London: Blandford, 1992).

29. John T. Emlen and David Archbald, *Quick Key Guide to Birds: Northeastern and Central United States and Adjacent Canada* (Garden City, N.Y.: Doubleday, 1967).

30. Merriam, *Birds of Village and Field*, 339, 346–47.

31. Hoffman, *Guide to the Birds*, 117, 145, 161–62.

32. Ynez Mexia, "Bird Study for Beginners by a Beginner," *Bird-Lore* 27, pt. 1 (January–February 1925), 69–72; pt. 2 (March–April 1925), 137–41.

33. Later authors made the same point. Birds varied somewhat by season and molt, light and background could change colors dramatically, and low light made even obvious patterns and markings effectively disappear. See Roger Tory Peterson, *How to Know the Birds* (Boston: Houghton Mifflin, 1949) 15, 26. E. M. Nicholson, *The Art of Bird Watching* (London: H. F. & G. Witherby, 1931; reprint, New York: Scribner's, 1932), 52–54.

34. Mexia, "Bird Study," 138, 139, 72. Chapman, *Handbook*, 10.

35. Kenn Kaufman, *A Field Guide to Advanced Birding: Birding Challenges and How to Approach Them* (Boston: Houghton Mifflin, 1990), 10.

36. See, for example, Ann Eisenberg, "Digital Field Guides Eliminate the Guesswork," *New York Times*, May 10, 2009, Sunday Business sec., 3.

37. On Chapman: "Boy Meets Bullfinch," *New Yorker*, March 4, 1939, 22. Ludlow Griscom, "Frank Michler Chapman, 1864–1945," *Audubon* 48 (January–February 1946), 49–52. Joseph Kastner, *World of Watchers* (New York: Knopf, 1986), 191.

38. *Bird-Lore* 1 (February 1899), 28; 1 (April 1899), 63.

39. Advertisement, in Chapman Papers.

40. Elliott Coues, editorial, *Osprey* 3 (February 1899), 94–95.

41. Wright to Chapman, October 2, 1903, and undated reply, both in Chapman Papers.

42. Merriam, *Birds through an Opera-Glass*, iii.

43. Editorial, *Bird-Lore* 15 (May–June 1914), 184. On listing policy see *Bird-Lore* 24 (May–June 1922), 166.

44. *Bird-Lore* 11 (January–February 1909), 7–8; 16 (July–August 1914), 275; 17 (July–August 1915), 288.

45. Frank Graham, Jr., *The Audubon Ark* (New York: Knopf, 1990), 101.

46. Australians relied on Neville Cayley, *What Bird Is That?* (Sydney: Angus and Robertson, 1931), New Zealanders on Perrine Moncrieff, *New Zealand Birds and How to Identify Them* (Auckland: Whitcombe and Tombs, 1925).

47. Roger Tory Peterson, Guy Montfort, and P. A. D. Hollom, *A Field Guide to the Birds of Britain and Europe* (Boston: Houghton Mifflin, 1954; London: Collins, 1954).

48. H. E. Parkhurst, *The Birds' Calendar* (New York: Scribner's, 1894). Jonathan Rosen, *The Life of the Skies* (New York: Farrar, Strauss, and Giroux, 2008).

49. For examples see Chapman, *Handbook*, 15–20, and *Bird Life*, 48–54; Wright, *Birdcraft*, 6–8; John B. Grant, *Our Common Birds and How to Know Them* (New York: Scribner's, 1891), 35–40.

50. Author's observations, undated. Jean Paquin and Ghislain Caron, *Oiseaux du Quebec et des Maritimes* (Waterloo, Quebec: Editions Michel Quintin, 1998), 186.

51. Chapman, *Color Key*, 5.

52. On this set and some changes, see "The Baltimore Oriole Is Back," *National Wildlife* 32 (February–March 1994), 24–27.

53. Merriam, *Birds through an Opera-Glass*, 171, 52, 60.

CHAPTER 3

1. Ludlow Griscom, *Birds of the New York City Region* (New York: American Museum of Natural History, 1923).

2. Griscom, *Birds of New York City*, 6, 7.

3. Biographical information from Joseph Kastner, *World of Watchers* (New York: Knopf, 1986), 192–94, and Edwin Way Teale, "Ludlow Griscom: Virtuoso of Field Identification," *Bird-Lore* 47 (November–December 1945), 349–58.

4. H. E. Parkhurst, *The Birds' Calendar* (New York: Scribner's, 1894), 11, 12.

5. Griscom's diary, quoted in William E. Davis, Jr., *Dean of the Birdwatchers: A Biography of Ludlow Griscom* (Washington, D.C.: Smithsonian Institution Press, 1994), 8.

6. Davis, *Dean of the Birdwatchers*, 8, 1–8. All information on Griscom here, unless otherwise indicated, is from this source.

7. Ludlow Griscom, "Problems of Field Identification," *Auk* 39 (January 1922), 31–41. On ornithologists' reliance on sight identification see Ludlow Griscom, "Modern Problems in Field Identification," *Bird-Lore* 38 (January–February 1936), 12–18, and *Modern Bird Study* (Cambridge, Mass.: Harvard University Press, 1945), 9–10.

8. Griscom, *Modern Bird Study*, 8–9, 11–12.

9. Roger Tory Peterson, "The Era of Ludlow Griscom," *Audubon* 62 (May–June 1960), 131.

10. Peterson was the first non-Bronx member; others included William Vogt, an ecologist and conservation official, and Ernst Mayr, who went on to become one of the twentieth century's great biologists. This account based, unless otherwise stated, on Davis, *Dean of the Birdwatchers*, 1–8; Roger T. Peterson, "In Memoriam: Ludlow

Griscom," *Auk* 82 (October 1965), 599–605; John Farrand, Jr., "The Bronx County Bird Club," *American Birds* 45 (fall 1991), 372–81.

11. John F. Kuerzi to Ludlow Griscom (LG), January 16, 1925, Ludlow Griscom Papers, Cornell University Library, Ithaca, New York.

12. Peterson, "Era of Ludlow Griscom," 102.

13. Peterson, "Era of Ludlow Griscom," 148.

14. Griscom to Henry Allen Moe, February 18, 1944, Griscom Papers. All quotes from this letter.

15. Peterson, "Era of Ludlow Griscom," 131.

16. Jared Diamond and K. David Bishop, "Ethno-ornithology of the Ketengban People, Indonesian New Guinea," in Douglas L. Medin and Scott Atran, eds., *Folkbiology* (Cambridge, Mass.: MIT Press, 1999), 17–45. Quote from 33–34.

17. Diamond, "Ethno-ornithology," 33–34.

18. Gilbert White, *A Natural History of Selbourne* (1788: reprint, New York: Penguin, 1977), 213. Roger Tory Peterson used this quote to head the preface to Peterson, Guy Montfort, and P. A. D. Hollom, *A Field Guide to the Birds of Britain and Europe* (London: Collins, 1954), v.

19. Eliott Coues, *Key to North American Birds* (Boston: Estes and Lauriat, 1887), 561.

20. Karen Harden McCracken, *Connie Hagar: The Life History of a Texas Birdwatcher* (College Station: Texas A&M University Press, 1986), 270.

21. Frank M. Chapman, "Birds of the Vicinity of New York City," guide leaflet no. 22 (New York: American Museum of Natural History, 1906).

22. Griscom, *Birds of New York City*, 5.

23. Griscom, *Birds of New York City*, 12, 7–8, 8–9.

24. Griscom, *Birds of New York City*, 7.

25. Griscom, *Birds of New York City*, 134, 206, 189, 108, 200.

26. Allen Cruickshank, *Birds around New York City: Where and When to Find Them* (New York: American Museum of Natural History, 1964), xi, viii.

27. Griscom, *Birds of New York City*, 195–96.

28. Chapman, "Birds of the Vicinity of New York City." Griscom, *Birds of New York City*. Cruickshank, *Birds around New York City*. John Bull, *Birds of the New York Area* (New York: Harper, 1964).

29. Griscom, *Birds of New York City*, 52.

30. *Bird-Lore* 34 (July–August 1934), 255.

31. Chapman, *Handbook*, 282–83, 287–88, and *Color Key to North American Birds* (New York: Doubleday, Page, 1903), 219, 177.

32. The male, as a friend pointed out to me, had a far higher value on the "ooh and aah" market. Kurk Dorsey, private communication, May 2009.

33. The rest came from the 66 accidentals (species only reported a few times), 21 irregular transients (18%), 18 casual visitants (5%), 20 irregular winter visitors (5%), 6 irregular summer visitors (2%), and the 12 extinct species (3%). Griscom, *Birds of New York City*, 18–26.

34. Florence Merriam, *Birds through an Opera-Glass* (Boston: Houghton Mifflin, 1889), 61.

35. *Bird-Lore* 15 (May–June 1913), 184.

36. Quoted in Davis, *Dean of the Birdwatchers*, 125.

37. Teale, *Ludlow Griscom*, 354.

38. Peterson, "Era of Ludlow Griscom," 102, 131.

39. Roger Tory Peterson, *Birds over America* (New York: Dodd, Mead, 1948), 19–20.

40. Joseph J. Hickey, *A Guide to Bird Watching* (New York: Oxford University Press, 1943), 147.

41. Hickey, *Guide to Bird Watching*, has many examples. One individual account of this kind of nature study is Lawrence Kilham, *On Watching Birds* (Chelsea, Vt.: Chelsea Green, 1988; reprint, College Station: Texas A&M University Press, 1997).

42. Peter Slater, *Birdwatcher's Notebook* (Sydney: Weldon, 1988), 70.

43. Frank M. Chapman file, Correspondence, Museum of Vertebrate Zoology, University of California, Berkeley (MVZ), provides evidence of pressures on collecting. Ray Wallace, "A Body in Twain? The Royal Australian Ornithological Union and the Events of 1969," M.A. thesis, University of Melbourne, 1970.

44. For examples of the deep hold of this culture in Britain, see Paul Fussell, "Arcadian Resources," in Fussell, *The Great War and Modern Memory* (New York: Oxford University Press, 1975), 231–69.

45. James Fisher, *Watching Birds* (London: Penguin, 1941), and *Bird Recognition*, vol. 1 (London: Penguin, 1947). *Bird Recognition* covered sea birds and waders in three volumes published in 1947, 1951, and 1955.

46. Mark Cocker, *Birders: Tales of a Tribe* (New York: Grove Press, 2001), 81, 82.

47. J. A. Leach, *An Australian Bird Book* (Melbourne: Whitcombe and Tombs, 1911); Neville Cayley, *What Bird Is That?* (Sydney: Angus and Robertson, 1931); Perrine Moncrieff, *New Zealand Birds and How to Identify Them* (Auckland: Whitcombe and Tombs, 1925).

48. The Vincent Serventy Papers, in the Archival Collections of the National Library of Australia, Canberra, contain many letters and columns, and Serventy maintained an extensive correspondence with many interested readers into the late 1960s. By contrast, Edwin Way Teale found writing a nature column in the late 1940s in American newspapers simply a chore. Edwin Way Teale Papers, Thomas J. Dodd Research Center, University of Connecticut, Storrs. Graham Pizzey, *Crosbie Morrison: Voice of Nature* (Melbourne: Victoria Press, 1992), sketches a career as a wildlife popularizer impossible at this time in the United States. E. M. Nicholson, *The Art of Bird Watching* (London: H. F. & G. Witherby, 1931; reprint, New York: Scribner's, 1932). On comparisons with Australia and New Zealand, see Thomas R. Dunlap, *Nature and the English Diaspora* (New York: Cambridge University Press, 1999), 111–13, 207.

49. P. A. Taverner, *Canadian Water Bird, Game Birds, and Birds of Prey: A Pocket Field Guide* (Toronto: Musson, 1939), and *Canadian Land Birds: A Pocket Field Guide* (Toronto: Musson, 1939).

50. An eloquent complaint about equipment appears in Aldo Leopold, *A Sand County Almanac* (New York: Oxford University Press, 1949; reprint, New York: Ballantine, 1967), 214.

51. Frank Graham, Jr., *The Audubon Ark* (New York: Knopf, 1990), 132.

CHAPTER 4

1. Roger Tory Peterson, *A Field Guide to the Birds: Including All Species Found in Eastern North America* (Boston: Houghton Mifflin, 1934).

2. Peterson, *Field Guide* (1934), 113.

3. *Peterson Field Guide to Birds of North America* (Boston: Houghton Mifflin, 2008), described on the title page as "First Edition."

4. Peterson never wrote an autobiography, though he often discussed his ideas and his history in talking or writing about his guides and his art. The first biography

appeared in 1977: John C. Devlin and Grace Naismith, *The World of Roger Tory Peterson: An Authorized Biography* (New York: New York Times Books, 1977). Two others appeared after this manuscript had largely been written: Elizabeth J. Rosenthal, *Birdwatcher: The Life of Roger Tory Peterson* (Guilford, Conn.: Globe Pequot, 2008) and Douglas Carlson, *Roger Tory Peterson: A Biography* (Austin: University of Texas Press, 2007).

5. Roger Tory Peterson, "Evolution of a Field Guide," *Defenders*, October 1980, available at Defenders.org/rtperter1.htm; Roger Tory Peterson, *Birds over America* (New York: Dodd, Mead, 1948), 5.

6. Frank Graham, Jr., *The Audubon Ark* (New York: Knopf, 1990), 130. William Zinsser, "Watching the Birds," in Roger Tory Peterson and Rudy Hoglund, eds., *Roger Tory Peterson: The Art and Photography of the World's Foremost Birder* (New York: Rizzoli, 1994), 18, 23. Peterson, "Evolution of a Field Guide."

7. Zinsser, "Watching the Birds," 23. Peterson, *Birds over America,* 12.

8. Zinsser, "Watching the Birds," 19.

9. Peterson, "Evolution of a Field Guide."

10. Remark overheard at dinner with Hickey and others, 30 or 31 August 1982. "Yes, we had some people who were really good at identification. Then somebody rang in this skinny kid from upstate New York who could identify *anything*." Other quote from Graham, *Audubon Ark*, 132.

11. Roger Tory Peterson, editor's note, in Kenn Kaufman, *Advanced Birdng* (Boston: Houghton Mifflin, 1990), v.

12. Roger Tory Peterson, "The Era of Ludlow Griscom," *Audubon* 62 (May–June 1960), 102 ff.

13. Peterson, "Evolution of a Field Guide." References are to Ernest Seton-Thompson [author varied name in this period], "Recognition Marks of Birds," *Bird-Lore* 3 (November–December 1901), 187–89. Quote from 188. The previous article was Ernest Seton Thompson, "Directive Color of Birds," *Auk 14* (October 1897), 395–96. Ernest Thompson Seton, *Two Little Savages* (New York: Doubleday, 1903). The duck plate is reproduced in Douglas Carlson, *Roger Tory Peterson: A Biography* (Austin: University of Texas, 2007), 5. Edward Howe Forbush and John Bichard May, *A Natural History of American Birds of Eastern and Central North America* (Boston: Commonwealth of Massachusetts, 1925; reprint, Boston: Houghton Mifflin, 1939).

14. Peterson, "Evolution of a Field Guide." William E. Davis, Jr., *Dean of the Birdwatchers* (Washington, D.C.: Smithsonian Institution Press, 1994), 109–10.

15. Peterson, editor's note, v.

16. Frank M. Chapman, *Color Key to North American Birds* (New York: Doubleday, 1903), 207.

17. Peterson, *Field Guide* (1934), xvii.

18. Peterson, *Field Guide* (1934), xix.

19. Zinsser, "Watching the Birds," 23.

20. First quote from his *Modern Painters*, vol. 4, chap. 4, quoted in Lawrence Campbell, introduction to John Ruskin, *The Elements of Drawing* (1857; reprint, New York: Dover, 1971), ix; second quote from Ruskin, *Elements of Drawing*, 27.

21. Mabel Osgood Wright to Arthur Allen, March 23, 1895, and June 23, 1895, Chapman Papers, Historical Correspondence, Department of Ornithology, American Museum of Natural History (AMNH).

22. Peterson, *Field Guide* (1934), 16, 44, 119, 75. Roger Tory Peterson, *A Field Guide to the Birds* (Boston: Houghton Mifflin, 1947), 171.

23. F. Schuyler Mathews, *Field Book of Birds and Their Music* (New York: Putnam, 1904; rev. and enl., 1921), xxi. Peterson, *Field Guide* (1934), xix.

24. Peterson, *Field Guide* (1934), 198, italics in original.

25. Chandler S. Robbins, Bertel Brunn, and Herbert S. Zim, *Birds of North America* (New York: Golden Press, 1966), 10–11.

26. Edwin Way Teale, *Wandering through Winter* (New York: Dodd, Mead, 1965), 148.

27. Frank M. Chapman, review of *A Field Guide to the Birds,* by Roger Tory Peterson, *Bird-Lore* 36 (July–August 1934), 253, 255.

28. Peterson, "Evolution of a Field Guide."

29. Donald Culross Peattie, "The Nature of Things," *Bird-Lore* 43 (July–August 1941), 346.

30. This appeared most recently in Mark Obmascik, *The Big Year: A Tale of Man, Nature, and Fowl Obsession* (New York: Free Press, 2004), 52. As early as 1909, Chapman said ornithologists knew North America's species and subspecies well enough that collecting served mainly as a way to train new ornithologists. Frank Chapman, editorial, *Bird-Lore* 11 (January–February 1909), 37.

31. Joseph Grinnell, director of the University of California's Museum of Vertebrate Zoology, held into the 1930s that collecting was an essential avenue to ornithology for young men seeking to enter the field. See Joseph Grinnell, "Conserve the Collector," *Science,* new ser., 41 (February 1915), 229–32, and his correspondence with Frank Chapman, Correspondence files, Museum of Vertebrate Zoology, Berkeley (MVZ). On sight identification in science see Ludlow Griscom, "Problems of Field Identification," *Auk* 39 (January 1922), 33. Joseph Hickey dated the end of the shotgun era to 1900 in *A Guide to Bird Watching* (New York: Oxford University Press, 1943), 51, 120.

32. Frank M. Chapman, editorial, *Bird-Lore* 36 (July–August 1934), 255.

33. Peterson, *Field Guide* (1934), xviii–xix.

34. Peterson, *Field Guide* (1947), x.

35. Roger Tory Peterson (RTP) to Chapman, September 19, 1934, Chapman Papers.

36. RTP to John Baker, September 28, 1944, Correspondence, Roger Tory Peterson Institute, Jamestown, New York.

37. RTP to Paul Brooks, October 11, 1944, Peterson Institute.

38. RTP to John Baker, November 17, 1944, RTP to Paul Brooks, March 6, 1945, Peterson Institute.

39. RTP to John Baker, November 30, 1944, RTP to Paul Brooks, October 11, 1944.

40. "Notes from Field and Study," *Bird-Lore* 39 (March–April 1937), 159–60.

41. Guy Emerson, "The Lure of the List," *Bird-Lore* 42 (January–February 1940), 37–39.

42. Griscom to Grinnell, January 15, 1929, Grinnell to Griscom, January 21, 1929, Correspondence, MVZ.

43. Emerson, "Lure of the List," 37.

44. Emerson, "Lure of the List," 37–39. Graham, *Audubon Ark,* 101.

45. Emerson, "Lure of the List."

46. Aldo Leopold, "Thinking Like a Mountain," in Aldo Leopold, *A Sand County Almanac* (New York: Oxford University Press, 1949; reprint, New York: Ballantine, 1966), 137–41.

47. Here see Christian Young, *In the Absence of Predators: Conservation and Controversy on the Kaibab Plateau* (Lincoln: University of Nebraska Press, 2002).

48. Herbert L. Stoddard, *The Bobwhite Quail: Its Habits, Preservation, and Increase* (New York: Scribner's, 1931).

49. "Feathered vs. Human Predators," *Bird-Lore* 27 (March–April 1935), 122–26; W. L. McAtee, "A Little Essay on 'Vermin,'" *Bird-Lore* 31 (November–December 1931), 381–84.

50. Warren F. Eaton, "Predators and Bird Preserves," *Bird-Lore* 37 (May–June 1935), 162–66.

51. Stoddard, *Bobwhite Quail.* Paul Errington, "Vulnerability of Bob-white Populations to Predation," *Ecology* 15 (April 1934), 110–27.

52. On extinction see Mark Barrow, *Nature's Ghosts: Confronting Extinction from the Age of Jefferson to the Age of Ecology* (Chicago: University of Chicago Press, 2009).

53. Charles Reed, *Bird Guide: Land Birds East of the Rockies* (Garden City, N.Y.: Doubleday, Page, 1912), 17; Reed, *Bird Guide: Water Birds, Game Birds and Birds of Prey* (Worcester Mass.: Chas. K. Reed, 1913), 30, 98.

54. Peterson, *Field Guide* (1939), 84; Peterson, *Field Guide* (1947), 128.

55. Chapman, *Color Key,* 123, 125.

56. Peterson, *Field Guide* (1934), 85.

57. Ludlow Griscom, *Birds of the New York City Region* (New York: American Museum of Natural History, 1923), 52.

58. Remark from John Farrand, Jr., "The Bronx County Bird Club," *American Birds* 45 (fall 1991), 380. Stanley A. Temple and John Emlen, obituary for Joseph J. Hickey, *Auk* 111 (April 1994), 450–52.

59. Griscom confessed to complete ignorance of common statistical methods in a letter to F.W. Preston, June 12, 1945, Ludlow Griscom Papers, Cornell University Library.

60. Carl B. Koford, *The California Condor* (New York: National Audubon Society, 1953; reprint, New York: Dover, 1966), 136.

61. Koford, *California Condor,* 135.

62. On science without formal study in this period see Thomas R. Dunlap, *Saving America's Wildlife* (Princeton, N.J.: Princeton University Press, 1988), 70–83.

63. Charles Elton, *Animal Ecology* (London: Sidgwick and Jackson, 1927). The popular account is Robert Porter Allen, *The Flame Birds* (New York: Dodd, Mead, 1947).

64. This history is common to recent books on the woodpecker. See, for example, Geoffrey E. Hill, *Ivorybill Hunters* (New York: Oxford University Press, 2007), 6–12.

65. T. Gilbert Pearson to Hoyes Lloyd, January 6, 1922, Whooping Crane files, Record Group 109, Records of the Canadian Wildlife Service, Public Archives Canada, Ottawa.

66. Ludlow Griscom's correspondence for these years has much on the frustrations of wartime birding. Griscom Papers.

67. Frank M. Chapman, editorial, *Bird-Lore* 33 (January–February 1931), 81.

68. Edwin Way Teale, "Ludlow Griscom, Virtuoso of Field Identification," *Audubon* 47 (November–December 1945), 349–50, quote 349.

69. *New Yorker,* May 4, 1934, 251; reproduced in the CD to the *Complete Cartoons of the New Yorker* (New York: Black Dog and Leventhal, 2004).

70. Gilbert White, *A Natural History of Selbourne* (1787; reprint, New York: Penguin, 1977), 214.

71. White, *Natural History of Selbourne,* 213.

72. A recent example is Kevin Karlson, "Birding by Impression," *Living Bird* 25 (summer 2006), 34–42.

73. Browsing and buying old guides for research I was struck by the practice, dating to the first generation.

74. Allen Cruickshank, *Birds around New York City: Where and When to Find Them* (New York: American Museum of Natural History, 1942), viii–ix.
75. On this era, see Robert E. Kohler, *All Creatures* (Princeton, N.J.: Princeton University Press, 2006).
76. Elliott Coues, *Key to North American Birds* (Boston: Estes and Lauriat, 1887), xxvi.

77. Alden Miller to RTP, September 13, 1940. RTP to Miller, September 24, 1940, Correspondence, MVZ.
78. Roger Tory Peterson, *A Field Guide to Western Birds* (Boston: Houghton Mifflin, 1941), 205. For a fuller account see RTP file, Correspondence, MVZ.
79. Peterson, *Field Guide to Western Birds* (1941), 203, 204.
80. For an example of popular names and their use in the previous generation's guides see Florence Merriam, *Birds of Village and Field* (Boston: Houghton Mifflin, 1898).
81. Roger Tory Peterson, "A Bird by Any Other Name," *Bird-Lore* 43 (September–October 1942), 277–80.
82. Donald Culross Peattie, "The Nature of Things," *Bird-Lore* 43 (November–December 1942), 349.
83. Peterson, *Field Guide* (1947), 258; RTP to Chandler Robbins, September 3, 1974, Peterson Institute.
84. J. A. Leach, *An Australian Bird Book* (Melbourne: Whitcombe and Tombs, 1911), 72, 74.
85. Moncrieff, *New Zealand Birds*; Dunlap, *Nature and the English Diaspora*, 98–99, 117–18, 201, 312–13.
86. Paul Ehrlich, blurb on slip around commemorative printing of the first edition, issued at Peterson's death (Boston: Houghton Mifflin, 1996). It came from Paul R. Ehrlich, David S. Dobkin, and Darryl Wheye, *The Birders' Handbook* (New York: Simon and Schuster, 1988), 563.

CHAPTER 5

1. The epigraph to this chapter is from Edward O. Wilson, *Naturalist* (Washington, D.C.: Island Press, 1994), 14.
2. Herbert S. Zim and Ira N. Gabrielson, *Birds: A Guide to the Most Familiar American Birds* (New York: Simon and Schuster, 1949).
3. Olin Sewall Pettingill, Jr., *A Guide to Bird Finding East of the Mississippi* (New York: Oxford University Press, 1951), and *A Guide to Bird Finding West of the Mississippi* (New York: Oxford University Press, 1953).
4. Roger Tory Peterson and James Fisher, *Wild America* (Boston: Houghton Mifflin, 1955).
5. For background, Marguerite S. Shaffer, *See America First: Tourism and National Identity, 1880–1940* (Washington, D.C.: Smithsonian Institution, 2001).
6. Roger Tory Peterson, *A Field Guide to the Birds* (Boston: Houghton Mifflin, 1947), viii, x.
7. Peterson, *Field Guide* (1947), xviii.
8. Roger Tory Peterson (RTP) to Ludlow Griscom (LG), July 14, 1947, Ludlow Griscom Papers, Cornell University Library, Ithaca, New York. RTP to John Baker, December 1, 1946, Roger Tory Peterson Institute, Jamestown, New York.
9. RTP to Frank Chapman, September 19, 1934, Chapman Papers, Historical Correspondence, Department of Ornithology, AMNH.
10. Peterson, *Field Guide* (1947), 186.

11. Peterson, *Field Guide* (1947), 245–72.

12. RTP to LG, July 7, 1947, Griscom Papers.

13. Chandler Robbins to RTP, July 8, 1947; Edwin Way Teale to RTP, July 2, 1947, July 10, 1947; Connie Hagar to RTP, August 27, 1947, Peterson Institute.

14. RTP to Paul Brooks, March 6, 1945, and for quotation, September 14, 1946, both in Peterson Institute.

· 219 ·

15. Careers can be traced through the National Union Catalog, longevity most easily by catalogs from Dover Publications.

16. See ad in the back of Chester Reed, *Bird Guide*, pt. 2, *Land Birds East of the Rockies from Parrots to Bluebirds* (Worcester, Mass.: Chas. K. Reed, 1906, 1909; reprint, New York: Doubleday, Page, 1912).

17. On interest in late revisions of the Reed guides see RTP to John Baker, November 10, 1944, and RTP to Paul Brooks, March 16, 1946, Peterson Institute.

18. Paul Brooks to RTP, September 19, 1946, Peterson Institute.

19. Roger Peterson, Guy Montfort, and P. A. D. Hollom, *A Field Guide to the Birds of Britain and Europe* (London: Collins, 1954).

20. Eleanor Anthony King, "Lady with Binoculars," *Audubon* 49 (July 1949), 202–10.

21. See RTP to Carl Buchheister, July 3, 1962, Peterson Institute.

22. Roger Tory Peterson, editor's note, in Kenn Kaufman, *Advanced Birding* (Boston: Houghton Mifflin, 1990), v.

23. RTP to Paul Brooks, May 3, 1947, Peterson Institute.

24. RTP to Paul Brooks, September 20, 1947, Peterson Institute.

25. Roger Tory Peterson and Margaret McKenney, *A Field Guide to Wildflowers* (Boston: Houghton Mifflin, 1968); Hal H. Harrison, *A Field Guide to the Birds' Nests East of the Mississippi River* (Boston: Houghton Mifflin, 1975).

26. Adolph Murie, *A Field Guide to Animal Tracks* (Boston: Houghton Mifflin, 1954).

27. RTP to Paul Brooks, April 26, 1946, Peterson Intitute. Leon A. Hausman, *Field Book of Eastern Birds* (New York: Putnam, 1946); Richard H. Pough, *Eastern Land Birds* (New York: Doubleday, 1946).

28. Richard H. Pough; all were published by Doubleday, Garden City, N.Y.

29. Pough, *Audubon Western Bird Guide: Land, Water and Game Birds* (Garden City, N.Y.: Doubleday, 1957), 67, 68.

30. Pough, *Western Bird Guide*, 158, 148.

31. Pough, *Western Bird Guide*, pl. 25.

32. RTP to Paul Brooks, March 6, 1945, Peterson Institute.

33. RTP to Paul Brooks, March 6, 1945, Peterson Institute.

34. RTP to Paul Brooks, July 5, 1945, Peterson Institute.

35. RTP to Richard Pough, October 7, 1947, Peterson Institute.

36. RTP to Guy Montfort, September 25, 1953, Peterson Institute.

37. RTP to Guy Montfort, April 4, 1962, Peterson Institute.

38. RTP to Guy Montfort, December 26, 1963, Peterson Institute.

39. A list is available at www.vintagepbks.com/gg-list_chrono.html.

40. Zim and Gabrielson, *Birds*, 6. That put it in the class of introductory guides, which had, from *Birds through an Opera-Glass* to modern flashguides, between 80 and 150 species, and it included all the material in adult guides. Frank M. Chapman, *Bird-Life* (New York: Appleton, 1897), 100 species; Florence Merriam, *Birds through an Opera-Glass* (Boston: Houghton Mifflin, 1889), 72 species; Merriam, *Birds of Village and Field* (Boston: Houghton Mifflin, 1898), 154 species; Edward Knobel, *Field*

Key to the Land Birds (Boston: Bradlee, Whitten, 1899), 155 species; *Local Birds of Central Texas* (Austin: Local Trading Company, 2004), 123 species.

41. Zim and Gabrielson, *Birds*, 7–15.
42. Zim and Gabrielson, *Birds*, 43, 63, 31.
43. Herbert S. Zim and Alexander C. Martin, *Flowers: A Guide to Familiar American Wildflowers* (New York: Golden Press, 1950), 95, 105.
44. Herbert S. Zim and Robert H. Baker, *Stars* (New York: Simon and Shuster, 1951).
45. John Bull, *Birds of the New York Area* (New York: Harper and Row, 1964).
46. RTP to Paul Brooks, November 1, 1964, Peterson Institute.
47. Bull, *Birds of the New York Area,* quote from 157; Roger Tory Peterson, foreword, x–xi, and Bull, introduction, 6, in Bull, *Birds of the New York Area.*
48. Pettingill, *Guide to Bird Finding East*, vii, ix.
49. Pettingill, Guide to *Bird Finding East*, viii, 348.
50. Peterson and Fisher, *Wild America*, 15.
51. Peterson and Fisher, *Wild America*, 368–69.
52. RTP to Frank Pitelka, February 23, 1953, Correspondence, MVZ.
53. Peterson and Fisher, *Wild America*, 250, 329, 133–34.
54. Peterson and Fisher, *Wild America*, 42, 46, 46–47.
55. Peterson and Fisher, *Wild America*, 36, 418.
56. Edwin Way Teale, *North with the Spring* (New York: Dodd, Mead, 1951, and *Wandering through Winter* (New York: Dodd, Mead, 1965). The other volumes were *Autumn across America* (1956) and *Journey into Summer* (1960), both published by Dodd, Mead, New York.
57. Teale, *Wandering through Winter*, 78.
58. Joseph J. Hickey, *A Guide to Bird Watching* (New York: Oxford University Press, 1943), 147.
59. Guy Emerson, "The Lure of the List," *Bird-Lore* 42 (January–February 1940), 37.
60. Roger Tory Peterson, foreword to Lyn Hancock, *Looking for the Wild* (Toronto: Doubleday Canada, 1986), ix.
61. Kenn Kaufman, *Kingbird Highway: The Story of a Natural Obsession That Got a Little Out of Hand* (Boston: Houghton Mifflin, 1997).
62. Hancock, *Looking for the Wild*, xiii. Scott Weidensaul, *Return to Wild America* (New York: Farrar, Straus, and Giroux, 2005), xvii.
63. Weidensaul, *Return to Wild America*, xix.
64. Foreword (1949) to Henry Beston, *The Outermost House* (1928; reprint, New York: Ballantine, 1971), x.
65. Hickey, *A Guide to Bird Watching*, 3. Roger Tory Peterson, *Birds over America* (New York: Dodd, Mead, 1948), 12. Laurence S. Cunningham, ed., *A Search for Solitude: The Journals of Thomas Merton*, vol. 3, *1952–1960* (New York: HarperCollins, 1996), 123–24.
66. Rachel Carson, "Help Your Child to Wonder," *Woman's Home Companion* (July 1956), 25–27, 46–48. Rachel Carson, *A Sense of Wonder* (New York: Harper Collins, 1965; reprint, with introduction by Linda Lear, 1999).
67. Rachel Carson, *The Sea Around Us* (New York: Oxford University Press, 1951), 166, and *The Edge of the Sea* (Boston: Houghton Mifflin, 1955), vii.
68. Carson, *Sense of Wonder* (reprint, 1999), 9–11, 54, 106, 101.
69. Peterson, *Birds over America*, 5.
70. Peterson, *Birds over America*, 6.
71. Kaufman, *Kingbird Highway*, 43–44.

72. Teale, *Wandering through Winter*, 84–85.

73. Linda Lear, *Rachel Carson: Witness for Nature* (New York: Holt, 1997), 312–16.

74. Author's interview with Lorrie Otto, February 18, 1974, tape in Wisconsin State Historical Society, Madison.

75. On endorsement, John Baker to Paul Brooks, December 9, 1946, Peterson Institute.

76. This account draws on Thomas R. Dunlap, "Organization and Wildlife Preservation: The Case of the Whooping Crane in North America," *Social Studies of Science* 21 (1991), 197–221.

77. Lynch memo, July 14, 1955, Whooping Crane Correspondence, 1955 Info—Corresp., Saskatchewan Museum of Natural History, Regina, cited with permission of Ronald Bordon, director, Saskatchewan Museum of Natural History.

78. Lynch to Hickey, December 12, 1956, Whooping Crane Correspondence, Saskatchewan Museum of Natural History.

79. Robert Porter Allen to Fred Bard, May 6, 1953, in Whooping Crane, Miscellaneous, pt. 3, Saskatchewan Museum of Natural History. On arguments about capture, see Faith McNulty, *The Whooping Crane* (New York: Dutton, 1966), 19, 136–39.

80. Carl B. Koford, *The California Condor* (New York: National Audubon Society, 1953; reprint, New York: Dover, 1966), 135.

81. Paul Ehrlich, blurb on slip around commemorative edition of 1934 edition. Roger Tory Peterson, *A Field Guide to the Birds: Including All Species Found in Eastern North America* (Boston: Houghton Mifflin, 1934; reprint, 1996). From Paul R. Ehrlich, David S. Dobkin, and Darryl Wheye, *The Birders' Handbook* (New York: Simon and Schuster, 1988), 563.

82. On the name "birding," the *OED* found the first use of "birder" in the modern sense of bird-watcher in *Audubon* 47 (1945), 212/2. It also cited a 1970 *Times* article on American practice, as birders, and a 1967 Boston Globe article about an Audubon club that had some years before, rejected the term "birdwatcher." The term "birder" became more accepted after 1970.

CHAPTER 6

1. Rachel Carson, *Silent Spring* (Boston: Houghton Mifflin, 1962). Chandler S. Robbins, Bertel Brunn, and Herbert S. Zim, *Birds of North America* (New York: Golden Press, 1966). Kenn Kaufman, *Kingbird Highway: The Story of a Natural Obsession that Got a Little Out of Hand* (Boston: Houghton Mifflin, 1997).

2. Carson, *Silent Spring* (New York: Fawcett, n.d.).

3. On Carson see Linda Lear, *Rachel Carson: Witness for Nature* (New York: Holt, 1997); also Mark Hamilton Lytle, *The Gentle Subversive* (New York: Oxford University Press, 2007); Alex MacGillivray, *Rachel Carson's Silent Spring* (New York: Barron's, 2004); and Priscilla Coit Murphy, *What a Book Can Do: The Publication and Reception of Silent Spring* (Amherst: University of Massachusetts Press, 2005).

4. Thomas R. Dunlap, *DDT: Scientists, Citizens, and Public Policy* (Princeton: Princeton University Press, 1981), 104–13.

5. Carson, *Silent Spring*, 8, 13, 277, 278.

6. William Darby, "A Scientist Looks at *Silent Spring*," 2, 1962. American Chemical Society, copy from Aaron Ihde.

7. Aldo Leopold, *A Sand County Almanac* (New York: Oxford University Press, 1949; reprint, New York: Ballantine, 1970), 262.

8. Lear, *Rachel Carson*, 33, 83–84.

9. Lear, *Rachel Carson*, 312–16.

10. Alexander Bergstrom to Ludlow Griscom (LG), July 28, 1944 (report referred to is *Time*, July 31, 1944, p. 72). LG to Bergstrom, August 8, 1944, Griscom Papers, Cornell University Library, Ithaca, New York.

11. Robbins to LG, March 31, 1945, Griscom Papers. John H. Baker, "The President Reports to You," *Audubon* 47 (September–October 1945), 309–15; press release, March 2, 1946, in the papers of Roland Clement, used with permission. Clarence Cottam and Elmer Higgins, "DDT and Its Effect on Fish and Wildlife," *Journal of Economic Entomology* 39 (February 1946), 44–52.

12. Roger Tory Peterson (RTP) to LG, July 11, 1949, Griscom Papers.

13. Dunlap, *DDT*, 64–68, 96.

14. Author's interview with Joseph Hickey, July 16, 1973, tapes in Wisconsin State Historical Society, Madison.

15. Hickey interview.

16. Derek Ratcliffe, "The Status of the Peregrine in Great Britain," *Bird Study* 10 (June 1963), 56–90.

17. Their report is Daniel D. Berger, Charles R. Sindelar, Jr., and K. E. Gamble, "The Status of Breeding Peregrines in the Eastern United States," in Joseph J. Hickey, ed., *Peregrine Falcon Populations* (Madison: University of Wisconsin Press, 1969), 165–73.

18. Joseph J. Hickey to Carl W. Buchheister, February 24, 1965, Roger Tory Peterson Institute, Jamestown, New York.

19. RTP to Olin Pettingill, September 9, 1964, Peterson Institute.

20. The following account relies on the author's interviews with Victor Yannacone, Maurice Van Susteren (the hearing examiner), and Lorrie Otto. Tapes in Wisconsin Historical Society.

21. Thomas R. Dunlap, "Organization and Wildlife Preservation: The Case of the Whooping Crane in North America," *Social Studies of Science* 21 (1991), 197–221.

22. On craft knowledge, New Zealand, where lack of money required using amateurs, provides the best examples. See David Butler and Don Merton, *The Black Robin: Saving the World's Most Endangered Bird* (Auckland: Oxford University Press, 1992).

23. Tom J. Cade, "The Breeding of Peregrines and Other Falcons in Captivity: An Historical Summary," in Tom J. Cade, James H. Enderson, Carl G. Thelander, and Clayton M. White, eds., *Peregrine Falcon Populations: Their Management and Recovery* (Boise: Peregrine Fund, 1988), 539–47. John H. Barclay, "Peregrine Restoration in the Eastern United States," in ibid., 549–58.

24. Roger Tory Peterson, *A Field Guide to the Birds* (Boston: Houghton Mifflin, 1947), 205.

25. Edward R. Tufte, *Beautiful Evidence* (Cheshire, Conn.: Graphic Press, 2006), 115.

26. Peterson, *Field Guide* (1947), 242–43.

27. Robbins, *Birds of North America*, 250–51, 80–81, 62–63, 128–29, 140–41.

28. RTP to Paul Brooks, April 12, 1964, December 5, 1964, Peterson Institute.

29. RTP to Paul Brooks, two letters, June 14, 1966, Peterson Institute.

30. Olin Pettingill to Chandler Robbins, June 6, 1966, Peterson Institute.

31. Paul Brooks to RTP, November 1, 1967, Peterson Institute.

32. RTP to Paul Brooks, January 1, 1968, September 18, 1968, Peterson Institute.

33. RTP to Paul Brooks, October 9, 1969, Peterson Institute.

34. Kaufman, *Kingbird Highway*, 16, xi–xii.

35. Roger Tory Peterson and James Fisher, *Wild America* (Boston: Houghton Mifflin, 1955), 15.
36. Kaufman, *Kingbird Highway*, 151–61.
37. Kaufman, *Kingbird Highway*, 2, 21.
38. John C. Devlin and Grace Naismith, *The World of Roger Tory Peterson: An Authorized Biography* (New York: New York Times Books, 1977), 52–61.
39. Kaufman, *Kingbird Highway*, 205.
40. Kaufman, *Kingbird Highway*, 21, 69, 24, 67.
41. Stuart Keith, "The '600 Club': America's Top-Ranking Birders," *Audubon* 65 (November–December 1962), 376–77.
42. Kaufman, *Kingbird Highway*, 307, 55, 163. On modern world bird tourism see Mark Cocker, *Birders: Tales of a Tribe* (London: Jonathan Cape, 2001; reprint, New York: Grove Press, no date), 196–213.
43. Kaufman, *Kingbird Highway*, 18.
44. James A. Lane, *A Birder's Guide to the Rio Grande Valley* (Denver: L & P Press, 1986), 25, 39.
45. Lane, *Rio Grande Valley*, 82–97.
46. Kaufman, *Kingbird Highway*, 100, 102.
47. Edwin Way Teale, "Ludlow Griscom: Virtuoso of Field Identification," *Bird-Lore* 47 (November–December 1945), 349.
48. Kaufman, *Kingbird Highway*, 154, 49, 81, 97, 294–95, 43.

· 223 ·

CHAPTER 7

1. The epigraph to this chapter is from Jonathan Rosen, *The Life of the* Skies (New York: Farrar, Straus and Giroux, 2008), 259.
2. American Bird Conservancy, *All the Birds of North America* (New York: Harper-Collins, 1997). David Sibley, *The Sibley Guide to Birds* (New York: Knopf, 2000), *The Sibley Field Guide to Birds of Eastern North America* (New York: Knopf, 2003), and *The Sibley Field Guide to Birds of Western North America* (New York: Knopf, 2003). Pete Dunne, David Sibley, and Clay Sutton, *Hawks in Flight* (Boston: Houghton Mifflin 1988). James D. Rising, *A Guide to the Identification and Natural History of The Sparrows of the United States and Canada* (San Diego: Academic Press, 1996).
3. Peter Alden, *Finding Birds around the World* (Boston: Houghton Mifflin, 1981).
4. *Local Birds of Central Texas* (Austin: Local Birds, Inc., 2004). On the American Birding Association, see its website, www.aba.org/. Quote from brochure for an Association birding tour, received by author in mail, January 10, 2007.
5. Examples of this phenomenon include Luke Dempsey, *A Supremely Bad Idea: Three Mad Birders and Their Quest to See It All* (New York: Bloomsbury USA, 2008). Sean Dooley, *The Big Twitch* (Crows Nest, NSW, Australia: Allen and Unwin, 2005). Mark Cocker, *Birders: Tales of a Tribe* (London: Jonathan Cape, 2001; reprint, New York: Grove Press, n.d.).
6. Donald Kroodsma, *The Singing Life of Birds: The Art and Science of Birdsong* (Boston: Houghton Mifflin, 2005).
7. Mark Obmascik, *The Big Year: A Tale of Man, Nature, and Fowl Obsession* (New York: Free Press, 2004). Dan Koeppel, *To See Every Bird on Earth* (New York: Penguin, 2005). For the Cornell Laboratory of Ornithology, see www.birds.cornell.edu; for the Fish and Wildlife Service, see www.pwrc.usgs.gov/BBS/.

8. Joseph Kastner, "Battle of the Bird Books," *New York Times Sunday Magazine,* April 15, 1979, 4.

9. RTP to Guy Montfort, September 24, 72, Roger Tory Peterson Institute, Jamestown, New York.

10. *"The* Emperor Strikes Back," *Birding* 13 (August 1981), 127.

11. RTP to Guy Montfort, November 30, 81, Peterson Institute.

12. Introduction to Henry Armistead, 116–18, reviews by Ron Naveen, 118–19, Claudia Wilds, 119, Will Russell, 120–21, and Lawrence Balch, 121–24, "A Response," by Peterson, 125–29, all in *Birding* 13 (August 1981).

13. Quotes from Wilds, 119, Russell, 121, and Kenn Kaufman, "The NGS Guide, 2nd Edition," *Birding* 19 (April 1987), 22.

14. Roger Tory Peterson, *Peterson Field Guide to Birds of North America: First Edition* (Boston: Houghton Mifflin, 2008).

15. Reader's Digest Editors, *North American Wildlife* (Pleasantville, N.Y.: Reader's Digest, 1998), front flap copy.

16. John Farrand, Jr., *The Audubon Society Master Guide to Birding*, 3 vols. (New York: Knopf, 1983), 1:9.

17. Farrand, *Audubon Master Guide*, 1:228.

18. Lawrence G. Balch, review of *Audubon Master Guide* by John Farrand, Jr., *Birding* 16 (August 1984), 173.

19. Guy McCaskie, review of *Field Guide to the Birds of North America*, by Roger Tory Peterson, *Birding* 16 (February 1984), 29.

20. McCaskie, review, 29.

21. National Geographic Society, *Field Guide to the Birds of North America* (Washington, D.C.: National Geographic Society, 1983), 156.

22. Rich Stallcup, review of *A Guide to Field Identification: Birds of North America,* expanded, rev. ed., *Birding* 16 (October 1984), 217.

23. National Geographic, *Birds of North America,* 4, 17. Farrand, *Audubon Master Guide,* 1:9.

24. RTP to Chandler Robbins, December 5, 83, Peterson Institute.

25. Edward S. Brinkley, *National Wildlife Federation Field Guide to Birds of North America* (New York: Sterling, 2008). Ted Floyd, *Smithsonian Field Guide to the Birds of North America* (New York: HarperCollins, 2008).

26. American Bird Conservancy, *All the Birds,* unpaged sec. after 62.

27. Kim Eckert, review of *Hawks* by William S. Clark, *Birding* 19 (April 1987), 17–19.

28. Kim Eckert, review of *Hawks in Flight,* by Pete Dunne, David Sibley, and Clay Sutton, *Birding* 20 (June 1988), 175–76.

29. Echert, review of *Hawks in Flight,* 176. Frank M. Chapman, *Handbook of Birds of the Eastern North America* (New York: Appleton, 1895), 10.

30. Kevin Karlson, "Birding by Impression," *Living Bird* 25 (summer 2006), 34–42.

31. Michael Harvey, "Which Species Is That?" *Focus on Citizen Science* 2 (winter 2006), 14–15.

32. Kenn Kaufman, *Kingbird Highway* (Boston: Houghton Mifflin, 1997), 307, 315.

33. Obmascik, *Big Year,* 63–65.

34. Obmascik, *Big Year,* 244, 247.

35. Alden, *Finding Birds around the World.*

36. RTP to Paul Brooks, November 1, 1964, Peterson Institute.

37. Paul R. Ehrlich, David S. Dobkin, and Darryl Wheye, *The Birder's Handbook* (New York: Simon and Schuster, 1988).

38. Kenn Kaufman, *Lives of North American Birds* (Boston: Houghton Mifflin, 1996). Chris Elphick, John B. Dunning, Jr., and David Allen Sibley, eds., *The Sibley Guide to Bird Life and Behavior* (New York: Knopf, 2001).

39. S. Podulka, R. Rohrbaugh, Jr., and R. Bonney, eds., *Handbook of Bird Biology* (Ithaca, N.Y.: Cornell Laboratory of Ornithology, 2004), i.

40. Pete Dunne, *Pete Dunne's Essential Field Guide Companion* (Boston: Houghton Mifflin 2006). Jonathan Alderfer, ed., *National Geographic Complete Birds of North America* (Washington. D.C.: National Geographic, 2006).

41. Jack L. Griggs, *All the Backyard Birds, East, West* (New York: HarperCollins, 2003).

42. The Waterford Press publications are listed at htpp://waterfordpress.com/regional/html.

43. *Birds and Blooms*, October–November 2007, cover; available at www.birdsand-bloom.com.

44. Peterson had been thinking along these lines for years. In 1960 he wrote Joseph Hickey, asking him to jot down authors and topics for a possible Houghton Mifflin series that would be "basically ecological," taking "certain land units and in a not too technical way pick them apart and explain them." RTP to Hickey, January 1, 1960, Peterson Institute.

45. Roger Tory Peterson, editor's note, in John Kricher, *Eastern Forests* (Boston: Houghton Mifflin, 1988), v–vi. Kricher, *Eastern Forests*, 2.

46. Kritcher fit Rene Dubos's description of the naturalist as "this eternal child—[who] never ceases to marvel at the peculiarities of each haunt of life." Rene Dubos, *Mirage of Health* (New York: Harper, 1959; reprint, Garden City, N.Y.: Doubleday, no date), 37.

47. Kricher, *Eastern Forests*, vii, vii.

48. Olaus J. Murie, *A Field Guide to Animal Tracks*, 2nd ed. (Boston: Houghton Mifflin, 1974) (originally published 1954), 93, 31, 71, 5–8, 4.

49. Sarah B. Landry, *Urban Wildlife* (Boston: Houghton Mifflin, 1994).

50. Landry, *Urban Wildlife*, 56.

51. Cover blurb to John W. Brainerd, *The Nature Observer's Handbook* (Chester, Conn.: Globe Pequot, 1986).

52. Brainerd, *Nature Observer's Handbook*, 129–35.

53. John M. Bates and Thomas S. Schulenberg, "In Memoriam: Theodore A. Parker III, 1952–1993," *Auk* 114 (1) (1997), 110. Adrian Forsyth, "Ted Parker: In Memoriam," *Conservation Biology* 8 (March 1994), 293–94.

54. The new sound technology also allowed a range of bird consumer gadgets, from bird call clocks (a different one each hour) to ringtones. (In most areas loon calls, giving better contrast with background sounds, should be preferred to songbird calls, as they reduce the chance of mixing up phone and fauna.) Donald Kroodsma, *The Singing Life of Birds* (Boston: Houghton Mifflin, 2005), with included CD. Les Beletsky, *Bird Songs: 250 North American Birds in Song* (San Francisco: Chronicle Books, 2006), with attached audio unit. On ringtones, Peter Cannon, personal communication, June 23, 2008.

55. Available at www.pwrc.usgs.gov/bbs/.

56. Quote and information from J. R. Sauer et al., *The North American Breeding Bird Survey Results and Analysis*, available at the website of the U. S. Fish and Wildlife Service, www.mbr-pwre.usfs.gov/bbs/genintro.html.

57. "The Laboratory of Ornithology at Cornell University, a center for Research and Cultural Development," typescript, Pettingill file, Chapman Papers, Historical Correspondence, Department of Ornithology, AMNH.

58. House Finch Disease Survey, available at www.cornell.edu/hofi/whatishfds.html.

59. Project details from wws.birds.cornell/edu/LabPrograms/citSci/index/html (May 29, 2006), and htpp://ebird.org/content/ebird/about/whatisebird.html (June 7, 2007). Statistic from "Winter Bird Highlights, 2006," *Focus on Citizen Science* 2 (winter 2006), 2–4.

60. Brian L. Sullivan, "eBird and the Evolution of a Birder," *Birding* 40 (January–February 2008), 48.

CONCLUSION

1. Even the guide as agent of conservation remained. A set of field guides for Brazilian birds, in preparation at the Bronx Zoo (formally the Wildlife Conservation Society) in 2006, was planned to encourage the idea of birds as a national heritage by marking endemics (birds found only in that region) with a tiny national flag beside the description. Author's interview with John A. Gwynne, August 3, 2006. This was done; see John A. Gwynne, Robert S. Ridgely, Guy Tudor, and Martha Argel, *Birds of Brazil: The Pantanal and Cerrado of Central Brazil* (Ithaca: Cornell University Press, 2010).

2. For a well-developed, nonbirding example, see Barry Lopez, "Learning to See," in Lopez, *About This Life* (New York: Knopf, 1998; reprint, New York: Random House, 1999), 232.

3. Aldo Leopold, *A Sand County Almanac* (New York: Oxford University Press, 1949; reprint, New York: Ballantine, 1966), 223–24.

4. Graham Pizzey, *A Field Guide to the Birds of Australia* (Sydney: Collins, 1980), 213.

5. Terry Tempest Williams, *Refuge: An Unnatural History of Family and Place* (New York: Pantheon, 1991; reprint, New York: Vintage, 1992).

6. Williams, *Refuge*, 281.

7. John Burroughs, introduction to Neltje Blanchan, *Bird Neighbors* (New York: Doubleday and McClure, 1898) viii.

8. Jonathan Rosen, *Life of the Skies* (New York: Farrar, Straus, and Giroux, 2008), 7.

9. Rosen, *Life of the Skies*, 14, 156, 15.

10. Leopold, *Sand County Almanac*, 261.

Bibliography

Alden, Peter. *Finding Birds around the World*. Boston: Houghton Mifflin, 1981.

Allen, David. *The Naturalist in Britain*. London: A. Lane, 1976.

———. "Tastes and Crazes." In *Cultures of Natural History*, ed. N. Jardine, J. A. Secord, and E. C. Spary, 394–407. New York: Cambridge University Press, 1996.

Allen, Robert Porter. *The Flame Birds*. New York: Dodd, Mead, 1947.

American Bird Conservancy. *All the Birds of North America*. New York: HarperCollins, 1997.

American Ornithological Union, ed. *Fifty Years' Progress of American Ornithology, 1993–1933*. Lancaster, Pa.: American Ornithological Union, 1933.

Armistead, Henry. "The Emperor Strikes Back." *Birding* 13 (August 1981): 116–18.

Atran, Scott. *Cognitive Foundations of Natural History*. New York: Cambridge University Press, 1990.

Bailey, Florence Merriam. *Handbook of Birds of the Western United States*. Boston: Houghton Mifflin, 1902.

Baker, John H. "The President Reports to You." *Audubon* 47 (September–October 1945): 309–15.

Balch, Lawrence G. "Review of *Audubon Master Guide*." *Birding* 16 (August 1984): 167–73.

———. "Review of Roger Tory Peterson's Fourth Edition." *Birding* 13 (August 1981): 121–24.

"The Baltimore Oriole Is Back." *National Wildlife* 32 (February–March 1994): 24–27.

Barclay, John H. "Peregrine Restoration in the Eastern United States." In *Peregrine Falcon Populations: Their Management and Recovery*, ed. Tom J. Cade, James H. Enderson, Carl G. Thelander, and Clayton M. White, 549–58. Boise: Peregrine Fund, 1988.

Barrow, Mark. *Nature's Ghosts: Confronting Extinction from the Age of Jefferson to the Age of Ecology*. Chicago: University of Chicago Press, 2009.

———. *A Passion for Birds*. Princeton, N.J.: Princeton University Press, 1998.

Bates, John M., and Thomas S. Schulenberg. "In Memoriam: Theodore A. Parker III, 1952–1993." *Auk* 114 (1) (1997): 110.

Beletsky, Les. *Bird Songs: 250 North American Birds in Song*. With attached audio unit. San Francisco: Chronicle Books, 2006.

Berger, Daniel D., Charles R. Sindelar, Jr., and K. E. Gamble. "The Status of Breeding Peregrines in the Eastern United States." In *Peregrine Falcon Populations*, ed. Joseph J. Hickey, 165–73. Madison: University of Wisconsin Press, 1969.

Beston, Henry. *The Outermost House*. 1928. Reprint, New York: Ballantine, 1971.

Blachley, Lou, and Randolph Jenks. *Naming the Birds at a Glance*. New York: Knopf, 1963.

Blanchan, Neltje. *Bird Neighbors*. New York: Doubleday, 1898.

Blum, Ann Shelby. *Picturing Nature: American Nineteenth Century Zoological Illustration*. Princeton: Princeton University Press, 1993.

Bonta, Marcia Myers. *Women in the Field*. College Station: Texas A&M University Press, 1991.

"Boy Meets Bullfinch." *New Yorker* 14 (March 4, 1939): 22–27.

Brainerd, John W. *The Nature Observer's Handbook*. Chester, Conn.: Globe Pequot, 1986.

Brinkley, Edward S. *National Wildlife Federation Field Guide to Birds of North America*. New York: Sterling, 2008.

Bull, John. *Birds of the New York Area*. New York: Harper, 1964.

Burroughs, John. *The Gospel of Nature*. Bedford, Mass.: Applewood, n.d. [1912?].

———. Introduction to Neltje Blanchan, *Bird Neighbors*, viii–x. New York: Doubleday and McClure, 1898.

Butler, David, and Don Merton. *The Black Robin: Saving the World's Most Endangered Bird*. Auckland: Oxford University Press, 1992.

Cade, Tom J. "The Breeding of Peregrines and Other Falcons in Captivity: An Historical Summary." In *Peregrine Falcon Populations: Their Management and Recovery*, ed. Tom J. Cade, James H. Enderson, Carl G. Thelander, and Clayton M. White, 539–47. Boise, Idaho: Peregrine Fund, 1988.

Cade, Tom J., James H. Enderson, Carl G. Thelander, and Clayton M. White, eds. *Peregrine Falcon Populations: Their Management and Recovery*. Boise, Idaho: Peregrine Fund, 1988.

Campbell, Lawrence. Introduction to John Ruskin, *The Elements of Drawing*. 1857. Reprint, New York: Dover, 1971.

Carlson, Douglas. *Roger Tory Peterson: A Biography*. Austin: University of Texas Press, 2006.

Carson, Rachel. *The Edge of the Sea*. Boston: Houghton Mifflin, 1955.

———. "Help Your Child to Wonder." *Woman's Home Companion* (July 1956), 25.

———. *The Sea Around Us*. New York: Oxford University Press, 1951.

———. *A Sense of Wonder*. New York: Harper Collins, 1965.

———. *Silent Spring*. Boston: Houghton Mifflin, 1962.

Cayley, Neville. *What Bird Is That?* Sydney: Angus and Robertson, 1931.

Chapman, Frank M. *Bird-Life*. New York: Appleton, 1897.

———. "Birds of the Vicinity of New York City." Guide Leaflet no. 22. New York: American Museum of Natural History, 1906.

———. *Color Key to North American Birds*. New York: Doubleday, Page, 1903.

———. Editorial. *Bird-Lore* 11 (January–February 1909): 37.

———. Editorial. *Bird-Lore* 33 (January–February 1931): 81.

———. Editorial. *Bird-Lore* 36 (July–August 1934): 255.

———. *Handbook of Birds of Eastern North America*. New York: Appleton, 1895.

———. "Review of 'A Field Guide to the Birds.'" *Bird-Lore* 36 (July–August 1934): 253, 255.

Cocker, Mark. *Birders: Tales of a Tribe*. New York: Grove Press, 2001.

Comstock, Anna Botsford. "Directions for Collecting and Preserving Insects." In *Cornell Nature-Study Leaflets*, ed. State of New York, 213–26. Albany: State Printer, 1904.

———. *Handbook of Nature-Study.* 2 vols. Ithaca, N.Y.: Comstock, 1911.

Cottam, Clarence, and Elmer Higgins. "DDT and Its Effect on Fish and Wildlife." *Journal of Economic Entomology* 39 (February 1946): 44–52.

Coues, Elliott. *Key to North American Birds.* Boston: Estes and Lauriat, 1887.

Cruickshank, Allen. *Birds around New York City: Where and When to Find Them.* New York: American Museum of Natural History, 1964.

Cunningham, Laurence S., ed. *A Search for Solitude: The Journals of Thomas Merton.* Vol. 3. *1952—1960.* New York: HarperCollins, 1996.

Davis, William E., Jr. *Dean of the Birdwatchers: A Biography of Ludlow Griscom.* Washington, D.C.: Smithsonian Institution Press, 1994.

Dempsey, Luke. *A Supremely Bad Idea: Three Mad Birders and Their Quest to See It All.* New York: Bloomsbury USA, 2008.

Devlin, John C., and Grace Naismith. *The World of Roger Tory Peterson: An Authorized Biography.* New York: New York Times Books, 1977.

Diamond, Jared, and K. David Bishop. "Ethno-ornithology of the Ketengban People, Indonesian New Guinea." In *Folkbiology*, ed. Douglas L. Medin and Scott Atran, 17–45, Cambridge, Mass.: MIT Press, 1999.

Dickey, Florence Van Vechten. *Familiar Birds of the Pacific Southwest with Size and Color Key.* Stanford: Stanford University Press, 1935.

Dooley, Sean. *The Big Twitch.* Crows Nest, NSW, Australia: Allen and Unwin, 2005.

Doughty, Robin. *Feather Fashions and Bird Preservation: A Study in Nature Protection.* Berkeley: University of California Press, 1975.

Dubos, Rene. *Mirage of Health.* 1959. Reprint, Garden City, N.Y.: Doubleday, n.d.

Dunlap, Thomas R. *DDT: Scientists, Citizens, and Public Policy.* Princeton, N.J.: Princeton University Press, 1981.

———. *Nature and the English Diaspora.* New York: Cambridge University Press, 1999.

———. "Organization and Wildlife Preservation: The Case of the Whooping Crane in North America." *Social Studies of Science* 21 (1991): 197–221.

———. *Saving America's Wildlife.* Princeton, N.J.: Princeton University Press, 1988.

Dunne, Pete. *Pete Dunne's Essential Field Guide Companion.* Boston: Houghton Mifflin, 2006.

Dunne, Pete, David Sibley, and Clay Sutton. *Hawks in Flight.* Boston: Houghton Mifflin, 1988.

Eaton, Warren F. "Predators and Bird Preserves." *Bird-Lore* 37 (May–June 1935): 162–66.

Eckert, Kim. Review of *Hawks,* by William S. Clark. *Birding* 19 (April 1987): 17–19.

———. Review of *Hawks in Flight,* by Pete Dunne et al. *Birding* 20 (June 1988): 175–76

Editorial. *Osprey* 1 (April 1897): 114.

Ehrlich, Paul R., David S. Dobkin, and Darryl Wheye. *The Birders' Handbook.* New York: Simon and Schuster, 1988.

Eisenberg, Ann. "Digital Field Guides Eliminate the Guesswork." *New York Times,* May 10, 2009, Sunday Business sec., 3.

Elphick, Chris, John B. Dunning, Jr., and David Allen Sibley, eds. *The Sibley Guide to Bird Life and Behavior.* New York: Knopf, 2001.

Elton, Charles. *Animal Ecology.* London: Sidgwick and Jackson, 1927.

Emerson, Guy. "The Lure of the List." *Bird-Lore* 42 (January–February 1940): 37–39.

Emlen, John T., and David Archbald. *Quick Key Guide to Birds: Northeastern and Central United States and Adjacent Canada*. Garden City, N.Y.: Doubleday, 1967.

Errington, Paul. "Vulnerability of Bob-white Populations to Predation." *Ecology* 15 (April 1934): 110–27.

Farrand, John, Jr. *The Audubon Society Master Guide to Birding*. 3 vols. New York, Knopf, 1983.

———. "The Bronx County Bird Club." *American Birds* 45 (fall 1991): 372–81.

"Feathered vs. Human Predators." *Bird-Lore* 27 (March–April 1935): 122–26.

Fisher, James. *Bird Recognition*. London: Penguin, 1947.

———. *Watching Birds*. London: Penguin, 1941.

Floyd, Ted. *Smithsonian Field Guide to the Birds of North America*. New York: HarperCollins, 2008.

Forbush, Edward Howe, and John Bichard May. *A Natural History of American Birds of Eastern and Central North America*. 1925. Reprint, Boston: Houghton Mifflin, 1939.

Forsyth, Adrian. "Ted Parker: In Memoriam." *Conservation Biology* 8 (March 1994): 293–l294.

Fussell, Paul. *The Great War and Modern Memory*. New York: Oxford University Press, 1975.

Gibbons, Felton, and Deborah Strom. *Neighbors to the Birds: A History of Birdwatching in America*. New York: Norton, 1988.

Graham, Frank, Jr. *The Audubon Ark*. New York: Knopf, 1990.

Grant, John B. *Our Common Birds and How to Know Them*. New York: Scribner's, 1891.

Gray, Asa. *How Plants Grow: A Simple Introduction to Structural Botany with a Popular Flora, or an Arrangement and Descriptions of Common Plants, Both Wild and Cultivated*. New York: American Book Company, 1858.

Griggs, Jack L. *All the Backyard Birds, East, West*. New York: HarperCollins, 2003.

Grinnell, Joseph. "Conserve the Collector." *Science*, new ser., 41 (February 1915): 229–32.

Griscom, Ludlow. *Birds of the New York City Region*. New York: American Museum of Natural History, 1923.

———. "Frank Michler Chapman, 1864–1945." *Audubon* 48 (January–February 1946): 49–52.

———. *Modern Bird Study*. Cambridge, Mass.: Harvard University Press, 1945.

———. "Modern Problems in Field Identification." *Bird-Lore* 38 (January–February 1936): 12–18.

———. "Problems of Field Identification." *Auk* 39 (January 1922): 31–41.

Gwynne, John A., Robert S. Ridgely, Guy Tudor, and Martha Argel. *Birds of Brazil: The Pananal and Cerrado of Central Brazil*. Ithaca, N.Y.: Cornell University Press, 2010.

Hancock, Lyn. *Looking for the Wild*. Toronto: Doubleday Canada, 1986.

Harrison, Hal H. *A Field Guide to the Birds' Nests East of the Mississippi River*. Boston: Houghton Mifflin, 1975.

Harvey, Michael. "Which Species Is That?" *Focus on Citizen Science* 2 (winter 2006): 14–15.

Hausman, Leon A. *Field Book of Eastern Birds*. New York: Putnam, 1946.

Hickey, Joseph J. *A Guide to Bird Watching*. New York: Oxford University Press, 1943.

———, ed. *Peregrine Falcon Populations*. Madison: University of Wisconsin Press, 1969.

Hill, Geoffrey E. *Ivorybill Hunters*. New York: Oxford University Press, 2007.

Hodge, Clifton F. *Nature Study and Life*. Boston: Ginn, 1903.

Hoffman, Ralph. *A Guide to the Birds of New England and Eastern New York*. Boston: Houghton Mifflin, 1904.

———. *Birds of the Pacific States*. Boston: Houghton Mifflin, 1927.

Hornaday, William. *Wildlife Conservation in Theory and Practice*. 1914. Reprint, New York: Arno, 1972.

Karlson, Kevin. "Birding by Impression." *Living Bird* 25 (summer 2006): 34–42.

Kastner, Joseph. "Battle of the Bird Books." *New York Times Sunday Magazine*, April 15, 1979, 4.

———. *World of Watchers: An Informal History of the American Passion for Birds—from Its Scientific Beginnings to the Great Birding Boom of Today*. New York: Knopf, 1986.

Kaufman, Kenn. *A Field Guide to Advanced Birding: Birding Challenges and How to Approach Them*. Boston: Houghton Mifflin, 1990.

———. *Kingbird Highway: The Story of a Natural Obsession That Got a Little Out of Hand*. Boston: Houghton Mifflin, 1997.

———. *Lives of North American Birds*. Boston: Houghton Mifflin, 1996.

———. "Review of the NGS Guide, 2nd Edition." *Birding* 19 (April 1987): 20–24.

Keith, Stuart. "The '600 Club': America's Top-Ranking Birders." *Audubon* 65 (November–December 1962): 376–77.

Kilham, Lawrence. *On Watching Birds*. 1988. Reprint, College Station: Texas A&M University Press, 1997.

King, Eleanor Anthony. "Lady with Binoculars." *Audubon* 49 (July 1949): 202–10.

Knobel, Edward. *Field Key to the Land Birds*. Boston: Bradlee Whidden, 1899.

Koeppel, Dan. *To See Every Bird on Earth*. New York: Penguin, 2005.

Koford, Carl B. *The California Condor*. 1953. Reprint, New York: Dover, 1966.

Kohler, Robert E. *All Creatures*. Princeton: Princeton University Press, 2006.

Krautwurst, Terry. "Field Guide Fever." *Mother Earth News*, June–July 2003, 17.

Kricher, John. *Eastern Forests*. Boston: Houghton Mifflin, 1988.

Kroodsma, Donald. *The Singing Life of Birds*. With CD. Boston: Houghton Mifflin, 2005.

Lambert, Mike. *Birds by Colour: The Simplest Identification Guide*. London: Blandford, 1992.

Landry, Sarah B. *Urban Wildlife*. Boston: Houghton Mifflin, 1994.

Lane, James A. *A Birder's Guide to the Rio Grande Valley*. Denver: L & P Press, 1986.

Leach, J. A. *An Australian Bird Book*. Melbourne: Whitcombe and Tombs, 1911.

Lear, Linda. *Rachel Carson: Witness for Nature*. New York: Holt, 1997.

Leopold, Aldo. *A Sand County Almanac*. 1949. Reprint, New York: Ballantine, 1970.

Local Birds of Central Texas. Austin: Local Birds, 2004.

Lopez, Barry. *About This Life*. 1998. Reprint, New York: Random House, 1999.

———. "Learning to See." In *About This Life*, 224–39. 1988. Reprint, New York: Random House, 1999.

Lytle, Mark Hamilton. *The Gentle Subversive: Rachel Carson, Silent Spring, and the Rise of the Environmental Movement*. New York: Oxford University Press, 2007.

MacGillivray, Alex. *Rachel Carson's Silent Spring*. New York: Barron's, 2004.

Mathews, F. Schuyler. *Field Book of Wild Birds and Their Music*. Rev. ed. New York: Putnam, 1921. (Originally published 1904.)

McAtee, W. L. "A Little Essay on 'Vermin.'" *Bird-Lore* 31 (November–December 1931): 381–84.

· 231 ·

McCaskie, Guy. "Review of *Field Guide to the Birds of North America.*" *Birding* 16 (February 1984), 25–32.

McCracken, Karen Harden. *Connie Hagar: The Life History of a Texas Birdwatcher.* College Station: Texas A&M University Press, 1986.

McNulty, Faith. *The Whooping Crane.* New York: Dutton, 1966.

Medin, Douglas L., and Scott Atran, eds. *Folkbiology.* Cambridge, Mass.: MIT Press, 1999.

Merriam, Florence. *A-birding on a Bronco.* Boston: Houghton Mifflin, 1896.

———. *Birds of Village and Field.* Boston: Houghton Mifflin, 1898.

———. *Birds through an Opera-Glass.* Boston: Houghton Mifflin, 1889.

Mexia, Ynez. "Bird Study for Beginners by a Beginner." Pt. 1. *Bird-Lore* 27 (January–February 1925): 69–72.

———. "Bird Study for Beginners by a Beginner." Pt. 2. *Bird-Lore* 27 (March–April 1925): 137–41.

Moncrieff, Perrine. *New Zealand Birds and How to Identify Them.* Auckland: Whitcombe and Tombs, 1925.

Moss, Stephen. *A Bird in the Bush: A Social History of Birdwatching.* London: Aurum Press, 2004.

Murie, Adolph. *A Field Guide to Animal Tracks.* Boston: Houghton Mifflin, 1954.

Murphy, Priscilla Coit. *What a Book Can Do: The Publication and Reception of Silent Spring.* Amherst: University of Massachusetts Press, 2005.

National Geographic Society. *Field Guide to the Birds of North America.* Washington, D.C.: National Geographic Society, 1983.

———. *National Geographic Complete Birds of North America.* 5th ed. Washington, D.C.: National Geographic Society, 2006.

Naveen, Ron. "Review of Roger Tory Peterson's Fourth Edition." *Birding* 13 (August 1981): 118–19.

Needham, James G. *The Natural History of the Farm.* Ithaca, N.Y.: Comstock , 1916.

Nicholson, E. M. *The Art of Bird Watching.* 1931. Reprint, New York: Scribner's, 1932.

"Notes from Field and Study." *Bird-Lore* 39 (March–April 1937): 159–60.

Nuttall, Thomas. *A Manual of the Ornithology of the United States and Canada.* 2 vols. Cambridge, Mass.: Hilliard, Gray, 1832–34.

Obmascik, Mark. *The Big Year: A Tale of Man, Nature, and Fowl Obsession.* New York: Free Press, 2004.

Paquin, Jean, and Ghislain Caron. *Oiseaux du Quebec et des Maritimes.* Waterloo, Quebec: Editions Michel Quintin, 1998.

Parkhurst, H. E. *The Birds' Calendar.* New York: Scribner's, 1894.

Peattie, Donald Culross. "The Nature of Things." *Audubon* 43 (July–August 1941): 346–48.

Peterson, Roger Tory. "A Bird by Any Other Name." *Audubon* 44 (September–October 1942): 277–80.

———. *Birds over America.* New York: Dodd, Mead, 1948.

———. Editor's note. In Kenn Kaufman, *Advanced Birding,* v–vii. Boston: Houghton Mifflin, 1990.

———. Editor's note. In John Kricher, *Eastern Forests,* v–vi. Boston: Houghton Mifflin, 1988.

———. "The Era of Ludlow Griscom." *Audubon* 62 (May–June 1960): 102–3, 131, 146, 148.

———. "Evolution of a Field Guide." *Defenders,* October 1980. Available at htpp://Defenders.org/rtperter1.htm (last accessed September 4, 2008).

———. *A Field Guide to the Birds.* Boston: Houghton Mifflin, 1934.

———. *A Field Guide to the Birds.* Boston: Houghton Mifflin, 1947.

———. *A Field Guide to the Birds: Including All Species Found in Eastern North America.* 1934. Reprint, Boston: Houghton Mifflin, 1996.

———. *A Field Guide to Western Birds.* Boston: Houghton Mifflin, 1941.

———. Foreword to Lyn Hancock, *Looking for the Wild,* ix–xi. Toronto: Doubleday Canada, 1986.

———. Foreword to John Bull, *Birds of the New York Area,* ix–xiv. New York: Harper and Row, 1964.

———. *How to Know the Birds.* Boston: Houghton Mifflin, 1949.

———. "In Memoriam: Ludlow Griscom." *Auk* 82 (October 1965): 599–605.

———. *Peterson Field Guide to Birds of North America: First Edition.* Boston: Houghton Mifflin, 2008.

———. "A Response." *Birding* 13 (August 1981): 125–29.

Peterson, Roger Tory, and James Fisher. *Wild America.* Boston: Houghton Mifflin, 1955.

Peterson, Roger Tory, and Rudy Hoglund, eds. *Roger Tory Peterson: The Art and Photography of the World's Foremost Birder.* New York: Rizzoli, 1994.

Peterson, Roger Tory, and Margaret McKenney. *A Field Guide to Wildflowers.* Boston: Houghton Mifflin, 1968.

Peterson, Roger Tory, Guy Montfort, and P. A. D. Hollom. *A Field Guide to the Birds of Britain and Europe.* Boston: Houghton Mifflin, 1954; London: Collins, 1954.

Ridgway, Robert. *Manual of North American Birds.* Philadelphia: Lippincott, 1887.

Pettingill, Olin Sewall, Jr. *A Guide to Bird Finding East of the Mississippi.* New York: Oxford University Press, 1951.

———. *A Guide to Bird Finding West of the Mississippi.* New York: Oxford University Press, 1953.

Phillippon, Daniel J. Introduction to Mabel Osgood Wright, *The Friendship of Nature,* 3–6. 1894. Reprint, Baltimore: Johns Hopkins Press, 1999.

Pizzey, Graham. *Crosbie Morrison: Voice of Nature.* Melbourne: Victoria Press, 1992.

Podulka, S., R. Rohrbaugh, Jr., and R. Bonney, eds. *Handbook of Bird Biology.* Ithaca, N.Y.: Cornell Laboratory of Ornithology, 2004.

Pough, Richard H. *Eastern Land Birds.* New York: Doubleday, 1946.

Price, Jenny. *Flight Maps: Adventures with Nature in Modern America.* New York: Basic Books, 1999.

———. "When Women Were Women, Men Were Men, and Birds Were Hats." In Price, *Flight Maps: Adventures with Nature in Modern America,* 57–109. New York: Basic Books, 1999.

Ratcliffe, Derek. "The Status of the Peregrine in Great Britain." *Bird Study* 10 (June 1963): 56–90.

Reader's Digest. *North American Wildlife.* Pleasantville, N.Y.: Reader's Digest, 1998.

Reed, Chester A. *Bird Guide: Water Birds, Game Birds and Birds of Prey East of the Rockies.* Worcester, Mass.: Chas. K. Reed, 1906.

———. *Bird Guide.* Pt. 2. *Land Birds East of the Rockies from Parrots to Bluebirds.* 1906. Reprint, New York: Doubleday, Page, 1912.

———. *Western Bird Guide: Birds of the Rockies and West to the Pacific.* 1913. Reprint, New York: Doubleday, Page, 1923.

Rhodes, Richard. *John James Audubon: The Making of an American.* New York: Knopf, 2004.

Rising, James D. *A Guide to the Identification and Natural History of the Sparrows of the United States and Canada.* San Diego: Academic Press, 1996.

Robbins, Chandler S., Bertel Brunn, and Herbert S. Zim. *Birds of North America.* New York: Golden Press, 1966.

Roberts, Charles G. D. "The Aigrette." In Roberts, *The Secret Trails,* 77–89. New York: Macmillan, 1916.

———. *The Secret Trails.* New York: Macmillan, 1916.

Rosen, Jonathan. *The Life of the Skies.* New York: Farrar, Straus, and Giroux, 2008.

Rosenthal, Elizabeth J. *Birdwatcher: The Life of Roger Tory Peterson.* Guilford, Conn.: Globe Pequot, 2008.

Ruskin, John. *The Elements of Drawing.* 1857. Reprint, New York: Dover, 1971.

Russell, Will. "Review of Roger Tory Peterson's Fourth Edition." *Birding* 13 (August 1981): 120–21.

Sauer, J. R., et al. *The North American Breeding Bird Survey Results and Analysis.* Available at www.mbr-pwre.usfs.gov/bbs/genintro.html(last accessed June 15, 2008).

Schmidt, Diane. *A Guide to Field Guides: Identifying the Natural History of North America.* Englewood, Colo.: Libraries Unlimited, 1999.

Scott, Charles B. *Nature Study and the Child.* Boston: Heath, 1901.

Seton, Ernest Thompson [Ernest Seton Thompson]. "Directive Color of Birds." *Auk* 14 (October 1897): 395–6.

Seton-Thompson, Ernest. [Ernest Seton Thompson]. "Recognition Marks of Birds." *Bird-Lore* 3 (November–December 1901): 187–89.

———. *Two Little Savages.* New York: Doubleday, 1903.

Shaffer, Marguerite S. *See America First: Tourism and National Identity, 1880–1940.* Washington, D.C.: Smithsonian Institution, 2001.

Sibley, David Allen. *The Sibley Field Guide to Birds of Eastern North America.* New York: Knopf, 2003.

———. *The Sibley Field Guide to Birds of Western North America.* New York: Knopf, 2003.

———. *The Sibley Guide to Birds.* New York: Knopf, 2000.

Slater, Peter. *Birdwatcher's Notebook.* Sydney: Weldon, 1988.

Souder, William. *Under a Wild Sky: John James Audubon and the Making of the Birds of America.* New York: Farrar, Straus, and Giroux, 2004.

Stallcup, Rich. "Review of *A Guide to Field Identification: Birds of North America, Expanded, Revised Edition.*" *Birding* 16 (October 1984): 217–23.

Steiner, Bill. *Audubon Art Prints.* Columbia: University of South Carolina Press, 2003.

Sterling, Keir B., Richard P. Harmond, George A. Cevasco, and Lorne F. Hammond, eds. *Biographical Dictionary of American and Canadian Naturalists and Environmentalists.* Westport, Conn.: Greenwood, 1997.

Stoddard, Herbert L. *The Bobwhite Quail: Its Habits, Preservation, and Increase.* New York: Scribner's, 1931.

Sullivan, Brian L. "eBird and the Evolution of a Birder." *Birding* 40 (January–February 2008): 48–52.

Sutton, George Miksch. *Bird Student.* Austin: University of Texas Press, 1980.

———. "Fifty Years of Progress in American Bird-Art." In *Fifty Years' Progress of American Ornithology, 1993–1933,* ed. American Ornithological Union, 181–97. Lancaster, Pa.: American Ornithological Union, 1933.

Taverner, P. A. *Canadian Land Birds: A Pocket Field Guide.* Toronto: Musson, 1939.

· 234 ·

————. *Canadian Water Birds, Game Birds, and Birds of Prey: A Pocket Field Guide.* Toronto: Musson, 1939.

Teale, Edwin Way. *Autumn across America.* New York: Dodd, Mead, 1956.

————. *Journey into Summer.* New York: Dodd Mead, 1960.

————. "Ludlow Griscom: Virtuoso of Field Identification." *Bird-Lore* 47 (November–December 1945): 349–58.

————. *North with the Spring.* New York: Dodd, Mead, 1951.

————. *Wandering through Winter.* New York: Dodd, Mead, 1965.

Temple, Stanley A., and John Emlen. "Obituary for Joseph J. Hickey." *Auk* 111 (April 1994): 450–52.

Tufte, Edward R. *Beautiful Evidence.* Cheshire, Conn.: Graphics Press, 2006.

W.A.J. "Review." *Osprey* 2 (February–March 1898): 91.

Wallace, Ray. "A Body in Twain? The Royal Australian Ornithological Union and the Events of 1969." M.A. thesis, University of Melbourne, 1970.

Weidensaul, Scott. *Of a Feather: A Brief History of American Birding.* Orlando, Fla.: Harcourt, 2007.

————. *Return to Wild America.* New York: Farrar, Straus, and Giroux, 2005.

White, Gilbert. *A Natural History of Selbourne.* 1788. Reprint, New York: Penguin, 1977.

White, Lisa, and Peter Dunne, eds. *Good Birders Don't Wear White.* Boston: Houghton Mifflin, 2007.

Wilds, Claudia. "Review of Roger Tory Peterson's Fourth Edition." *Birding* 13 (August 1981): 119.

Williams, Terry Tempest. *Refuge: An Unnatural History of Family and Place.* 1991. Reprint, New York: Vintage, 1992.

Williamson, Sheri. "Choose Your Wardrobe Wisely: Good Birders Don't Wear White." In *Good Birders Don't Wear White,* ed. Lisa White, 33–37. Boston: Houghton Mifflin, 2007.

Wilson, Edward O. *Naturalist.* Washington, D.C.: Island Press, 1994.

"Winter Bird Highlights, 2006." *Focus on Citizen Science* 2 (winter 2006): 2–4.

Wright, Mabel Osgood. *Birdcraft.* New York: Macmillan, 1895.

Young, Christian. *In the Absence of Predators: Conservation and Controversy on the Kaibab Plateau.* Lincoln: University of Nebraska Press, 2002.

Zeller, Suzanne. *Inventing Canada.* Toronto: University of Toronto Press, 1987.

Zim, Herbert S., and Robert H. Baker. *Stars.* New York: Simon and Shuster, 1951.

Zim, Herbert S., and Ira N. Gabrielson. *Birds: A Guide to the Most Familiar American Birds.* New York: Simon and Schuster, 1949.

Zim, Herbert S., and Alexander C. Martin. *Flowers: A Guide to Familiar American Wildflowers.* New York: Golden Press, 1950.

Zinsser, William. "Watching the Birds." In *Roger Tory Peterson: The Art and Photography of the World's Foremost Birder,* ed. Roger Tory Peterson and Rudy Hoglund. New York: Rizzoli, 1994.

· 235 ·

Index

tourism, 84, 123, 178

Wallace, Alfred Russel, 29–30
White, Gilbert, 33, 76, 112
wild, 59, 87, 108, 120, 144, 169
wild America, 31, 82, 94, 121, 138–42, 159
Wild America, 120–21, 135–40, 168–70
Williams, Terry Tempest, 205–6
Wilson, Alexander, 29–30
Wilson, E. O., 27, 117

women
    in Audubon movement, 31–34
    in birdwatching, 22–24, 83, 87, 123, 172
    conservation, 31–34, 142–43, 155–56
world birding, 188
Wright, Mabel Osgood, 22–24, 32–33, 46, 56, 98

year-list, 57, 105–06, 120, 137, 139–40, 168–71

Zim, Herbert, 121, 129, 163